FIFTY MILES WIDE

JULIAN SAYARER has made many journeys by bicycle and as a hitchhiker, along the way recording a passing view of the world's roadsides. After breaking the 18,000-mile world record for a circumnavigation by bike, he went on to write his first book, *Life Cycles*. He is a past fellow of the Royal Literary Fund, and winner of the Stanford Dolman Travel Book of the Year award for his book, *Interstate*, and its depiction of a less-seen USA. *Fifty Miles Wide* is his fifth book.

FIFTY MILES WIDE

Cycling through Israel and Palestine

Julian Sayarer

A

Arcadia Books Ltd
139 Highlever Road
London W10 6PH

www.arcadiabooks.co.uk

First published in the United Kingdom 2020
Copyright © Julian Sayarer 2020

ISBN 978-1-911350-75-0

Map illustrations are by a Palestinian illustrator who wished to remain anonymous.

Typeset in Garamond by MacGuru Ltd
Printed and bound by TJ International, Padstow PL28 8RW

ARCADIA BOOKS DISTRIBUTORS ARE AS FOLLOWS:

in the UK and elsewhere in Europe:
BookSource
50 Cambuslang Road
Cambuslang
Glasgow G32 8NB

in USA/Canada:
BookMasters
Baker & Taylor
30 Amberwood Parkway
Ashland, OH 44805
USA

in Australia/New Zealand:
NewSouth Books
University of New South Wales
Sydney NSW 2052

For Yasmin, for Yasmin.

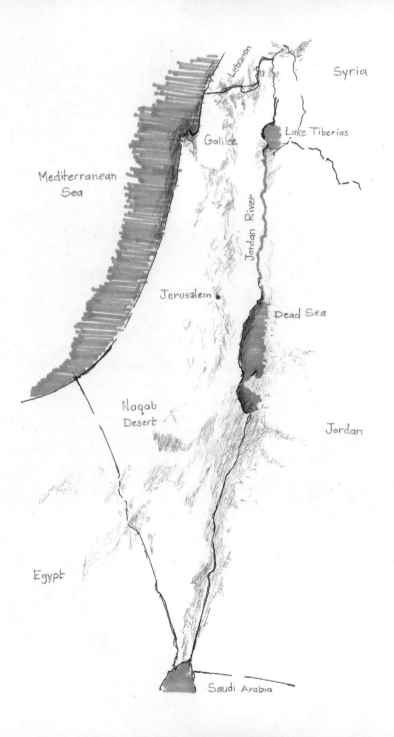

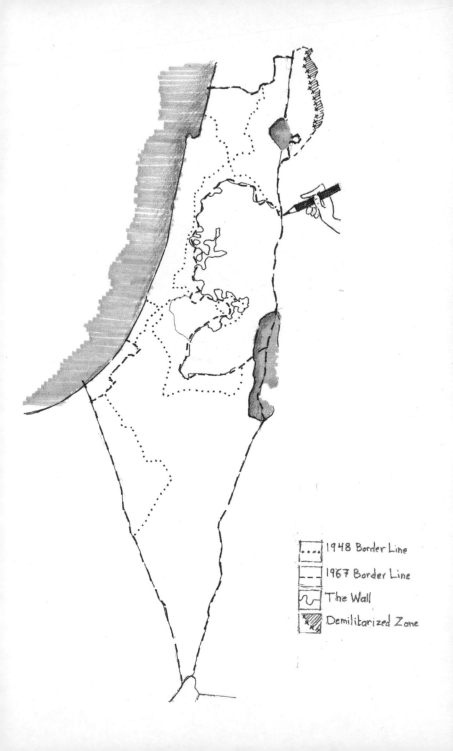

1948 Border Line
1967 Border Line
The Wall
Demilitarized Zone

Contents

Prologue

Offhand I had said it, to an author from Israel, seated beside me in a grand square at the Edinburgh Book Festival. I said that the bicycle seemed to bring out the best in people. I said that it cut through to something deeper and, in so doing, showed the truth of a place. And her face had taken on a serious expression, as if here was a thought that required her full attention.

'You should go to Israel then. On a bicycle I think you'd see it all. The land, the checkpoints. Palestine and Israel, the root of the problem is in the land.'

And at times I would damn her for it and at times feel a profound gratitude, but in all the many emotions that took me in those thousand miles, never was she wrong.

⁜

Sometimes in life it happens that an idea you first held only in passing becomes steadily stronger, until finally you realise that it has come to possess you. That single idea grows in prominence until it has you working for it, it makes you its keeper, until maps, notepads and books scatter your desk in homage to a once-vague thought, and your every waking moment pours into forming the plans, at first so small, that unwittingly you have become. So it went with that idea to ride a bicycle through Palestine and Israel, and if it would be too strong to suggest that it began as only a single casual suggestion, still, I never expected to wind up doing it, nor to be so convinced that indeed there was no better place to learn about this world than from the seat of a bicycle. Dragging yourself across a landscape, one pedal stroke at a time, if you can take that theory and test it in the heart of the Middle East, in the guts of history that you find there, if the bicycle can navigate some sort of truth in even that tangled place, then there is no knot or idiosyncrasy it cannot unpick.

How it does that I do not know, and I can only make the guesses of a student, someone who spent years pedalling roads and watching what the roadsides showed me. Riding a bicycle served as something of a leveller, a vantage point that reminded me of the basic sameness of streets and roads everywhere, for these are simply the venues in which people set quietly about the work of building their lives and their dreams. Whether I was pedalling the Middle East or my route into the city of London, the surrounds of each and news of both places reached me as if filtered by the same strainer of my spokes. Aboard a bicycle, I felt so keenly that what passed in one place would eventually come to pass in the other, for it is only with time that the many separations of our world are proven false. Through all the miles, the bicycle came to represent in my mind the best of us. It was our ability to live in harmony with the laws of physics, with ourselves, our better natures, and by which, when riding, the world seemed like it might just about be OK. Perhaps. In my bowed head above the handlebars, sweating through the pilgrimage of a long mountain pass, only in the bicycle have I found a place where all beauty, ecstasy, anger, hate and joy could collide together in chaos but still come out the other side as something recognisable. Even as something positive. My vehicle is the bicycle, always the bicycle... for when I ride, still to this day and just like the first time, it feels like I am reading a love letter.

But for all that that is so, I never rode so that I could write about the cycling. To me, the best thing of the bicycle was the way it allowed me to see better and so write better of everything that was around it. The bicycle's main gift was the way it was willing to take me great distances, relying on few but myself, and to ask in return for almost no mention of its service. The bicycle is simultaneously a telescope and a cloak, it reveals and it hides. It shows you details that you would not normally see for haste, for barriers, for your own cluttered thoughts. And at the same time it shelters you from the world, concealing those causes for cynicism and for suspicion that adults acquire in their instinctive views of one another. So that somehow, miraculously, at the end of it, you are left only ever as a human being, riding on a bicycle. Innocent. Arriving by bicycle, people see their young self once learning to balance. Arriving by bicycle, people see their children at play. And if you can take that energy into encounters with checkpoints, with walls, with soldiers, with both the wretched and the wronged, then by bicycle, I swear, you go fortified forever with that most potent of defences, a smile.

Part I

ENTRY

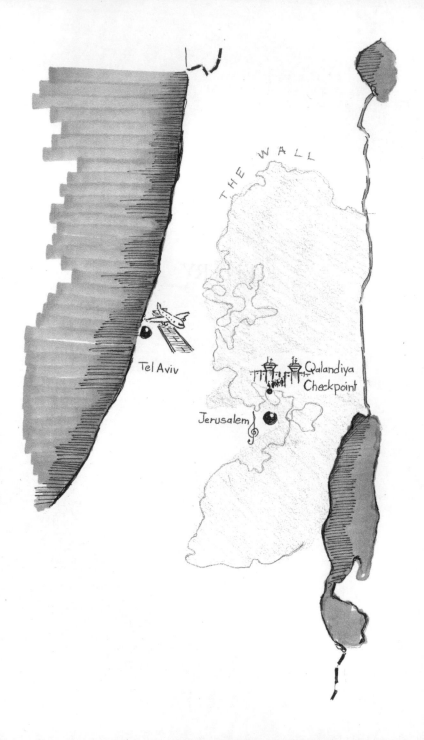

Best-laid Plans

In my room I make final preparations, eyes weary from the screen. Its light projects my shadow onto the wall over my shoulder. A few people have forewarned me, to be on the safe side, of the intrusions of Israeli interrogations at the border. I have been told that my phone might be searched, messages read, family background and family photos unearthed on or prior to arrival. To save us all the trouble, I sit and I search. I trawl my histories. *Palestine*. Select. Delete. *Palestinian*. Delete. *Gaza*. Delete. *West Bank*. Delete. With a half dozen clicks I wipe all mention of where I'm headed, a removal that feels unnerving in its ease. In a totalitarian instant that shows how the age of the internet can erase people as readily as it might liberate them, I abandon the Palestinians. They vanish from the record of my communications and I begin to move out of the digital and back into the analogue world. I turn off the computer and, there unsearchable, put ink to paper.

⁜

The fluorescent bulb, covered in a plastic casing, casts the centre of the ceiling in a pool of pale light. It flickers rapidly, and my eyes blur as if trying to watch an out-of-focus television. Midnight comes closer. Into the otherwise sterile room, a fly has made its way, moving through the levels of light, then in and out of the shadows. Immigration at Ben Gurion Airport envelops me on all sides. In three orderly lines we stand, waiting for a border guard to call us up.

A new official has just come on duty, takes her time setting out her stall inside a booth. She makes us wait. I'm third in line. Person One fidgets with the cordon between us and the next queue. Eventually she waves him over, and I play guessing games at how his entry will pan out. I watch the psychology from afar: borders, where humans aspire to be machines that follow policy, but do so through a filter of our flesh-and-blood judgements. Person One stands there skinny in a pair of shorts and a polo shirt, looking like he never had an incriminating thought in his life, flustered, doesn't realise that his only crime was to be her warm-up act. She gives him a hammering. She looks at the passport, looks at him, keeps hold of the thing as – tentatively – he reaches as if it's on its way back, but no. His facial expression changes, grows concerned, the guard putting him under such suspicion he looks ready to start suspecting himself, like maybe he did do something wrong after all.

Five minutes later, with a sigh, he goes clear. Person Two is up: a woman, perhaps the same middle age as the official, similar build, plain haircut and a pull-along suitcase. She leans on the counter. The official looks at her and at the passport. I catch her face through the glass of her booth, peering down her nose as she appears, obscured, from round the side of the head of Person Two. Minutes pass, she's taking some time, holding her up, getting into her stride. Some minutes later, Person Two gets ushered in. Here we go.

I've been told I should be fine. It's my first visit, I'm not returning to anything. I'm not a *James Smith, Stephanie Wilson* or any of the other middle England names they wave through, but my name is only part-foreign, so perhaps it'll be easy. Getting closer, I see an unhappy face, as if maybe she is starting to regret a few of these years in uniform at the border. I feel a familiar sensation coming over me, because me and authority never really got on. For I desire authority over no other human, and the reverse of that, childish as it may seem, is that I can abide no other human holding it over me. Still, this time there's work to be done, and as my body takes its last steps towards the red line that indicates my first frontier in this land chock-full of frontiers, I hear my brain, whispering instructions to my lips and to my soul.

'Don't say anything dumb. Make like she's the horizon, neither bad nor good, it's just there and we need to roll over it.'

She takes my passport. Leafs pages. Looks at me with what resembles distaste, but perhaps I'm just being sensitive. She speaks in a thick accent, her tongue scuffing the words.

'Your name. What is it?'

'Turkish.'

She looks at me. 'Turkish?'

I nod.

She looks at me. 'You go to Turkey?'

I nod again.

'You like it there?'

I keep my eyes level, mouth a silent prayer to Atatürk. Please forgive me.

'It's OK,' I shrug.

She snaps closed my passport. I reach for it, a smile appearing on my face, this whole thing easier than I thought. That wasn't so bad after all, fairly painless and they're only doing their jobs. I reach for the passport just as she removes it from sight, shakes her head firmly with a look that says *no chance*. She points.

'Over there. That room. Wait.'

▓

More than an hour I've been waiting, sitting in the bucket of a chair surrounded by people a mixture of angry, sullen, anxious.

I wonder what it was that set me here. The surname, the middle name from a Sufi poet? Perhaps the Turkish stamps in my passport. Which of those many journeys landed me in trouble, which of those family or friends shouldn't I have visited?

All around me, characters shift in and out. Border officials, security guards, then travellers landing curiously into this psy-ops exercise I have been warned can range from minor to major, with all of us hoping we wind up on the right side. They call it a random screening, which saves everyone the awkwardness of asking if it is only a racist one. One piece of advice I received was that I might be held for hours with no chance of food, brain softening and patience fraying so that hunger does the first part of the interrogation for them, primes you, sets a tongue and temper ready to give careless answers. And so I came prepared, and at Ben Gurion Airport, Tel Aviv, I've three Eccles cake from Lancashire, baked with pure butter and just waiting in case of emergency. They could interrogate me for hours before hunger showed up in this belly.

Together, we all wait. Two rows of chairs face one another in this peculiar choir of unwitting deviants and dissidents. Football plays on a television above us on the wall. Opposite I see Russians, or so I suspect from their language. There is a boyfriend and girl-friend, and a young girl on her own. Right now I don't understand what they're all suspected of, but someone waiting down the road will explain to me Israel's problem with human trafficking of Russians and Eastern Europeans for the sex trade. They come over in a couple, the girl gets left behind.

Next to me sit two Africans, Ethiopian perhaps, their crime in a racist world more obvious. The other side of me is a man in trainers, jogging bottoms, comfortable flight clothes. He takes out a notepad and I eavesdrop with my eyes, want to write too but fear incriminating myself, so I keep it all in my head. The man scribbles on his pad: *Marketing plan. Beta phase. Investment Approach. Venture*

Capital profile. I laugh to myself: maybe it is random after all? This guy will be out soon enough. None of us is given any information, there is no window by which to see any light of day, and from each agitated face I get the suspicion that Israel is intensely relaxed about the idea of everyone here deciding, aggrieved and insulted, never to come back. All of us are expendable to however this nation is to grow and whatever it aims to become. I consider whether this is about security, and then decide that, more likely, we are just not really welcome.

Opposite me are photos of the country outside: flamingos on the edge of desert, city walls in East Jerusalem, seafront in Akka, snorkelling and coral in Eilat. I look again around the sterile room in which we're held. Israel sure looks better in photos. Sitting beneath the flamingos are a couple, a particularly sad case. He must be Israeli, speaks Hebrew to our guards and makes his displeasure known. He and his wife have sheaths for their passports, matching sheaths. *Just Married* is printed on the front of them in gilt, the honeymoon off to a bad start or finish. He has long black stubble growing sparse. Large eyes behind thick-rimmed glasses, black hair, thin, receding at the temples: a studious look, like he might have read too many books for his own good and also wound up under suspicion.

'Enough,' he says softly to his wife, a voice fatigued and distant. 'No more time in this airport. Never again. The first time, OK. The second, is enough. The third, I don't know. The sixth. No more.'

But most of all it is his trainers that catch my eye, for embroidered into the upper of the right shoe is a word in Hebrew, and on the upper of the left, I suppose, its English translation. One word: *Equality.* And in all the thousand miles of road waiting up ahead I promise to remember this guy, as I ride under walls that sever Palestinian villages, as I meet Palestinians afraid to ride their bicycles because of checkpoints across the roads. I will remember this Israeli who cares so much and so overtly as to have trainers spelling out his political view.

'Julian?'

A man peers at me. I'm up.

⁞

Another room. Two officials behind a desk. A young man with fair hair and a goatee beard sits half behind a computer, an older woman stands silently at his side. They both examine me.

'First time in Israel?'

His accent is international English, placeless but vaguely American. His hair shines, gelled in short spikes. His eyes smile, real bright, like we're new pals, but in a way that feels hard to trust after two hours detained at his border.

'Yes.'

'You're Turkish? Mother, father?'

'My father.'

'You go there a lot?'

'A bit.'

'What are you doing here?'

'Cycling.'

'Cycling? You got your bike with you?'

I nod as he increases the cadence and goes speeding up on the questions, leaving me to wonder if this is a tactic, if it is intended to unnerve in the way it does. The woman at his side stays silent, mute and unmoving. Her job seems to carry a high risk of automation, maybe even a cardboard cut-out to fill her shoes. I decide that a person of innocent intent should probably sound more taken aback than I do at why all this is happening, less ready for it, less resigned.

'Why are you questioning me?'

'Just procedure. But don't ask questions. Do you know anybody here?'

I nod.

'Where you staying tonight?'

'In Tel Aviv.'

'With someone?'

'Michael.'

'Who's that?'

I don't want to get anyone in trouble.

'There's a community, touring cyclists. They host other touring cyclists.'

The surface smile in his eye goes a shade deeper. Bicycle has touched him.

'That's super cool.'

I look right back at him.

'After that?' he asks.

'I'm not sure.'

And here we step to dangerous territory, for if he asks if I mean to travel into the West Bank, Palestine, then either I have to tell the truth and prolong this interrogation, or I must lie and risk worse. Here, in these opening hours that feel so very long, is the first time in this land that I will meet with the accountancy of the soul. In a country where so much harm gets justified or excused, where life itself and right and wrong become a grey area, here, face-to-face, there still exists some oddly clear distinction between good and bad, so that I too know in my heart that I should not lie. In this procedure, I know that if I lie then I have sinned, I will have broken some eternal moral law of the playground, a thing that puts me clearly and distinctly in the wrong. And so I must play the game: Do not tell the truth. But do not lie. Think politician.

Brain steps up and into gear, wracks itself to remember what it was Leon told me. Leon was a friend back in London: Northern

Irish but from a Catholic town that, having been occupied by the British, always held solidarity with the Palestinian cause. Softly spoken, gentle in his opinions but curious for the world, Leon had grown up with a Palestinian flag flying from a mast outside his school. Unionists in the town down the road had an Israeli one. He visited Israel before me, told me of an evening at a bar in Tel Aviv. There had been an Israeli girl, border official out for a night on the town, part-way drunk, her tongue talking. She'd explained the screening system, said that being non-Western, from a country like Turkey, a man, on your own, all that was a red flag and would mark me as a hazard. That much couldn't be helped, but, 'If they think you're in the bad bracket, but that you're *doing* something in the good bracket, like just going to the beach, then that surprises them. They like that.'

My pause has gone on too long. Their eyes are intent, I think even the female official at the interrogator's shoulder just moved slightly. I go for it, make a decisive move.

'I might cycle down the coast a bit.'

And that's the truth. I don't need to mention a plan to go to any hill above Gaza. If he doesn't ask, then I don't need to lie, and my man here now only needs to hold up his end of the bargain, keep mum and think bike.

'And what do you do in the UK?'

A breath. 'I'm a writer.'

He looks, suspicious. 'What do you write?'

'I write about cycling, cycling culture.'

'What does that involve?'

I go for barefaced.

'Fashion accessories. Health and fitness. That sort of thing. Lifestyle. Very lifestyle.'

The face of the border looks at me a moment, then smiles.

'Cool, very cool.'

I look at my interrogator, leave my eyes glasslike, lifeless but for that same insincere smile he has for me, reflected back at him. And I smile at the border, I smile at him like he's the horizon and I'm just gonna keep my calm and roll right on through.

'Yeah,' I nod, 'it's cool.'

Pushing Off

The bicycle plunges down into the highway as dawn approaches. Four lanes lie mostly empty, only the occasional taxi with a driver firing a horn to relay messages I cannot decipher as I pedal towards the city. Another shrill blast comes at me, filled with whatever emotion is being felt inside that metal box. Whether by a tailwind or the gradual decline towards the sea, the road comes kindly, as if I'm meant to be going where I am going, as if no obstruction shall be presented, even if I am unclear of both my destination and my route to it. From under the road comes a smell of sewage, or at least of stagnant water. The wind breathes it clear, only to blow in with the new stench of refinery beside the domed fuel tanks of the airport.

At the roadside, I suppose, is Israel. Beyond the high and rising bank of the expressway run train tracks and freight platforms, then the equipment of a maintenance crew working the rails: a digger loaded on to a train deck, then the carriage carrying aggregate, small cubes of rock, then the bollards and lamps that will be switched on to show men at work. Concrete sleepers are stacked up, waiting for workers to awake. In everything there is a sense of industry, of mission, and beside me on my other side run uniform rows of red and green runway lights. A few planes are lifting off or landing, but somewhere out of sight, so that their only presence is the sound of engines pummelling at the sky I ride beneath.

Leaving the quiet motorway for a smaller trunk road, the earth sprouts its first razor wire, and beyond it an imposing building with blue lights then security gates that reveal *Israel Aeronautical Industries*. Pedalling on, I take it all in as the sky begins its day and lights the world anew. I look back over my shoulder, due east behind me, where a kind of blue is coming upon the black, dimming the three-quarters waning moon lying on its back. At the roadside rises an orchard, where trees are trapped beneath broad nets to protect the fruit, but the identity of those fruits is hard to make out. The familiar scrub of a universal roadside fills my vision: fencing, overgrowing grasses, piles of earth excavated then left for unknown purposes of the future. Eucalyptus trees weeping. There is something odd about finding a land so contested, so fought over, in the same banal and part-derelict state as land the world over.

The outskirts of metropolis begin. And like always, I can feel it coming, with sky lightening another shade to shine a stage light on a set. And I do not see the face that says it, and cannot make out the voice that I will hear so many times in the coming weeks, but over the rooftops and as I ride towards the waking city, I hear the question:

'What do you want to learn, and what do you expect to find?'

A band of yellow, perfect bright yellow, cuts direct above the black outline of the earth. A water tower, houses, trees. The hills behind me I keep looking round at, drinking them in with my eyes. Over my shoulder they rest, so vast and yet so gentle, calming, that they seem to lift, breathing. Yellow-black day rises into a purer yellow still, like the striped abdomen of a hornet that throbs with waiting sting. In a sudden gust of scent and the coming light, I see the fruit trees again. Citrus fills air and lemons hang from branches. Two men, Arab-Palestinian, lean against a small van with three seats up front, a door open as they wait for a third worker to make his way across the road with a rucksack and one strap falling down a shoulder. Warehousing begins: a timber merchant, planks of wood stacked up on racking outside a hangar door newly unlocked and pulled open. I ride beneath an overpass where men sit – knees up – with all their earthly belongings in bags beside them. From the shadows of a small bus shelter rolling quickly by, I realise in the corner of my eye that inside it are three faces – all Arab, Palestinian – watching the road and waiting in work overalls as they fulfil that immutable law of economics and life, that the poorer you are the earlier you must get out of bed.

A run-down concrete house, crumbling and part shuttered by sheet metal, takes up with the next hue of dawn, my favourite company. Pink does a turn on the colour wheel of this new day, and cylinders of compressed gas litter the garden to the ruin. The silhouette of the house stands flanked by palm trees, leaves fall flat down trunks grown fat and an aeroplane suddenly lowers onto the scene from on high, roaring as it comes in to land. Between railings above a doorway, a cat looks out, watching me, eyes as wide as saucers, with that word finished by its tail looping into a perfect *S*. From over the top of a wall, a clutch of vines escape, throwing themselves out of another derelict building where the leaves catch light or cast shade so that the wall becomes marbled, speckled black and green. I watch the wheel turn in front of me, the tyre humming as it makes its way along the white stitches of road markings in the quilt of black asphalt. The lights of the city shine on the metal, the alloy face of the rim. The glimmering reflection makes its way down the stainless steel of the spokes to flash on the ever-turning hub, locked in motion, stationary but constantly moving as together we roll into the city. Delivery vans line up in a narrow track leading to a depot, and as with cities everywhere – whether in its workers or provisions – the lifeblood of Tel Aviv-Jaffa is stored at the less costly margins, to be transfused invisibly to the centre each morning.

Steadily the rows of low-rise housing begin, taking over from sporadic roadside tower blocks. Restaurants appear among them, signs of leisure, of life lived. In the gutter a crow pulls at two slices of old pizza still hinged at the crust, so that pizza and bird hop down the road together. A door opens, producing a dog on a lead that pulls its owner out into the street. At a bus stop sits a man with fair hair turning grey, dressed in an old coat and old jeans. On his nose rests a pair of spectacles, a length of string attached as substitute for a chain across the back of his neck. He places a box of food back inside a bag beside him on the bus stop bench. His legs are crossed one over the other, out in front. He closes his eyes, his head resting on the back of the bus shelter. I look at him and I sense he is important, that I am about to start dealing with humans where before was just abstractions. For there he sits, tired, with a lunchbox of the food he will eat, perhaps to save the money of buying a meal, and waiting at a bus stop to go to work and support his family, or perhaps just a partner, or perhaps only himself. One way or another, this stranger I will never see again reminds me of an old faith that there are few sights more tender than a person who sleeps while on or waiting for public transport. Only now, and in my empathy for him, am I ready to begin. For here sits an honest man, tired at his early start, and – whatever my opinions, which in life can come and go so fast – the most important tool in writing is a deep and unshakeable faith that everybody is in fact good, that we were not born sinners, but innocents.

The traffic grows and the sky goes almost fully dressed in daytime. It ties a belt of cloud around its middle, a few ribbons of pink, and in its brightness comes the sense that not much further from me, the sea will open, the Mediterranean, the western border of this land that looks backwards towards the Jordan River at its eastern frontier. The sea and the river, the only two irrefutable things that make sense of all that falls in between. Over a small rise in the road, the horizon appears, opens, and I lift over it.

Michael

Catching the morning light, blue sky shines in the hub, glistening, rolling. Onwards it goes, as sun casts through the spokes that cut the shadow of the wheel, rolling beneath us on the boulevard. The tyres purr, rubber soaking with the morning heat, and my eyes move up the metal frame towards where Michael's hands rest gently on his handlebars. I follow him down the streets, his curly hair white from the sun, black-framed spectacles on his nose, in a loose vest and excited to be introducing me to his city.

'This was where it all started, the city's first bike path.'

We navigate past a coffee kiosk, people on chairs outside, newspapers unfurled and dogs tied to table legs.

'It was all parked cars and gravel, there was some crime, but they cleared it, put in the bike tracks, and it came to life. Then you got the dog walkers, the skateboarders, then the cafés, buskers, now you have people coming here for meetings, protests.' Michael smiles. 'But it all started with the bicycle.'

We roll along, pass a young woman reading a book in a hammock, a child on a scooter, a well-built man examining his biceps as he runs, dripping sweat. I look at Michael, leaning over his handlebars, his thin hair falling to just above the lenses of his glasses.

'It's really nice,' I say. 'How long did it take to happen?'

'Long enough. When we first started campaigning for cycle paths, they laughed. Said it wasn't possible. They said Israel was too hot. People didn't cycle. It was the Middle East, the wrong culture.

"People want cars." Now we've got bikes everywhere and the mayor can't stop talking about how he wants to make Tel Aviv a cycling city. The protests worked.'

We weave around a rutted section of the path, where a metal dog bowl sits, and an electric scooter glides the other way. Michael's bike is an old Dutch model, with a mudguard and pannier rack that rattles, but the handlebars are swept back so that he sits comfortably upright, regal-looking. His face is long and slender, and he gives a warm expression of humble pride as he explains their victories.

'I was thinking we could go to a place in the Yemenite Quarter for food.'

'Lead the way.'

Michael points and we pick up the pedalling into a side street. A group of African men sit on stools or squat in a huddle around a street corner. One man is washing an electric bicycle with large batteries on the frame, and wing mirrors and streamers attached to its handlebars. A bucket waits beside where he stoops, knees out and a puddle of water and suds before him and the gleaming bicycle.

'You're still involved in campaigning?' I ask.

Michael shakes his head. 'My bicycle activism is kinda over. It became this quite middle-class thing. Kinda safe. There are enough people in that movement now. The issues you're talking about, the Palestinians, people take less of an interest in.'

We pedal on in silence. Michael catches his breath.

'Where do you think you'll ride to from here?'

'I'm not sure yet. Probably Jerusalem, into the West Bank and Jericho. I think I'll go up to the north first, then down to the south. Everywhere really.'

'Sweet. You'll probably see some birds, migrating cranes flying down through the Galilee, the Jordan Valley, on their way to Africa for winter. It's really something.'

I nod politely, more curious about what he said before than any ornithology.

'I'm looking forward to getting out on the road,' I say, but then, 'What do you mean, about people not taking an interest in peace?'

'I dunno, but the word even, "*peace*", it became a cliché. Activism in Tel Aviv now it's all sexuality, animal rights, gender, being vegetarian. These days, people are more likely to go on a demo about veganism than peace.'

⠿

Opposite one another we sit with a table of bowls laid between us. The purple skin of an aubergine, charred and blackened, slumps while its insides fall out and onto my plate. Under a short boardwalk two cats fight, hissing and spitting at one another, claws out. All around us a large construction site casts its shadow, maybe a dozen stories high and curtained off behind dark mesh netting, waving with wind from the sea like the sail of an old ship. Michael pushes a bowl towards me.

'This one's *shakshuka*… it's like a tomato and egg mixture.'

I lever out an egg with my spoon and place it beside the aubergine.

'We have it in Turkey, too.' I say with a smile. 'It's *menemen*.'

Michael gestures to the restaurant, 'They do it well here.'

Together we eat in silence a while, cyclist appetites, a sort of polite vigilance about how much is on the other's plate, how much food remains unclaimed. Over speakers attached to the wall outside the café, music plays… a romantic, sentimental pop but with strings gliding through it, a wind instrument playing a charm.

'The music sounds pretty Turkish too.'

'This is becoming fashionable now. These Arabic, Middle Eastern influences and these old styles. It wasn't the case until very recently. It wasn't OK to like the traditional, like it was backward or something.'

'Same in Turkey. Neo-Ottoman they're calling it now.'

'Nostalgia, right?' Michael laughs. 'Nostalgia everywhere.'

'You think it can be good? Make people think more about history?'

'Maybe for some people. History's a strange thing. I mean, when my mother arrived here it was from Poland, right after the Holocaust, with only one suitcase. Her family were put into the large house of an Arab family in Haifa. So they were refugees here, and their home created new refugees. I always wanted to know what happened to that other family. We lost a lot of history in that time, everybody did. The Jewish people who came from Europe, they also started again, had to take new surnames, Hebrew ones.'

'That's like Turkey, too, when Atatürk said in the 1920s that everyone should take surnames to be like a Western country. A lot of Arabic words were removed from Turkish to create this new, secular language.'

'For us it was the whole thing. Hebrew, this dead script, it was resurrected from religious texts. Whatever you think about Israel, it was an amazing feat, with lessons and education to get everyone speaking it, from Arab Jews to a Jew from Hungary. European Jews had to give up their language, their Yiddish, so they left their roots behind. Really it was two cultures that got lost when they created the state of Israel. The Palestinian, but also the Yiddish.'

'Same in Turkey, sort of. People say secular Turks were ashamed of their Turkish culture, that it got lost in the change.'

Michael watches me thoughtfully from over a fork of aubergine.

'I never knew so much about Turkey, but, I mean, Israel and Turkey sort of share a history. Both new nations, under a hundred years old.'

I think about it for the first time.

'And I suppose they both have a pretty small middle class who want the country to be secular,' I suggest, 'but a population that is more religious, with politicians who manipulate that.'

'Right. And when Ben-Gurion was planning to make Israel, he was studying Turkish law, the Turkish constitution. He thought he was going to have to work with Ottomans, not the British, to get Israel. Then World War I happened and it all changed. The Ottoman Empire collapsed, the British were in control.'

'Do you think the land and the state stuff is the main problem with Palestine, or is it the religion?'

'It's both, and it's confused. I mean, some Palestinians say they're the Jews from the Old Testament. They say they were the original peoples of the land, but that they converted to Islam in the four-teenth century.' Michael points to his long, straight face with a smirk. 'They just see me as some guy from Poland! But then we don't look Polish either. You see photos of Jewish Poles, from the twentieth century, and they've got black hair, dark eyes. Polish faces are rounder, you know, like central Asian or something.'

'I guess long faces are maybe like Ethiopian, Northeast Africa.'

Michael shrugs, and maybe for a moment we both think how bizarre this curiosity about the shape of a head is. The conversation exists only because borders of a land were drawn in a certain way, and people were not permitted to move as they wished, leaving the oddity of discussing which shape of head belonged where on a map.

'The Zionists, when they first came, tried to deny that the Pales-tinians were here. They tried to say it was empty, they called it "the land without a people for the people without a land".'

'I heard "maximum land with minimum Arabs" was another one.'

Michael gives a part-shrug, part-nod. A silence returns, and for a first but not last time I feel remiss, as if I perhaps took it too far, broke the conversation, the strands of understanding that allow people to talk across their awkwardness and differences. Michael sips at a coffee, and I sense that here is the sort of guy more at home in questions than answers, the sort who knows enough about the world to prefer keeping his wisdom to himself. Finally, he goes on.

'We're divided. You have the Palestinians and us, but then we Israelis are also divided. Ashkenazi, Mizrahi…'

I look at his words, familiar-sounding but my brain in need of a reminder. Michael obliges.

'The Mizrahim… the Arab Jews. Ashkenazi, like me, that means "Northern Person", it's the Jews who came from Europe. Then you have the Sephardim too, the Jewish who were expelled from Spain. And then there are the Palestinians who live as citizens of Israel. Things change, like it's cool now in Israel to like Arab culture and stuff, but it all happens really slowly.'

Over the remains of a meal that appears so similar to so many waiting for me, at various grid references behind different lines, Michael hands over another piece of a jigsaw that I didn't know I was looking for.

'The Torah says: "*Am Israel, Eretz Israel, Torat Israel*. One people, one land, one book". Jewishness understood itself as a national project all along. The Palestinians are just starting to, because they had to when we arrived. But here, in Israel now, it feels like there's nothing to challenge the identity of nationalism, based in nation states. Something that lifts people out of that? It's hard, man, it's hard to see where that could come from.'

Armistice Road

Out into the hills, east I ride. Up to where the city can be seen in its white haze, shimmering beneath pylons lined with pigeons that first watch me and then fly their perch with a clap of wings. Beyond the last of the traffic, a liberty takes to my wheels, moving with the rhythm and reliability of each twin orbit. The bicycle works its regular spell, constructs surroundings that exist irrespective of destination or location. Uphill I climb, pedalling into a place defined by motion, where new things become possible, a place that reminds me again that the bicycle is its own country.

All around are the red earth and soft green foliage of the olive groves. Over my shoulder stand the skyscrapers so garish, the city so unapologetic and indiscreet, urging me further out, encouraging me to abandon the belongings left temporarily at Michael's, to head for Palestine and its villages clustered in the folds of the hills. However pleasant, I felt an imprecise sense that the streets of Tel Aviv held an oddness in them. There was something strange about being in Palestine, or Israel, or whatever anyone wanted to call it, but with the Palestinian existence so quiet, removed, and where Israel had made itself Palestine's gatekeeper. In Israel was the high ground of the first impression, the opportunity to moderate the opinions, people and information permitted to pass in the direction my wheels now finally roll.

Lightly I pedal, moving easily but by the same terms regretting the panniers left in the city, so that I know in advance this ride will be brief. Over the brow of a hill I see the concrete white of the 1948 Armistice Line stretched, brutal but ignored, all across the edge of Palestine. A white arrow on the road, a traffic marking, points boldly east, inadvertently also signing the direction of Israeli advance since then, its arrival in Palestine marked always by one determination: keep on pressing on. Moving steady, watching the scar of the Armistice, I recall that small North Arctic island, uninhabited but technically in the Danish waters of Greenland, and also the waters of Canada. When the Danes first claimed it as their own, it was with their flag and a bottle of liquor, which the Canadians periodically replace with their own flag and a bottle of whisky, as the territory changes hands and awaits a final settlement. I consider whether this land into which I ride might eventually be settled thus, perhaps with a bottle of olive oil from either side, left in offering for the other. One day, one day.

Standing up on my pedals, the late afternoon heat cooling, I see small, huddled houses in the distance. Impatience again wills me on, whispers to go further, across the Armistice, across Israel's wall beyond that: '*Head for Palestine*' it says, again and again, whistling up from the spokes. But a force restrains me, pulls me back and makes first my pedalling and then wheels hesitate. A sense in the back of my mind reminds me that now is an age of haste, where we hurry and so things are done too fast, and where causes get accidentally separated from their consequences. Together with the bicycle, I take just a look at what waits ahead. The tyres sniff at the road. But no, not yet, there is more for us to learn in the city, and in the wide arc of a crescent, I turn back west. One more night in the metropolis and then we will take properly to the road.

Burners

From inside his kiosk in the shopping mall he looks at me, wears a fashionable few days' stubble. The man is scrawny, sticking out of the sleeves and neck of a loose shirt, and all around him are large posters boasting the deals he offers. Unassuming though he looks, in today's world, it is this man who can best provide me with communication all across the Holy Land, and in the perfect words of neoliberal communion he welcomes me. *Yes, we have deal for you!* He gets out a clipboard with a grid on it, turns the Hebrew page and points to the English one displaying days, data, cost. I make an agreeable face in approval of the final figure for the middle option. He pulls out a cardboard pouch with a plastic card in it, a panel of silver paint to scratch away with a shekel and reveal my number: my key to the world.

'It works everywhere?'

'Everywhere!' he booms, throwing up his arms. 'All Israel.'

'I'm going to Ramallah, the West Bank. It works there too?'

'It works everywhere!' he repeats. '*All Israel.*'

'OK, sure. But I'm leaving Israel, to go to Ramallah. It works?'

He rolls his eyes, levels them on me, amused but irritated at my stubbornness. He's not going to consent to what I'm insisting.

'All Israel,' he goes on flatly. 'One country.'

'Ramallah is Palestine,' I smile. 'One day… you'll know I'm right.'

He rolls his eyes again, our disagreement total, but my money

---

appears on his counter and eases the friction. I watch as he takes a pin to the side of my phone, ejects a tray and fiddles with the SIM card to make it the right size. The two of us are under a large air-conditioning unit. At a nearby stand are lines of cupcakes and, further on, women's hosiery, stockings and tights hugging plastic mannequins standing on tiptoe, making a crook of one leg.

In some ways, I think, this man is simply unfortunate. Most of the rich world gets away with having its third world kept under military control thousands of miles away, where here in Israel it is but a few dozen distant and harder to ignore. This man is guilty of a total, racist indifference to the existence of Palestinians, but indifference is a crime of which many are guilty. I wonder how the rest of us would fare, if we saw the barbarism in which we are complicit not only on the news, but just over a nearby wall of our own construction. For though most of us like to think we would act bravely against the injustice, history suggests otherwise.

Watching the man as he thumbs at my phone a little clumsily, and despite his denial of Palestinian existence, he is not totally unlikeable. At least towards me, he is on some level pleasant, and looking at him, I realise that – just like the man dozing at the bus stop – I need him. Human society is a strange mixture of those who don't know about its ills, and those who do. That second group, though, splits again into those who know and care, and finally – the majority – those who know but don't care. This man is in the last of the categories, and by far the most dangerous, for in him is found the possibility of evil. To commit evil is bothersome, whereas to permit or turn away from an evil that nobody troubles to question is the easiest thing in the world. However differently he does it, very quickly this man, and without realising it, teaches me every bit as much as Michael. I watch him prepare my phone, and somehow I sense that here I am standing together with the key to peace. For he does not care enough to change a single thing, but nor is he actively bad.

⠿

Back outside, I restart the phone, wait for the name of a new service provider to appear. Bars of signal are found, then increase. Messages bleep, I am welcomed, and I join this new network for however long my journey will last. I find the page in my notepad with the number she had once scrawled in a nonchalant invitation. I tap it in, and wait. It rings, then clicks with connection as strangers go on walking by me, heading into the mall. A familiar voice in an unfamiliar language comes through.

'Shalom?'

'Hey, Dorit?'

'Julian? Julian, that you?'

'Yeah, I got here eventually.'

'Great, let's meet up.'

Dorit

We had to see one another, two years since that grey afternoon among the stone houses of Edinburgh. It had been Dorit's idea to begin with, after all, and though we had argued when we first met, we had argued kindly, with some shared sense that the questions of Palestine we bickered over would eventually be resolved. Her Israeli perspective clashed often against my Turkish one, and long into the night we had talked, at first with an Irish writer fresh from walking the border between Ireland and Northern Ireland. As day passed to evening, the three of us shared the same worry that lines upon maps could have come to hold such weight in the heads of those that lived inside them.

Dorit was an author from Tel Aviv, but living once as a student in New York, she'd fallen in love with a Palestinian. He was a young painter, an artist from the West Bank who'd trained in Baghdad, and there in Manhattan the two of them began a relationship impossible in their home cities only a few dozen miles apart. Her book, the story of their romance, caused a controversy when it was published in Israel. 'Promoted assimilation', they said. Risked inciting romance between Israelis and Palestinians, they said. In response the Israeli government had taken the only option they felt open to it. The text was banned by the Ministry of Education. And in that ban, the government proved there is no advert quite so good as state censorship. Dorit became a sensation.

In her blood she was an Iranian Jew, though where Farsi might once have been was now Hebrew. Whatever her ethnic background, Dorit was Israeli and that was that. Her mother and father had moved from Iran in the early days of Israel, helping to build the Jewish state, and so Dorit was a child of that new world within the Middle East, while her parents still remembered the old one. You could see the lineage maybe most of all in her proud airs, that posture of Iranians who have in them the regal sense of a country that retains some connection to the idea that, once upon a time, it had an empire and ruled over all of the world that was deemed worth ruling.

Dorit sits on her leather couch, feet up. Waves of black hair are over her shoulders and she holds her chin in her palm, thinking. Dorit's face was never far from an expression of thought, it was as if thought was how she relaxed. She trails off a comment about politics, then lightens, smiles.

'But enough of that, how do you find us Israelis, so far?'

'Yeah. You're quite direct.'

She laughs, guilty as charged.

'We are very good at being quite blunt and quite arrogant.'

'I knew that, but I didn't expect to find it so strong right away. Is it like this because as Jews you feel you're chosen people, something like that?'

'No.' Dorit pauses, enjoying the examination. 'If that was the reason then we wouldn't be like this with each other.'

I laugh. 'Is it a feeling of superiority about the country?'

'We worked hard for seventy years and now you see the fruits, that's all.'

'You got quite a lot of support from outside.'

'Look at our borders. We have a rough neighbourhood.'

I can feel us, right away slipping back to the dynamic of our first meeting.

'If Israel didn't like the neighbourhood, why move here? Egypt,

Jordan, Syria, Lebanon. Being here wasn't a great idea if people were going to have a problem with Arabs.'

Dorit sighs.

'There were twenty Muslim Arab states around here and no Jewish one.'

'Palestinians are Christians too.'

We look at one another, resolute. For a moment I am reminded that Dorit has contracted *nation-state*: that condition where, once seen somewhere, it appears everywhere. But, more than that, *nation-state* relies on others seeing the world in such a way too: that an Arab from Damascus or Cairo won't mind sharing their neighbourhood and country with an Arab removed from a home two hundred miles away, because the person who removed them decided they were the same people. The person removed from that home apparently might not mind either, because they were put among Arabs.

'You see these nice fire balloons they're now sending up from Gaza, balloons filled with gasoline? The south of Israel is burning because of them.'

'Don't settlers set fire to Palestinian crops? And your army snipers killed a hundred people in Gaza this month. What did you expect?'

'Like I say, we live in a bad neighbourhood. If it was the UK, it would have been seven hundred.'

I'm sceptical. Dorit maybe senses it.

'We are a divided country. My taxes are paying for these settlers to occupy Palestinian land. I hate it, with every drop of my blood. Many of us are fighting it. But most of these radicals and activists, believe me, have it easy. They just talk to people who already agree.'

I back down, remember the similar ease by which I can arrive with my views and leave with my views, and only be burdened by this conflict to the extent of my own choosing.

'I'm sorry. I know it must be intense.'

Dorit nods. 'And you? Are you nervous at all about riding through this place?'

I shake my head, think genuinely that it should be OK.

'I think people see bicycles, and it brings out the best in them.'

Unheard by either of us, fate is laughing at me, softly.

'I like your optimism.'

'It's the easiest way to be,' I say, and then find myself asking, naively but perhaps inevitably, 'Do you think there's any solution here? Any chance of one?'

Dorit shifts in the sofa, the leather gives a padded sigh.

'The solution, if there is one, is always one that nobody likes. Both sides have to hate it.'

I must look confused at her logic.

'Because if both sides hate it, then it means they both had to give something up. They both let go of something they said they never would let go of. Only then can it be balanced.'

Geraniums

That night was the first during occasional returns to the city that I spent in a sleeping bag on Michael's balcony. It was those rides with Michael around his city, and our conversations together, that helped me begin to understand this place. He gave me the framework to start building on, offered to make introductions, and of all the Israelis I spoke to, there was nobody I came to trust as much as him to strip away all personal ego and social graces in telling me the truth of a situation. There was a mixture of awkwardness and warmth to him, bicycles and a certainty about the equal value of people everywhere seemed to be his entire worldview, and something about that awkwardness had maybe safeguarded him as that rare sort of person who long ago gave up on the popularity contests of social life and instead just spoke of the world as he saw it.

Some of the things that he said stayed with me, returning again and again as I made my way through the changing landscapes of Palestine and Israel. Often I considered his warnings of nationalism, and so too his words about the Tel Aviv activism of sexuality, animal rights, gender, veganism. I wondered if such individual and emotional rights were where the future lay. Would Israel, and indeed the whole world, be able to forge individual and cosmopolitan identities – based on bicycles, consumerism, diet, animals or the world's climate – identities that were so strong they could transcend the need to be associated with place, and so do away with the abuses committed by nations? Or would it transpire that those cosmopolitans were content to live their liberties inside of nation states and cities, speaking the language of the universe from inside the suburbia of borders?

On some levels I was optimistic. I liked to imagine a love of animals, of body and mind, so strong that it could create new levels of empathy with the downtrodden of the world. At other times, more sceptical, I imagined a future in which animals and trees inside wealthy borders were afforded rights and accorded values higher than those given to actual people outside of them.

Still more than that, the thought I returned to most was that of the end of the Ottoman Empire, and the idea that Ben-Gurion had expected to find himself dealing with Turks rather than Britain in the creation of Israel. Something told me, and I wanted to believe, that it could all have been so different. I imagined if that new country demanded by the arriving Jews had been brokered by a culturally Muslim power of the Middle East, and not by white, culturally Christian powers from the distant west, those for whom the people of the Middle East had often been seen as only foes to be fought, or simply as lesser and to be shunted around. But it was no good wondering, for history is always just a series of unfolding accidents.

⠿

The evening before my departure for the West Bank, Michael worried for me. Didn't I need more stuff, what about planning my route more carefully? Did I know where I'd stay that night?

'I'm fine,' I'd said. 'I never really plan too much.'

He laughed. 'I'm the opposite. I go crazy planning everything. I guess I'm an over-thinker. That Jewish thing, worrying a lot.'

'Where do you think it comes from?' I asked.

'I don't know. We're just brought up that way. Obviously there's the stuff about being persecuted, but also our culture. I guess we just analyse everything. Right down to the Seder meal every week before Shabbat. We ask, "Why is tonight different to the other nights?"'

And as he said that, his Jewish culture reminded me so much of the Muslim one, enamoured with an idea of a spiritual universe, almighty and beautiful, that vested into the everyday both great meaning and an all-powerful sense of destiny.

Next morning, waking again on Michael's balcony, just as on each visit before and after it, I marvelled that a place of such peace could exist in a land of such animosity. I watched the leaves of the mulberry tree cast wide parasol shadows on the wall of the apartment, while the petals of geraniums blushed red against blue sky. Along the balcony ledge a cat picked its way, moving through the leaves of jasmine, tail curling upwards to disturb a stem holding a few white flowers that left their fragrance on the morning, still cool. I closed my eyes to darkness, to nothing, and thought to myself that this was some rare moment in which the sight of the world was actually somehow more restful than that of nothing. Were such colours really not enough to right the wrongs that take root in the hearts of men and women? A bird sang in a nearby tree, the breeze set free once again with the scent of the jasmine, and a few clouds drifted on the sky overhead, printing contentment in the briefly passing shadows they cut from the hot sun.

Jerusalem

As if a scroll, the tarmac parchment unrolls the geography of this land, showing a place where only the truest and most permanent of stories take root. Hungrily I pedal, eking out my beginning, the start of this, the first in all the miles to come. History crackles in the pebbles that tumble with the passing cattle or startled lizard down each contested rockface. And forgive me, I am loath to do it, because nothing will show the world as it is quite like those conversations coming at this roadside, but as we pedal I feel that I must give some short history of this land, a history penned as if it were watched from either another planet or the safe neutrality of a time many hundreds of years distant.

In the mid-nineteenth century the Jewish of the world began to arrive in ever greater numbers in Palestine, then part of the British Empire. This arrival was met mostly with the indifference of those Arabs who already lived here, but as numbers grew, and with them the chance of tension, some Palestinians began to warn that this would not end well, that indifference to ever-increasing newcomers would lead to the loss of their own homes. The Jewish, under the banner of the project they called Zionism, determined to organise and fight for a nation state of their own, and their paramilitaries waged a campaign regarded as terrorist by British overlords, who knew it was fought with the sole intention of driving them out.

Back in Europe the twentieth century raged. Ever more Jews arrived in Palestine for fear of their rising persecution in Europe, a tide of hate that led to the Holocaust, the Shoah, the evil that drips haunting from what the Jewish Romanian-German poet, Paul Celan, called simply '*das, was geschah*': 'that which happened'. The old continent, steeped in the horror that it had perpetrated or permitted such a thing, gave Palestinian land in compensation for European guilt, with a deal done in 1948 to grant half Palestine for a Jewish state. War followed immediately as Israel's neighbours invaded, only to be repelled, but Israel continued to expand outside those agreed borders, until eventually Arab neighbours waged, and lost, further wars in 1967 and 1973.

Come the end of those battles, all the land of Palestine up to the Jordan River was under Israeli control, along with a Palestinian population that had been made refugees by the ongoing Jewish arrivals. In the 1990s, with Israel having violated more United Nations resolutions than any other country on earth, the Oslo Peace Process was set in motion to help deliver that statehood the Palestinians had always been denied, but in the end – with a half-hearted international community, and a Jewish nationalist assassinating his own prime minister for trying to make peace – the process became a fig leaf. Israel pleaded peace even as, behind that leaf, the country went on building ever more settlements in Palestinian territory, and so undid the conditions for peace itself. Often the situation through which we will ride together is described in a language of 'both sides', and that is right, for there are two sides here, only they are not equal. One side is militarily weak, the other strong. And one side has done wrong, while the Palestinians, who are only civilians caught up in war and ethnic cleansing, have been wronged.

Believe me but it is reluctantly that I write such things, when new histories are being made every day, and these miles ahead will give you your own version of events. Humans and their pathways through the universe are complex, it is true, but that does not alter the fact that politics, often, is in fact quite simple. Be that as it may, these details aren't what you're here for, and some will always disagree with even the most careful version of events. Come now, let us take up the road.

Qalandiya Checkpoint

Razor wire cuts black diamonds out of the sky, and the diesel plume of a military jeep rises past me as the engine throbs and tyres tear dust up from the track. I see fences, walls. All sign of human life this last hour of cycling has been shut inside cars, in a road sunk like a pipe along the bottom of a concrete trench. At the end of an empty service road, where old gates fall open on their gateposts, up ahead I see a mobile home used as an office, and beside it an armoured gate, one that means business and is rolled across the road that should lead on to Palestine. A window opens, reveals a security official in a baseball cap.

I point ahead, asking, 'Beitunia? Ramallah?'

He shakes his head, points at a truck pulled in at a gravelly roadside. 'Here only freight.' He waves his arm in the other direction. 'That way.'

In the heat, I begin to pedal, doubling back on my kilometres towards the crossing, realising that this inconvenience is my first encounter with the obstructions, bureaucracies and detours by which the life of Palestine and its people has been cut up. Riding back to the main road, Israeli traffic continues flooding in its walled trench, and ever more razor wire sprouts out of the earth like man-made scrub formed from blades and rust. Another security official, dour-looking, waits at a junction, and though I am sure that now I must go left, and shortly after take a new left, I ask the way.

'Qalandiya?' I say, pointing the way I'm heading, seeking confirmation.

He shakes his head and I repeat.

'Qalandiya? That way?'

He looks at me, but in a way that appears strange, unfamiliar. It is as if he is blank, or not hearing the question. Qalandiya is the largest crossing into Palestine and I know that, wherever it is, it must be but a few miles from here. It is to the north and so it must be to our left and very soon. How could he not know? We continue looking at one another. He shakes his head and I pedal away, unsure of what it is that I am learning here, but sure that I am learning something. Riding on, a scattering of green number plates appear next to me in the cars waiting ahead: green for the Palestinian Authority, that other legacy of an old peace process, hosted in Oslo, where the Palestinians were to get control for licensing vehicles in their own state. The process forgot about the state, pulled up short, but they got the vehicle licensing.

All that though, the detail… let me leave it for another time. For now, my wheels take me on, purring at tarmac while the scene imprints itself on me in flashes. Thistles shoot from rocks, their flowers in hard, spiked explosions of harsh but beautiful violet. On the top of the barrier wall waits a line of crows, some lifting and some sitting, some flying free to circle, jet black against blue sky, the nine-metre-high concrete partition nothing but a perch to them. As I ride, I smell the earth, that Mediterranean earth of hot rock and fertile red soil, where nature conjures so many new herbs and smells, and the wind blows warm scents into your nose, as if the elements are trying calmly to speak of the magic of the world you inhabit.

At last, Qalandiya rises ahead, the nearest Palestinian camp to East Jerusalem, refugees still waiting for return since back when they were cleared from their homes: 1948, the Nakba, Arabic for 'catastrophe'. I pull in at the roadside, where a young boy kneels, buckling under the weight as he regains the finger-hold of his small hands around three plastic bags full of onions that he ferries to a kitchen somewhere. From a crumbling kerb, another boy steps down without looking, right into my path so that I swerve to avoid him. Our faces meet, only he doesn't see me, looks straight through, and I suspect that with my shorts and short-sleeved shirt, with my bicycle and its look of leisure, to him I am just another damn Israeli getting in his way. There is a difference between this place and everywhere else, though; around here, even if it is the edge of a refugee camp, beside a pile of watermelon husks and smouldering rubbish, here at least is somewhere resembling his own place, and he'll be damned if he's going to break stride for me.

Cars pull in front, one rocking on its axles and with rosaries and a cross hanging on a rear-view mirror: a first reminder that Palestinians are Christian, are Muslim, are fair-haired or Arab in appearance, are a people who have been recast as homogeneous – Muslim, brown-skinned – because the world is a racist place where it became easier to commit injustices against those who match that description. On the edge of the tarmac, where grass and earth prepare to break apart the road, lies the giant head of a sunflower, swollen with the summer, its seeds all fallen free to leave only the grey comb, as if a swarm of bees has fled its hive. I smell the dusty stones of aggregate for construction, smell the cement, smell the fumes, and then from somewhere else, from that different place called normal life, a man and a woman cross a road with a quick burst of cologne… a couple, perhaps with a date tonight, finishing their shift on the other side of the crossing, arriving here at the end of another day in Palestine.

Dressed all in black, a soldier, semi-automatic rifle pointed at the ground, stands beside a red-white sign warning Israelis they are prohibited by law from going any further. The checkpoint throbs in the heat, the thing like thrombosis in this artery out of the Middle East's heart, an organ by which you can come to understand the whole body. Lines of traffic crawl, trucks with smoke stacks burp black diesel, uniforms with weapons, and then he reappears and all I see again is the knock-kneed boy and his bags of onions making their way home to the other place. Off to one side spin turnstiles, holding pens, where women in headscarves and long coats walk hurriedly through, clutching at a shoulder bag as if the entire situation has caught them indisposed, as if any minute they could be mugged by fate in this wretched place, somewhere they were never supposed to be, returning to the home they keep as best they can but first marched through this. Laboured, deadpan faces brush up and press, one against the other, as people shut in turnstiles pass through the sealed membrane that holds Israel. Tired eyes fall closed, tired faces conserve energy, conserve dignity. Within concerned expressions are flashes of indignation, embarrassment, like this is not who they are, like they were given the wrong damn role in the play, were misassigned in the sorting office of the universe, presented with these lives when they were meant to have had ours. I see a father go through, his child behind him, and then the turnstile jams, so that the young boy is trapped by its iron hand, his father the other side in dismay, but powerless beside its metal and latch.

All around the wall runs nine metres painted with murals of martyrs, slogans of freedom, the graffiti tags of Western artists. In a section high above my head I see winches start to spin, hauling at a steel cable which in turn – *clunk* – hauls a heavy iron-panelled gate ajar. It slides, lifting out of the concrete to reveal the headlamp eyes of an armoured jeep. Below the menace of a radiator grille, the wheels pull forward with tails of dust, making their way towards the camp where an army monitors a perimeter holding refugees behind concrete walls. With a punch in the stomach you first realise and then feel on a deeper level that 'dystopia' is in fact only a word that describes a present somebody else is already living.

Beneath everything, together, me and the bicycle roll quietly through the margins. The bicycle and me, same as always: half man, half machine. For by its metal tubes and cogs, this vehicle locates me inside the mechanical world, and so I stick to the road rather than the turnstiles, but I glide by the waiting traffic because the drivers and the guards can see I am in fact really only a human on a bicycle, faintly ridiculous to them, and pedalling. I make to stop beside another soldier, another semi-automatic held to an overfull belly. The man is dressed in black rather than the green fatigues of the Israeli army, meaning that he is private security, mercenary. In his black shirt, combat trousers and boots, this man belongs to a new age, one without need of conscripts, where states can raise a force, go to war, or run an occupation without troubling the sons and daughters of their voters. Just pay the invoice and in you go. Me and the mercenary look at one another, alien species in search of common ground: his semi-automatic faces my bicycle, his flak jacket meets the orange checkers of my open shirt. We look at one another. 'Passport?' I mouth, doing his work for him, saying something to stop the heavy silence. He almost sneers at me, so that I realise right away that he is not interested in me, that it is easier to get out of Israel than to get in, and then, quietly, I read a thought spoken silently in his mind but loud in the way he looks at me:

'Why are you doing this?'

And though I do not quite have an answer, and though I reject the sneer in his glance, on some level, I can't help but feel the question is a good one.

⠿

Through the crossing, through the chaos, a semblance of peace settles in the air. Bustle begins, the music of village life, bringing the sights of daily errands and the sound of things fitting back into their rightful order. Drenched in heat, I pull to a halt beside a stall, below a billboard advertising a Palestinian mobile phone network that knows before I do that the man selling SIM cards in Tel Aviv told a lie, and mine will not work beyond these walls. Under the billboard stands a man in a fez and red waistcoat, tending to three large buckets kept in a puddle of shade.

'*Tamer, Tamer, Tamer*,' he calls out, coming at me with a plastic cup he fills from a tap with a little brown liquid. I drink, sip, taste herbs and some sugar, but mainly I taste cold and that cold it tastes so sweet. I point to the other buckets, ask their contents with a lifted eyebrow.

The man points to one. '*Lemonade*.' He points to the other. '*Kharoub*.'

And I shake my head uncertainly, so that he opens the tap and in another plastic cup gives me two fingers of a second rich brown drink. I sip, the flavour comes slowly and he repeats – *kharoub, kharoub* – as the possibilities of this chocolaty liquid run through my mind and then lead me with a look of recognition to the right word, hidden in plain sight: *carob*. I go for lemonade and the man reaches again for a new tap, letting flow a yellow liquid with soft chunks of yellow-white fruit floating through it. He hands me the cup and I sip, gasp happily, a chunk of lemon making its way into my mouth, but its sharpness all gone and soft to chew as I drink it down and feel my eyes smile.

The man smiles back, a proud bartender with a satisfied customer. He tosses away the plastic cup in which I tried the *kharoub*. Over his shoulder it sails to settle against a rock with all the other cups, plastic bottles, gnarled metal drinks cans and cardboard boxes falling away where the natural scrubland meets one of human litter.

I consider this a moment: a refugee camp, the people displaced from their homes, from the homes of their parents and their grandparents, living under military occupation but me belonging to a world so peaceful we were left with the luxury of time to worry about plastic waste. Habits die hard and, just because there's an occupation to deal with, well, it wouldn't harm to keep the place a little cleaner, and this could be such a pretty roadside. With a smile I lift up my palms, gesture towards the empty plastic cup, now full of sunlight where it rests on the earth, a gentle *whaddyadoing?* sort of expression on my face.

'Do you have a bin?' I laugh, holding up my lemonade in my hand, making a circle of my arm and dropping the cup through it to try and illustrate my quandary.

The man looks back, meeting my smile with his own, a playful roll of his eyes but also a nod, as if he gets my point and has been meaning to get round to it, but really, haven't I heard? He makes a sort of gentle look... *what's a guy to do?...* and as the guns stroll by, the turrets watch over us and the razor wire flows down the hill, his kind look reminds me that round here, they have had bigger things to worry about.

Mohammed

My bicycle is on its stand outside the café: just a few tables with stools where people drink tea. At the adjacent table a man sits, dressed in a light rain jacket with a high, rigid collar. It looks windproof, waterproof, good gear. He's young, has a full beard, wears a baseball cap, and beside him leans a bicycle with a tapered frame for downhill riding: off-road but the thing well kept, shining under the lights. Unashamedly we look at one another's bicycles, then at one another, smile a look of recognition, family. He introduces himself. Mohammed. We lean across, shake hands and he gestures at my bags.

'How long have you been riding here?'

I stutter in answer, for I think that Mohammed can sense that I just arrived *here*, beyond Qalandiya, but that is not exactly what I'm being asked. I prepare to say that I got to Israel some days ago, yet the word 'Israel' sticks in my mouth, like I know the weight it carries. The land between the river and the sea is broadly what he must mean by *here*, and 'Israel' is certainly not *here* but, if anything, *there*, and is not the question I have been asked. I compromise.

'I got to Tel Aviv a few days ago.' I smile, content that there is no dispute that there exists a city called Tel Aviv, before remembering the Arabic part of its name.

'Yafo, I mean.'

'Jaffa?' Mo corrects me with a smile that understands these distinctions are crucial but also trivial. 'How long are you in Palestine?'

'I'll probably ride around for a while, then back to Israel, and then more in Palestine.'

I wonder if this is more acceptable, to mention Israel in this way, as someplace else. I will ride *back to* it precisely because it is not *here*.

Mo sips his tea, amused at it all, like he knows my thoughts. I wonder what is better: *to Israel*, as if it were a distinct place, a destination ... or *into Israel* as if the land were just that, land, territory, and no different to how I would ride *into* the mountains or *into* trouble.

He says it gently: '"Israel" is a problematic word for us.'

I nod my understanding and then Mohammed changes the subject, gestures at my bike.

'Nice wheels.'

'Thanks. It seems like there are a lot of bikes here.' I pause again. 'And there. Like cycling is really popular.'

'It's growing. I think more people are riding these days. The Giro d'Italia came to Jerusalem last week.'

'I saw. Was that a big deal for Palestinian cyclists too?'

Mohammed scoffs. 'It didn't come *here*. An Israeli billionaire paid for it to happen. They wanted to show Jerusalem like it was one city, an Israeli city.'

'Did many Palestinian people go to watch?'

'I know some people with travel permits. They went to watch it finish in the city.'

'Did you?'

Mo shakes his head, smiles. 'If I am honest, if I was allowed to travel to see it, I would have gone. It is a big bike race and I love cycling. I thought it was an OK thing. We have a cycling club, near here in Ramallah, so someone from Dutch media interviewed me about it. But I was tricked, they said they would tell both sides of the story, but when they made the edit, they just showed me saying it was good, that I would like to see it. I also said many things about how we can't cycle because of Israel's checkpoints. About a cyclist in Gaza who was shot in the leg, by Israel, the day before the race. The TV people tricked me, and then the Palestine cycling community got angry at me.'

Mo waves a resigned hand, dismissive.

'Were there protests at the race?'

'The Palestinian Cycling Union did not say anything about it, so as a cycling community we had no message. Last month, some riders from Israel and Palestine went to Europe, the Alps, and because again we had no statement, we were also used. They call it "Peace Ride" or something. Like it's all about peace, never the cause of the conflict. Some people wrote a letter to the union, saying how we need to be more anti-normalisation.'

He says the words as if the meaning is obvious.

'What's that?'

'Anti-normalisation?' Mo checks with me. 'Some people want to pretend the occupation is normal, and we just need peace.' Mo gestures towards the fortifications around the camp. 'But living like this is not normal. How can we have peace like this?'

A part of me is impressed to hear that Palestine has a cycling union, that there are cyclists irritated that their union isn't representing their views adequately. A part of me is impressed, but soon, with these encounters piling up, it will stop being so, and I will realise that this reaction of mine patronised the Palestinians and misunderstood their cause. For Palestine already has all of the institutions, rights, expectations and organisations of a state, only no state to put them in. They can have a cycling union, grievances, angry letters, but still no state.

'Is cycling popular all over Palestine?'

'There is a strong community, yes, I would say so. Go to Hebron, there are good riders there. You should meet my friend, Sohaib. He started a club.'

Mo takes out his phone, takes pen and paper, writes down a number and hands it over.

'And with Israel? Do you think cycling can help bring people closer, build relations, maybe through the cycling community?'

'I met Israelis. When we were riding on trails. I had some experiences that were good, but most, almost all, were bad. I don't want to say things about it, but some were really bad. People always say things about us.' He makes a shooing gesture. '"*Arabs go away!*" they say. For us it is safer to ride trails than roads, because there are no military, no checkpoints.' Mo looks wistful. 'It would be nice, road cycling.'

I look at him, something in him sort of punk, another of the rebels of this world who somehow, believing it could all be different, find their way to the bicycle. He gives a smile.

'A few times we got into settlements with our bicycles. These are the most dangerous places for us. Most settlers are armed, security could come, but because we had modern bicycles, clothing, I think people think we are from the settlement. We rode last weekend, in a group, we started early morning in the settlement. We were all very quiet, it would be dangerous for us to speak Arabic, but the trail we wanted to ride started there, so we went.'

'Why didn't you just pick up the trail in,' I pause, 'open country?'

Why I ask it I am not sure, and I am instinctively embarrassed even to have done so, suggesting Mohammed sneak around like a fugitive in his own land, as if it were he who was illegal. Mohammed looks at me, steel in his glance, but checked by politeness. He knows the answer. I know the answer. I believe he knows that I know his answer and so too does he guess correctly that it would be the exact same one as my own. He looks at me. Straight. A pure rider.

'Because I wanted to ride the whole trail. From the start.'

———

⁜

Pedalling slowly south along the road to Jerusalem, thinking back on Mohammed's words, I realised the occupation had forced every Palestinian to become an activist, a lobbyist, a minor political thinker, and for the simple reason that politics was everywhere. Compared to people in Tel Aviv, there was something different in the way Mohammed had spoken. Intuitively you could sense not who it was that was in the right and who in the wrong of this conflict, but who had the power. As I thought about it, even that word seemed wrong. For what waited all around felt less like a *conflict* and more like a chokehold, where everything was locked, static and unmoving. In Israel, there had been an ease to the way people spoke of the occupation. Even if they were opposed to it, still there was a liberty with which they were willing to talk about it, to stretch their mind and exercise thoughts for its being there. The idea of its existence or its resolution was like a walk on a weekend afternoon… a minor exercise, perhaps even an exertion, but not too much of an inconvenience.

Beside all that, I considered Mo, saying that he did not want to talk of the insults he suffered, of the bad experiences out on the trail. In Palestine it was different, there was little desire to mention it, and where the subject arose, it would come only slowly, with the beginnings of trust, as if life demanded a great and constant labour with this burden anyway, and so why would anyone incur the fatigue of talking of it again? The occupation was Israel's to discuss because it was also theirs to alter, while in Palestine, people had simply to persevere.

Neta – West Jerusalem

That night I made for the home of an old friend living in West Jerusalem. Neta and I had first met a decade earlier, back when she spent her days waiting tables in a north London café and in the evenings would make her way to gigs around the city, a keyboard strapped to her back and an amp on a pull-along trolley. Determined to make it in London's music scene, she'd created for herself a stage name, Stella, and sometimes she'd call herself by that name and other times by her own… she'd tell me that Stella was feeling down lately, but things with Neta weren't so bad. In all ways, she was a character.

We became friends in that café, and though we'd mostly lost touch across those ten years, we'd once bonded over a shared fondness for Tom Waits. In one another's eyes I think we each became one of those people that you sense – however far away – you'll always be able to travel alongside, because you have something in common that goes beyond the passing of the everyday life events you no longer share. When I got in touch to say I'd be riding through Israel, Neta told me she'd be around, gave me her address and phone number to pass to immigration if they started giving me trouble at the border, asking who I was visiting and why. She'd guessed how it might go, had always alluded to what Israel was like on the inside, but it was only seeing her there that I realised the extent of her understanding. From all the years outside it, as maybe is often so, she had come to know her country well.

We sit in the kitchen, the room is cool, an old Arab house made from large stones. The Colonial Quarter. Baka. The lower floor of the apartment is set half below ground level, perfectly attuned to its climate so that the shelter of the earth wards off the day's sun. Wide tiles stretch from the kitchen to the far end of the living room, where a grand piano – white – is waiting with its lid raised. Strings, springs, hammers: it all stands ready with the anatomy of sound, of pre-sound. A ledge is set into the long wall of the house, runs its length and holds a few colourful pebbles, the branch of an olive tree, perfectly smooth and aged grey. A lamp is made from a triangular frame with a canvas shade. At the window are the shapes and shadows of bougainvillea, its flowers bright, the sky a hot and dusty blue beyond them, that hue that in Greece they call *Attica sky*, a blue washed white by heat and which exists unique, unmistakable, all across the Mediterranean. Outside a rare breeze comes, a petal breaks from its flower, pink flutters down.

'I lied,' and Neta's wide, dark eyes look so innocent. 'I said I was an Orthodox Jew, and so I couldn't go to the army. I knew I couldn't do it.' She gestures to her piano. 'I'm a musician, and it might sound crazy, but I couldn't be part of these things. But my brothers, they went.'

Neta pauses, offering the service of her siblings to reassure me of something, or to demonstrate why her instinct was as it was. She takes a thick bang of black hair and places it behind an ear with a pearl in it. A smile hides and her eyes sparkle with the look of an artist or a fantasist, trying to keep her spirit in a land that casts her on the side of the oppressor.

'I can't remember what year my first brother went. But now they both have trauma.' Neta says it so matter of fact, like it was as inevitable as going out without an umbrella and getting wet.

'They were serving during a war, an incursion, into Gaza. And their battalion was at the front, so that every day they were made to be ready. Shouted at, prepared, waiting, every morning. Face paint, camouflage' – she paints it on with her fingers – 'everything ready. Waiting, all day, day after day.'

'And then they went in?'

Neta shakes her head, places her fingertips down on the marble tabletop, slides a bowl of pistachios and salted almonds towards me.

'They spent all that time just waiting, like it was about to happen, like they could go to war any minute. It is common. My house-mate, Aharon, will tell you about the army. He is a nice guy, now he is trying to start a gardening business. A bit crazy, but a nice guy.'

'Crazy in what way?'

'From the army,' Neta says nonchalantly. 'He has trauma.'

She gives a shrug, suggests that's enough of an answer for how trauma happens. Without saying so, I wonder if the experience of her brothers is in fact that of all Israel, perhaps more literal, but in essence no different. Everyone just waiting for the war to come.

From the next room a phone rings, and Neta unpeels herself from the chair, covered by the pluming black folds of a long skirt. She skips over the tiles, a sparkling pair of slippers flash over the stone. Passing the piano, lazily she lets her fingers release some latent energy, trailing a hand along it. Hits two keys, a third. Inside the grand instrument, strings pull, hammers strike. Doh– re – mi. The notes lift, linger, rising up to the low ceiling, expanding to fill the air where they hang and reverberate.

'Shalom?'

She answers, walking up and down the far room as I wait and play with the shell of a pistachio on the tabletop, the pink skin of the green nut falling from its case. Neta paces, appearing and disappearing, and I consider whether all this talk is too much, if she is burdened by these thoughts and would rather forget them.

She puts down the phone and the sound of slippers steps back to me, slapping the tiles gently. She lifts back on to her chair, knee up, arms holding it towards her so that she hugs at herself. Her eyes are kind, asks where we'd got to.

'That was my costume designer. We have to make a very important dress, with paper swans floating on it, for a concert performance later this year.'

She enjoys the extravagance of it and I smile, thinking that Neta is perhaps not your typical Israeli, but then that she is not your typical anyone.

'Do you ever feel like you don't really belong here?'

'I was born in Argentina, remember?'

I shake my head. I'd forgotten.

'My family is from there, so the start of my life was not here. Then, when I was twenty, I lived for those years in London, working those cafés, playing my music.'

'What happened to that in the end? I guess we lost touch.'

She laughs. 'I was going to get a passport, I had even done my citizenship test for your Queen, everything, and then I had to leave.'

'How come?'

'I'm not good with numbers, and in the UK you put the number of the day and month the other way round to us. It was stupid of me, but I got confused and overstayed a visa, so I had to leave. And then when I went back to my application there was that immigration offence, so I lost my years.'

The words 'lost my years', so accidentally full of the bureaucratic punishment that fills the space between borders and life. She sucks in her lips, cheeks pursed with a sad smile of no words worth saying. I feel for her. But here we sit, in such perfect surroundings, a skylight shooting a column of light down to skewer the turquoise of an Iznik tile in the floor.

'Is it so bad here?'

Her face answers, straightforward but at the same time apologising for itself, as if she'd rather not make a fuss.

'The racism is. Here people walk down the street being racist: about Arabs, Muslims, black people. Whoever. That would not happen in London, it is not normal, someone would say something. When I moved to this house, I saw an advert for a removal company, hiring. *Hebrew speakers only* it said, which is discriminating against Arabs. So I will never use this company. I know someone who owns a house that she finds hard to rent because people know her politics is on the left. My last relationship ended because my boyfriend had worked in security and he wanted to keep a gun in the house.' She gives a nervous laugh, 'And maybe it is just my Jewish mind that worries, but I wasn't comfortable with that. The children here are all medicated, because of life like this. I give music lessons now, and you can tell when they come for piano class if they have had high doses, because they can't focus. Drugs are the easiest way to control their minds.'

Neta points to her record collection.

'I am sensitive to noise here. When I first came back, I listened to a lot of Bach to clean my ears. I couldn't listen to music with lyrics. People want to pretend that what is happening is not so strange, but it is. Yes, we should stop people in Gaza putting gasoline in balloons and sending them over the wall to burn farmland, but to stop that, first you ask why they are doing it.'

'Is there enough momentum for that inside Israel?'

'Some try. I have a friend, his child was killed by a Palestinian bomb, fifteen years ago maybe. It made him an activist, he organises a lot against the occupation, demonstrations, together with Palestinians. He gave his whole life to it. There are people like this.'

'Did you ever go to anything like that, in the West Bank?'

'Once, but Israel makes it illegal for us to go there, so it is difficult. I remember being in the car and I was so afraid when we stopped at the checkpoint.'

'What do you do in that situation?'

'You hope they don't catch you. People have their tricks for driving there, they tune the radio station to a nationalist Israeli one, the one the settlers listen to. And they told me to take off my shoe and put my foot up on the dashboard,' Neta laughs at my expression. 'Apparently that is how the settler girls sit.'

It strikes me, as Neta looks at me, willing to face whatever change takes, that others I spoke to and will speak to seemed more afraid than she: afraid of the future to such an extent that they could tolerate the now. Neta, meanwhile, smiling soft, her eyes shining as if she comes from another place and none of this makes sense anyway. Neta, I realise, is the opposite. She is unafraid, and she will risk the future because she cannot tolerate the present.

'When the occupation ends, in the end, it will happen so fast. But… I think it will have to come from outside.'

'Like you need the outside world to help you see yourself?'

Neta ponders my words. She uncurls her knee and resettles herself as if to look clearly at the concept, square in the face. Finally, she gives a small nod of approval, as if my words will do.

'You should go out, explore a little. See for yourself.'

I nod, but find myself asking that last large question, almost timidly.

'What do you think will change things? What would make the difference?'

Her answer is right on the tip of her tongue: 'Sanctions.'

Home Truths

Out of Baka I rode steadily up the hill, beside a disused railway line converted to a walkway and a string of uniform cafés trying hard to give some sense of personality. A sign in front of a bar sported the US and Israeli flags with the word *JerUSAlem* large through the middle. A crowd came gliding towards me on two-wheeled platforms that gave out the buzz of battery power. Young people rode along, smiling smiles of perfect teeth and each one motionless, holding a handlebar raised in front of them as they went cruising at the head of that electrical hum. They wore sunglasses, US accents called back and forth to one another, and as we passed I saw their emblazoned T-shirts and matching backpacks with the words *Birthright Israel* across them: the organised tours that paid to bring those with any Jewish connection to visit Israel, and perhaps then move to the country for good. Over their smiling faces, flown in from far away, I imagined the refugee village at Qalandiya… barely a dozen miles distant and over half a century since the arriving Jews had first cleared the Palestinians.

Jerusalem, I soon found, was nothing like Tel Aviv. Hasidic Jews in hats and long black jackets walked the streets, read from religious texts while they waited for trams, and stood pressed together in crowded buses. Guns became more present, too, and the olive-green uniforms of Israeli conscripts huddled around public transport, while the large boxes of X-ray machines and metal detectors checked each bag going into a bus terminal or shopping mall.

Set back a little from the road, I saw the ornate stone wall of the Damascus Gate, leading down into the old city of East Jerusalem, the Palestinian half of the city, but its entrance policed by Israeli security forces stationed inside a booth. I watched as they called a young Palestinian boy to their position, had him take off and unzip his rucksack, inspected it a while and interrogated him before allowing him return to his day. The boy hurried on, and I watched as he sprang down through the gate, moving by a line of old Palestinian women, dressed despite the sun in snug woollen cardigans and holding wicker baskets, from which they sold yellow plums and bunches of sage tied with twine.

Riding onto the main road, working slowly up a long hill as cars moved by, I saw the King David Hotel, with palm trees outside and the ornamental stones of the façade soaked with sun. In its golden letters the name jumped out at me, for that very hotel had once housed the British Authority in Palestine, blown up in 1946 by Jewish terrorists determined to win their own freedom and state. Nearly a hundred British staff had died in the bombing, and in 1948 the goal of the terrorists was achieved and the state of Israel founded, at which point, I supposed as I pedalled on, they became freedom fighters.

iii

Outside of the café I drink my coffee, break from pedalling the hills of Jerusalem, which tire my legs while the tension of a divided city weighs in my thoughts. The café garden is mostly quiet, but the voice of one man keeps grabbing my ear, speaking English in an Israeli accent. My chair is facing the opposite direction, but out of the corner of my eye I can make him out, just, seated with a friend. Olive skin, bald head, an unrelenting baritone not exactly loud but with a force to it. Sun is shining through the leaves on to our café forecourt and the shadows of branches are across his face. The companion says something I don't catch, looking down the barrel of the hairdryer he sits opposite, gently roaring in his face. A half-century friendship and you suspect from the body language that every week this guy roasts him just like this, tells him the world as he sees it. The speaker sips from a glass cup of black tea, his friend in a baseball cap, back to me.

'He's a corrupt bastard.'

I can't help but glance round. The speaker looks grandfatherly, like some sort of a mafia don. Round belly, clubs for forearms. A warm face that seldom smiles but you sense that, when it does, it's real good, real kind. Gandolfini. The guy has Mediterranean blood and a pitch of passion that is nonetheless delivered in measured fashion. His voice is deep, angry, but reassuring, in a way that somehow feels under control. He goes again.

'He's a corrupt...' he pauses, meticulously, to let that word settle before again adding the second: 'Bastard.'

Then he runs with it.

'Netanyahu took a lot of money because apparently the family doesn't make enough from the government already. He's a corrupt bastard, that's what he is. A corrupt bastard.'

The man's partner in coffee says something inaudible.

'He's not strong, we're not. In 1967, in six days, we destroyed the nations of six countries. Now we can't even destroy Hamas. We are not strong, but we have no threats and there is no opposition to stand against him. When I was in the army we had Iraq. Gone. Jordan. Safe. Syria. Gone. Now we have no threats, they are all imagined, while he corrupts the country. *Steals!* The Health Minister – *is a Rabbi!* Why? Every prime minister of Israel, left or right, always cared about Israel. Bibi Netanyahu is the first one that cares only about himself. He's corrupt. He uses fear and the religions for himself. Palestinians, the conflict, it is just to distract from the corruption. If the occupation could be ended tomorrow, he still would not choose to do it.'

Shuffling in my seat, considering the number of reports I'd have to read to get to this sort of insight. Make this guy a minister already. Mark my words, it will not always be found there, and for every soothsayer will be a half dozen mavericks, but no truth can ever take hold until it has been spoken with feeling over coffee in the morning. I steal another glance their way: the day's paper has been bought but scarcely read, is hardly even a prop, reduced to lining the furniture like a tablecloth, to stop forearms sticking in the humidity to the hot metal. In figuring out the truth, there is a careful equation by which daily news must be read but also ignored and this guy has the balance just right. It's to be digested rather than swallowed. News is like food… if you don't chew it a little for yourself, you get problems in your guts.

Turning away, I try and regather my own focus. I should control myself. Looking over my shoulder so much, shuffling in my chair, notepad open, so clearly tuning my ears to their conversation. The guy's going to think I'm undercover, a cop, like Mossad has staked out the café and sent a man with a bicycle to eavesdrop. The corner of his eye watches the corner of mine. All the blood is in my ears, setting off sirens and letting him know what I'm up to, but my brain is desperate not to drop a single word he says.

His back to me, the silent partner in coffee says something, inaudible. Edgeways he gets a word in, before his friend resumes.

'I'm not saying there's a solution, but even if there isn't, why keep sending more settlers, more troops? Why go creating hate for propaganda, why go on TV every time making us look dumb. He doesn't care about Israel. Why aggravate it all? Let them be I say, let them be!'

Damn, someone give this guy a radio show. The man's voice is aggrieved, a little irate but nonetheless persistent because the human brain carries an innate aversion to being patronised or deceived. In an instant, I realise it, it passes in one complete and single swoop. Blow me, but if politics in the modern age is merely the act of defining an in-group and defining an out-group, and telling your righteous in-group that they're threatened by the unrighteous out-group, then, suddenly, shit. But it all makes sense. The occupation, I just realised, but is it… surely not… only the ultimate act of political theatre?

Hizma

All that day I spent riding, heading through Jerusalem, out of it and back in. Aimlessly I followed roads that orbited and fed the city, unaware of how time and the daylight went drawing in. To the north I saw Israel's vast settlements, like holiday homes on the Costa del Sol. To the east, shut away behind concrete and sheet metal, I passed refugee villages where Palestinians' shacks were clustered inside walls. The Israeli wall, its concrete with occasional razor wire and watchtowers, loomed over everything so that only the crows passed above, their black bodies floating down, wings spread and hanging against the bright blue sky. Over valleys and hillsides I rode, seeing across the land those outlying settlements built right up on the crests of hilltops – blatant, staked-out and walled-in – as if the settlements had been thrown up by crusading armies. That was the first day the religiosity of the land itself became clear to me, as I realised that I was riding a road, up to the high hill of Jerusalem, that had been coveted for centuries. Below and to my east began the desert, and at the horizon I saw the future plan for Israel, where there was intention to build a swathe of settlements stretching so far east that the West Bank at its narrowest point would become scarcely the width of a road. In this expanse of an annexed and sprawling city, Jerusalem would serve almost as an urban roadblock, a city checkpoint, stationed between Hebron in the south and Ramallah and Nablus to the north, finally making a Palestinian state unviable.

Winding around a wide bend, way up high and level with the opposite settlement of a far hill, I stopped and drank the last of my water. The road was carried on concrete stilts struck deep into the meeting point of three hills that formed a small gully. A rusty chain-link fence threw a shadow net of diamonds on the ground below, where a few blades of dry grass shot through the gaps. A fig tree stood lonely on the hillside, the last of its windfall shrivelling perfectly on the crash barrier where it had dropped like dried fruit at a forgotten market stall. Cars swarmed back towards Jerusalem as I looked over the distant land, spreading in shades of yellows and greens. A few clouds, pulled thin, moved over the sky on winds high up. Here gathering and there pulling apart, they formed arrows and diagrams, like borders, rivers and townships all set on the drawing board of the sky, a bright blue stretched with thoughts waiting to be manoeuvred into shape.

Below me were a couple of small buildings attached to a home that looked makeshift but as though it had been there a long time. Two veins of brown earth trickled down to it, a track, where the scrub had worn thin and then been cleared by a lifetime of a family in their comings and goings. I saw the broad leaves of a plant beside a tap, where someone had emptied a bucket rinsed of plaster, so that the leaves were all painted with a heavy dust. Next to one of the outbuildings with a sheet-metal roof was a run of golden straw bedding, which a small horse with a white-grey coat and a black mane trod at slowly. I watched as the animal shook its mane and tail to disturb flies visible only by its movements. A young girl stepped out of the home, picking over two old bicycles that lay rusting on the ground, and turned a tap and pulled a hose towards the horse's water trough. I watched her, this girl that I suppose I must describe to you, to paint this picture, as Palestinian, but only because the contours of this struggle demand the label. Really, she was just a girl: Palestinian, Israeli, Arab, American, British, German, Iranian, Chinese. By each name, she was just a girl.

Looking down at her, as the settlers on their hilltops must have looked down on the Palestinians, I realised then how much of the architecture of Israel – its roads and its housing settlements – was constructed higher than the Palestinians, elevated. For a moment, I remembered life as a courier in London, where delivering up in the skyscrapers of bankers, the supremacy of altitude left you to look down at the little people of the city, all of them just dots, somehow hard to care about as they carried on with their small, inconsequential lives, way, way down.

⠿

Kids with guns are hanging around as I crest a final hill, longer than all the rest, the sweat of my body forming silver rivulets on my shirt. The troops look uninterested, stand in green-conscript and black uniforms. Some seem to look right through me, like I can pass; others tip their heads and take a second glance at the bicycle. Eventually I will realise that checkpoints are really just the weighing scales of entitlement, of privilege. If you can roll up with enough of the stuff, don't consider stopping because, well, why would you … then you're through. It takes a Palestinian an awful lot of front and nerve to reach that weight, to smuggle themselves past, while the Israelis are born into chutzpah. Someone once told me that if you're approaching a checkpoint, you should always go to the gate of the white male soldier, the Ashkenazi man, for he is the one with most privilege in this society, and so it is he who least itches to either demonstrate loyalty or exercise power, things so encased within his being that he scarcely notices them. The Mizrahi male or female soldier, even the Ashkenazi female soldier, all have a lesser place in the hierarchy of Israeli society and so, humans being what they are, will take his or her checkpoint moment to flex a little authority over someone above whom they now enjoy supremacy.

Israelis have told me that this explanation was reductive, nonsense, but then so were the checkpoints. Not once did it prove untrue.

Slowing my pedalling, I half-focus at the soldiers through the sweat in my eyes. The hill has been long, the heat unrelenting. A taller guy in a black uniform, private contractor, mercenary, strides out of a booth towards me. The dark gunmetal of his semi-automatic points down from where it hangs, ugly jewellery, heavy at his neck. He waves his hand, though makes no eye contact, and I cannot tell if he waves down at the ground to halt or on at the road to go, and his scowling face and the semi-automatic both raise the stupid stakes in this rotten place and make it important not to guess incorrectly.

I call over, through the engines idling, the heat reflecting back off desert metal, everything so loud and uncomfortable.

'You want me to stop?'

He waves his hand some more, still unclear, shouting Hebrew while my body's muscle memory is still grappling with the hill just finished. Head fuzzy from traffic and heat, guns weren't meant to be on my mind. He waves again, still unclear, then shouts. 'ID!'

I stop, presume he means passport, but I do have a photo ID nearer to hand, British flag and all, so I hand it over. He takes it without acknowledgment, walks off, walks tall, but with his shoulders hunched in his black polo shirt, combat trousers, combat boots. I wait, watch as he returns from a gathering of officers, steps out of the huddle with a child in olive green fatigues and another semi-automatic. The arrival in green is public sector, a dumpy kid but raised well, carries a slight air of maybe being the superior to Black. He walks up. Full, rosy cheeks, a military haircut but a gentle face hiding in there. Shame about the gun. He comes up, stammers at me politely in decent English, kinda eager to help.

'Travel documents. You have visa? Passport?'

I go into my bag, watching the two similar but distinct species of combatants as they watch me. I consider this child soldier in green: he's a soldier of the occupation, but then, also only a kid who inherited the sins of his parents, no different to the rest of us. I wonder what he will do with that inheritance. If he will again pass it on? Does he want to change it, and even if he does, is that even still possible? My fingers fidget on a bag buckle, Black talks to Green, Tweedledum to Tweedledee and the kid in green so much more likable, mannered, I suspect educated. A good upbringing is stamped all over him and now shines a little from the calm in his eyes. One day I know he will be gone from this place, national service over and he on his way to better prospects. These days will become nothing but memory and nostalgia. Black: born of a different neighbourhood, from a different school and story… he just needs a job and has found one here in the security economy that relies on the occupation. He'll still be around, manning this checkpoint, surly and bad-tempered for no reason more than the fact that, push comes to shove, his is a shit job. In Israel he is just a poor kid, but with the help of Palestinians and a checkpoint, he gets to be a big shot.

As I retrieve my passport, looking at both of the young faces, I see clearly that the occupation reproduces itself, that it reproduces its own mental pathways. I wonder what hope there is for Palestinians when the only Israelis they meet are those that police them. And I wonder what hope for the Israelis when each new generation, boy and girl, has instilled in them the opportunity-cum-duty to corral and patrol the Palestinians as a rite of passage in their formative years.

I step up to them, passport in hand, leafing through pages and looking for the barcoded slip the border control gave me instead of a stamp on entry, so as not to compromise future travels in those nations of the Middle East that do not recognise Israel. I try to leaf through the pages, but my hands are still set to grip handlebars and help me heaving round on pedals. Body was not thinking of fine-motor skills like picking one page from the next in search of that damn slip and the sudden change of task is somehow too much. The pages move on the wind, dance away from my reaching fingers, moving forward and back uncertainly. Green looks up at me, concerned, 'Why are you shaking?'

Internally I roll my eyes: bicycle beside me, sweat all through and obviously nobody told him Jerusalem was a city on top of a hill. The guns, for whatever reason, don't bother me anymore. I've already seen enough in the last few days and Brain, cerebral as always, has been desensitised to the image of lethal force on street corners, has learned how to see guns as only part of the uniform. Body, that said, is the one that'll feel hot lead if things get confused, and is currently preoccupied just by the simple task of standing upright, isn't a fan of anything that fires expanding bullets designed to pierce skin, flesh, artery, organ. Brain understands the situation is nominally safe, but Body knows innately the potential for death, and nothing's changing that. The last thing we need is a soldier thinking me jumpy, unnaturally nervous, something to hide. Here, I am learning the force of the checkpoint, where the ruination of lives waits more than anything in the gaping *maybe* and the trailing *what if* that haunt each moment.

'You don't have to be afraid,' says Green, his voice kind over the barrel of his gun.

Part of me – Soul – so flecked with pride, resents that this boy thinks me afraid when really I'm just annoyed and tired. Part of me – Brain – feels this a not unhelpful misunderstanding in circumstances such as these: I'd rather they think me afraid than suspicious. The kid looks at me all full of pathos, and we hold one another's eyes as finally I find the slip and hand it over with my passport. He hands it right back, without looking at it, a shake of the head as if to say that this is now unnecessary. Past his uniform and gun, I look at his beardless skin, smooth and shining with sweat around pale red lips. And for a short moment, his eyes betray some regret and shame at this entire situation and what it must say of his country, and what that must say of him. Right away, he follows up with more reassurance.

'It's OK, you can go through.'

And then he pauses. His hand moves to the gun at his side, swaying on its heavy cotton strap, but the words from his mouth are so damn human.

'You want water?'

I have to smile. '*Mayim?*' I reply, giving him one of the few words of Hebrew I know, for 'water' is the most important word when travelling in foreign lands on a bicycle. I present it to him as a sort of gift, a peace offering in his own language.

He smiles back, nods in confirmation. I got it right. '*Mayim.*'

Green leads me to a cabin off to one side, up on short props and entered by three metal steps. Inside is a sink with a large steel cup hanging there, two-handled with some words engraved on it. A water fountain waits in the corner and on it, before Green leaves me be, he presses a button to demonstrate that it works. With an apologetic wave he goes, excuses himself, honouring some fundamental sense of a human's right to some privacy as they revive. I cup my hands under the tap, take water to the flaming candle that is the top of my head, extinguish it as *mayim* runs through my hair, down neck and brow, washing more salt into my eyes so that they sting a little before the salt dilutes and my vision returns. Clearly now, I see the dark inside of the cabin, with a square of light on its floor where sun slips through a small window. I think of the words just exchanged, of *mayim*, so similar to the Arabic for water, *ma'an*, and both perhaps just-so because the sound of *M* is one of the first that a baby's mouth and tongue can hold and can form. My mind travels from one thought to the next, guessing that this must also be why that sound, represented by its various letters and characters around the globe, also begins the word '*mama*', and the many other versions of that word we humans form as babies to speak to the woman who once brought each of us into the world. *Eema* in Hebrew, *Um* in Arabic.

There is a wastepaper bin and a roll of paper towels that I unreel to mop the floor clear of the puddle around my feet. I look around, see a short stool in the corner, and wonder who sat there before me, and if they received such kindness.

Headlights

A few times more I cycled past the wall, though in reality it wound so capriciously that I often did not know which side of it I was on. The agreed border between Israel and Palestine is some 300 miles. The wall is 600, constructed in and out and according to those stretches of land Israel claims for itself. The wall was not built to create safety; it was built to create real estate. Every one of its winding meanders makes more enmity in return for the parcel of land it grabs. Some spurs of the wall, those spreading furthest from agreed Israeli territory, are called 'fingers', and each one reaches out and gathers up more of the cloth that was Palestine.

With the last light, Bethlehem nears, and I watch the hills rolling to the east, moon rising to the west. The sky shifts to a darker blue, light fails. Rolling down the hill I see the best-known section of the wall, where graffiti by local artists meets graffiti of famous artists who have visited from the West. Painted rope ladders lead over the concrete to the other side. A girl floats up on a balloon. There is a painted hole, the concrete torn to reveal scenes of an imagined life lived prosperously beyond it. Then the simple words: *Make hummus not walls.* Beside that an escalator makes its way up over the wall. Messages of solidarity abound. So much of it is written in English, and for a moment I wonder if this might be the future that I'm seeing: political tourism in the West Bank, with revenues into Israel's treasury in return for no change at all. Only an exhibit. In front of me a tourist stands cradling his lens, shoots, and with the camera held like the conscript's gun on a strap over his shoulder, I watch him walking away, wondering, hoping, what that photo will go on to achieve.

Out of the town I loop around, take up the highway, the last of my roads back towards the south of Jerusalem and Neta's place. In the roadside undergrowth I see the red lights of a police jeep, pulled off the road. At the time the image doesn't even enter my mind, only the red light. The tarmac is roaring, cars bound for the city on one of the mixed roads where Palestinian and Israeli vehicles drive together, where the people can apparently coexist, but only if they have the metal of the bodywork and the scream of an engine to hold them apart. Beyond a junction, traffic thins, and in silence the dusk grows thick. Two headlamps are in the near distance, far side of the road and coming towards me. My mind wanders and I think of the *fingers* of the settlement building and the wall. I remember that Winston Churchill described the long, narrow country of The Gambia as Britain's 'finger up the backside of French West Africa', so that colonisers always see land in ways that sugges—

The car flashes by so fast, headlights gouge the dusk. From the corner of my eye a large, grey shape disappears out of sight but then suddenly I know exactly where it is because – Damn! Ouch! Shit! *What?* – I've been hit on the head with a rock.

Whose Hand?

That's right. Hit on the head, with a rock. A perfect description of events. Bravo, Julian, bravo. *Fuck!* Stinging. Road spins a little. *What!?* Brain gathers up the information along with the spreading pain, but it turns out rocks impede logic. Steel yourself, don't pass out. That's my first and most crucial thought as I look down between my arms at the front wheel and handlebars, watching to see if I'm about to tip, but no. Steel yourself, don't pass out. I cling to the instruction like it was a tree trunk, a lamp post. Dependable I hold to them, stay upright. My front wheel continues, rolls, centred. I'm not toppling, balance is good. Vision OK. I know what happened. The stone pinched under the car tyre, propelled straight at me. But no, that's not it, the trajectories were wrong. The stone was too high, the flight path was flat, not rising. I've seen stones pop a hundred times from tyres and this wasn't that. I know it. No stone so big would shoot so fast from under a tyre. I see my old worries, that I'd be mistaken for Israeli. That rock was shot. Slingshot. From the bushes? From the car. I consider what to do. I should stop. Stop while the going's good, get off before you fall off. Good call. But no, Brain interjects. There are people round here who want to see how a rock looks in your face. It's a good point. Whatever you do, don't stop. Keep going. I want a safe place, I need a safe place. But there is no safe place, here there can be no safe place.

I pedal, my head spins faster than my wheels. I'm lost. I'm

stranded. The accountancy of my circumstances goes into over-drive, someone smashed the abacus. This land, of such cursed and constant arithmetic. Who did this? Who is my enemy here? A plague on both their houses! The image of the rock repeats in my mind, I see it coming again. And then, night falling, yellow moon up and nobody around, I feel my heart beating, and Brain quickly goes through the available information again. That rock just glanced you, you're fine. It was at the wrong trajectory – flat, level with your head – to have begun its journey under a car tyre at that sort of distance. And then Brain sees the memory of the police patrol unit, the jeep with the haze of red lights in the bushes barely a mile or so earlier, watching for people in the undergrowth. I feel my heart thump, crack. Then I can hear it coming: the knock, *knock, knock*. Footfall, like a headmaster making his way down a corridor, echoes ominous, and all this is going only one way from here. The crack of heels accelerates and, shit, suddenly he's coming, running right for me. My heart is off the rails. There's a tingling hand that spreads from the impact across the back of my head. Logic is found in the prefrontal cortex of the brain but I am not in my prefrontal cortex. Prefrontal cortex is gone. I'm an animal and someone is hunting me, someone just shot a rock at me, someone in this accursed place thinks I'm the enemy, but can't they see what I'm doing? And dusk, with the moon rising over the purple sky and the aching hills, replies:

'They cannot see.'

So I pedal on, pedal hard, but my head is swimming through options and only adrenaline's keeping me vertical. I can feel the pain spread from the sting at its epicentre, scurrying out to set the back of my scalp aglow. I still haven't fallen off, the air from the hills is cooling. I feel breaths landing in my lungs. I'm going to be OK, just need to get out of here. But that's the next problem – how do I get out of here, where is *here*? My map said *here* was on the 1948 line, or did it? And either way, which side of it? But even there, that's not important, because the Israelis built their wall where they pleased, and the line exists only on a map and knows nothing of the reality they constructed. I double back, turn and head for Bethlehem, the crossing point in the wall there.

For one moment, I think like an Israeli. I actually believe the wall will keep me safe, that its charmed concrete will stop the stones. Then I pause and think: did the rock hit me on the Israeli side anyway? Because that side is shared with a quarter of the population who are Palestinian–Israeli, who had their city annexed, who have both the right to be here but also a bond to their brothers and sisters in Gaza, with those who were shot in the head with sniper bullets so that, all things considered, in this strange place – and not that it feels much like luck right now – it's a mark that you belong to the lucky and the powerful if it is only rocks that are cast at you. For a moment, as I pedal frantically, I wonder if it was maybe an Israeli, and this is perhaps the bottom line, because really, I don't care who cast the rock at my head so much as the fact that someone cast a rock at my head in this stupid country or countries or land, whatever you want to call it. Palestine. Israel. Pal-Is. Palestine & Israel. Jerusalem. Occupied East Jerusalem. All I want to do is to leave. To hell with it. At the same time, something in this moment tells me it is important, that I need to hold on to the pain and what caused it because the immediacy brings with it a perspective as clear as the stinging at the back of my head.

▦

Finally, I stop at a bench by a busy road with people walking along it. I look up at the firmament, trapped like the rest of us beneath the stars. All I trust right now is people, not individuals, but that people in plain sight of one another do not harm other people. My chest eases, my heartbeat begins to calm and I watch the people strolling by, unaware of what's inside me just as I am unaware of what trouble or joy it is that they walk with this evening. The rock just glanced the back of my head. I was lucky. The rock was only a rock and not a bullet, and so I was lucky. Still, I imagine the ten centimetres that separated it from my face, the five from my temple. I feel that hypothetical impact, I see how fast it travelled, the size. I imagine my face in the mirror, caved in. The danger to Body, somehow it makes everything clearer. It gives me my lessons, right there in front of me as I stare at the night.

Where the language of rationality has failed, people move into the language of hatred and force. Where people are made to suffer as if they were not human, then those who inflict the suffering are no longer seen as human either. If you make a person's life unbearably hard, then their heart will become unbearably hard. Finally, if there is no discourse and no chance of concession – and this last realisation bears down on me – then violence becomes logical. Under state violence – snipers, surveillance, drones and airstrikes – a rock is the last option to which the Palestinians have been driven. I'm lucky. It missed. I'm lucky. It was only a rock. The Palestinians have agency: a Palestinian arm cast that rock and is at fault. A Palestinian cast that rock at someone who, with each bone in his body, wants victory for their struggle. And so whoever threw it was not only to blame but also acted unwisely. And yet were the Israelis, I think hard and ask myself, also guilty? Did they not push that arm down to pick up the rock?

Aharon

The sound of water bubbling in a small pond, bougainvillea flowing down the side of the building and into the garden where I watch the stars above. It all feels so far, so tranquil against the unknown hostility of the highway. In truth, I just want to leave this city without another story, but Neta's flatmate, Aharon, he said things, things that were important. He walks out of the house and into the shed, his loose sandals fall off his heels and scuff the floor as he passes. I hear rummaging, and he appears with a bucket, rattling with a trowel and small garden forks in it. I already know that I won't tell him what has happened, just as I considered never telling you of it either. I refuse to provide him a fair cause for unfair prejudice.

He gives a lazy wave as he puts down his bucket, comes over to me on the wicker furniture and somehow I feel a little trapped, like I can think of nothing but the rock. The sweet tingling of impact still lodged in the back of my head. He stands over me, a smile showing in the light from the house, his curly hair thick on top of his head, stars in the sky behind. He fans his shirt a little, cools himself, then he lifts a hand towards me in offering.

'So, my friend… how was your day? Neta said you went riding.'

I clasp his hand and he gives it a vigorous shake, sinews winding up towards a large bicep stuck inside a thin arm. Everything in his manner is so large and expansive, so – I don't want to say it but – Arab compared to the quiet, restrained Ashkenazi gestures. He sits beside me as I give an agreeable nod.

'Yeah, it was good.' I go British, talk about weather. 'It was so hot! How was yours?'

He sighs. 'Working! I have to go again tomorrow, really early, gardening for a friend. Our landlord here he wants to increase the rent, it's stress, man.'

'Landlords, always the same.'

'He's some French guy, lives in France. Every month, I work just for him.'

Quietly, I smile. Give me a choice between a tenant and a landlord and I'll take the tenant's side each time but, despite that, I can't help but enjoy an Israeli lamenting the injustice that an outsider took his land.

'How long have you had your gardening business?'

'It's new. After I came out of the army in Hebron, first I travelled, I went to your country, to Europe, then I went out into my own country. I needed a time to think. I want to know my language, to know myself.' He puts a hand on his chest. 'My father is Moroccan. I am an Arab. And I want to know more of this land. I went out into the desert for a long time. It helped.' He points behind us. 'I made that.'

I follow his arm to a piece of shaped wood on a ledge. The thing is solid but twists upon its own internal axis, like a bent propeller illuminated by a small lamp. I smile, for it is so impossibly elegant, innately beautiful.

'What is it?'

'It is a seed case, you know, from a palm tree.'

I lift it, turn it over in my hand, the thing so light for its size. Inside run the tiny hollows of tubes where water once moved inside the pod. Aharon gets back to his feet, stoops beside his bucket and withdraws a roll of clear plastic bags. He talks over his shoulder.

'I shaped it with tools. Sandpaper to bring the colour. I took it out into the desert to work it like this.'

Aharon goes through his bucket of belongings. His curly hair stands up on end, his brown skin shining with beads of sweat in the night humidity. There is a peculiar spirituality to the love of nature and gardens that this country's military seems to have induced in this young man as a coping mechanism. There is a poetry to it, but a sad one, for I sense from his smile that it has not really worked. It doesn't work, it never will work. Unwinding a bag from the roll, shaking it into shape, he picks up a tiny net and steps over to the pond. I walk over as he presses the plastic below the surface of the water.

'What are you doing?'

'The house where I go tomorrow has a pond. But it's getting mosquitoes, so he needs fish. It's balance. The water in this pond, I never disturbed it, so it is full of good bacteria, small fish, eggs. It has the right balance. Come.'

He hands me the tiny net and I stoop. The cool water and a practical task calm my mind. Our arms disappear through green algae, poking holes in the surface so that small fish appear, darting, scales a silver flecked with orange.

'Maybe if you catch them in the net or move them to the bag...'

Our hands follow one another's, up to our elbows, algae hanging on skin.

'How many fish do we need?'

'At least two.' He smiles. 'You always need two to start again.'

The two of us follow a fish, tail flickering, Aharon with his bag moving under the surface. He lifts it a little, the top of the bag above the surface but the fish holding position, oblivious to having been caught.

'What did you think of your ride in Palestine?' he asks.

'I didn't go far, not yet. I'll leave tomorrow, head north.'

Aharon gives a nod of supportive enthusiasm, and I ask, 'Do you think there's a solution here, to your struggle with the Palestinians?'

He frowns and waits silently.

'The Palestinians missed their chance. Their leaders fucked it up. When I think how serious we were, in the sixties, and how much we were going to give up. And they were so proud, and they said no.'

He nods towards the street beyond the gate, a few illuminated buildings higher than the garden wall.

'Now we're here, we're making it work. We're doing this. Now we're not going anywhere. They missed their chance.'

The pond bubbles, the sound of water rippling gently with our movements, but Aharon with more to add, always a chest to get stuff off of.

'After the Holocaust, we were down, man, we knew this was our last chance and we had to make it work. We built this, we had to be the best. And we did, because we are the smartest bastards in the world.'

'*The* smartest?'

He gets suddenly self-conscious, laughs at himself as I catch a fish in my net and move it towards him.

'Maybe not the smartest! But we are some smart bastards.'

He pushes up from the pond, ties a knot in the bag with the fish and spore and bacteria, resting it up among the rocks and lilies. He looks at my face as if momentarily embarrassed at being so brash. His soul talks over his ego.

'People's thinking is so small when they talk of this land. The Middle East, it is big. If you make peace… you have made more land.'

I enjoy the eloquence of his solution, the simplicity, the fact that he's right. Aharon, you can tell, has some sort of a trauma still inside him, and yet it feels like it has been cauterised, quarantined. He has trauma, but will not transmit it to anyone, he's not contagious. A carrier, not a transmitter.

'I don't see this land as ours and as theirs… it belongs to all of us. I don't feel jealous about this land, I don't want more of it. But I feel responsible to it. I love this land.'

'Do you have any hope for sharing it?'

'Hope? I don't think like this. For me, hope is to be in the desert and to plant trees. That is my hope.'

'But you will plant trees with the Palestinians?'

Aharon he looks at me, deadly serious.

'Of course with the Palestinians.'

First Cut Is the Deepest

My bags are packed. We spoke late but still I woke early, and right away my head started moving, thoughts racing, plans forming and reforming in a sense of panic. Perhaps the whole journey wasn't such a good idea, the occupied territories less safe than I'd imagined. There were other things that Aharon said last night, about the army and the city of Hebron, hard things to listen to politely. I'll tell you about them, but not now, later, when you can see for yourself. Now is not the time. With this new morning I just want to get out of the city, where the heaviness of Jerusalem sits on me. I no longer know if the tingling in the back of my skull is real or imagined, perhaps the numbness is only the projection of those fears and their nearness. I wait to leave, wait for Neta to rise as I sit at the stool in front of the piano, aimlessly press its keys. Neta in a calico dress unwinds the short, stone spiral of the stairs and walks over, sits beside me on the stool.

'Is that Ravel?' she asks, flattering me that my pressing of keys has in its accidental beauty been mistaken for music.

'Just playing,' and she places her hand a few keys away from mine, picking a tempo and order of notes to move with my own.

She leans over, 'You should learn scales. Do as I do.'

And I lift my hand away as she plays scales, her fingers babbling across keys like water over rocks in a stream.

'Doh-re-mi,' she sings and I watch. She takes my wrist and moves it to the correct position. I follow, my fingers stretching into this new configuration, the pathways of my brain unaccustomed to directing a part of my body in a way that is not so out of the ordinary, yet entirely alien. Falteringly, I press the keys, fingers hesitant as I put new memory into the movement of bones and muscles. And as they follow it, a kind of music comes.

'This is your *ostinato*, it is your melody.'

Neta says it to me as my fingers go again and again through the scale that begins to sound so sweet, even at the end of my own fingertips, and I am moved to believe that – like riding a bicycle or believing in justice – our mind can accustom so quickly to new thoughts, where those thoughts are sweet and have in them their own sort of harmony. Her hand moves away from mine, further down the keys, begins to play a pair of notes as I continue. She plays repeatedly back and forth, low and plodding in contrast to mine.

'*Dom-dom. Dom-dom.*'

She sings, and the pulse of her keys takes up the melody of mine and one supports the other as if they were meant to be together.

'And this is your *basso continuo*.' Neta looks to me as I go through my scales and wait on her explanation. 'It's the rhythm section, it accompanies an *ostinato*.'

Together we sit at the piano, plodding through our new music and I miss a key, resettle my fingers.

'You make... mistakes.'

Playfully she chides, the musical pause in her comment a reminder that a little silence allows us to hear words all the louder. She smiles, enjoying her role of teacher.

'You make mistakes... because you are going too fast.'

⁛

In the doorway we hug goodbye. Neta stands with a small smile, coy, always slightly entertained by what's happening.

'You be careful out there.'

I nod and the two of us stand, a little awkward, ready to part. The rock is in my mind, and the road outside feels like it will be long, while this home with its piano is so nice. I will leave this shelter, this comfort, and at last take that step into the open book of where I'll sleep each night, that thing Westerners have the luxury to call 'adventure', but is really only the voluntary dabbling in a hardship under which so much of the world's population lives each day. It always begins the same way, a basic formula: known to unknown, abundance to less. Looking back, it's never such a big deal, but at the time the threshold always rears up at you.

Next to us, on a ledge in the stone of the wall, is a brass bowl that shines bright in the morning sun. In it is a solid length of hardwood, resting on its edge, like a musical pestle and mortar. I pick it up and give the brass a tap that prompts a short ringing. Neta takes the bowl gently from my hand, rests it on the ball of her palm, fingers stretched back. She strikes the bowl once, hard, so that a chime rings out loud. She takes the length of wood and, slowly, begins to stir the bowl so that the sound lifts, as if it jumped across from the bowl to the bar of wood, then rises, ringing, up into the stone ceiling of the house where, lost in that sound, all my worries abate. Rhythmically, smooth, the distance perfect between the two objects, she stirs the stick around the bowl. She makes the bowl sing, ringing, enchanting until – abruptly – she stops it with her other hand and passes it back.

'Do as I do.'

I take it. I do as she does. I strike it, a ringing opens quickly but then falls back down flat. Neta takes back the bowl, gives it a firm strike.

'The first hit is the important one. You give it space, so that it can speak, so that it can ponder the sound. You must always have this space to ponder, Julian, or nothing new can be understood or created.'

And she stirs it again, so that the singing starts up. Then she stops it. She hands me back the bowl, realises that she has stumbled upon a lyric, and so her voice falls into song in that way she likes to let it. *'The first cut is the deepest...'*

Across from her, I strike the bowl and she watches me steadily. It rings deep as I lower the bar to the rim, stirring, stirring at it so that the vibrations of the bowl jump out to the stick conducting it, stirring around, taking up their note and pointing the song higher, up to the ceiling, stirring as Neta smiles and we prepare to part, nodding that I got it, that the sound is there as I turn the bar around the bowl, turning, and the sound ringing true, all of those random notes falling into a single pitch, breathing like a gasp of music that makes such sense, reaching up and turning, turning, turning as the wheels move beside the white line painted at the roadside that leads down and into Palestine, where all those notes go turning inside my head.

Part II

WEST BANK

Abu Bakr

The car comes alongside, windows down, the white bodywork shining with the sun and each pane of glass speckled with red dust. From the driver's seat, a man is waving through the passenger window, waving enthusiastically into his vehicle, shouting Arabic at my politely confused expression, then moving into English. *Welcome, Welcome!* I return a wave and keep riding, hills up ahead and a long way to go, scarcely out of the city. The car drops behind me and then I hear it stop, handbrake on. Door opens.

'Hey, hey!' he calls at me, leaning up out of the door.

I stop.

'Where you go?'

'To Ramallah!'

'You cycle? To Ramallah?'

I nod.

He points at the car, then speaks, walking my way, gesturing to stay calm, like whatever my ordeal is, it's over and things are now under control.

'My name is Abu Bakr. I take you. Come, come.'

I laugh, 'Thank you, but I'm OK.'

Abu Bakr stands there in a pair of baggy jeans. He's short and with a paunch, well-fed, his hair is cut close and he wears a polo shirt spotted with white paint – all told, he looks a picture of kindness. I get from my bicycle and we shake hands.

'No, my friend,' he shakes his head. 'You can't cycle to Ramallah. Come, I take you.'

He leads me round to the back of his car, opens the boot to reveal gardening equipment, trowels and buckets. He points in to it, then looks at me like his answer is the obvious one.

'No, really it's OK.' I protest. 'I want to cycle.'

'You *want* to cycle?'

And at that notion this Palestinian man shoots me a look of amazement I've not seen since Texas, where one pickup after another was stopped by drivers eager to save me from needless travel by bicycle.

'Really! I want to,' I nod eagerly. 'After Ramallah, I cycle north to Golan, then south to Eilat.'

Abu Bakr's eyes open wider. 'It is like… your journey?'

'Yes, it's my journey,' I laugh, then ponder this profound title and put a hand, reassuring, on his shoulder.

'Really. I take you?' He invites me once more, like it really would be OK to say 'yes'.

'Thank you,' hand to my heart, 'but I cycle.'

He gives a final nod, one more pat to my shoulder as he closes the boot, returns to the wheel of his car and I walk back to my bicycle. I try to give a further look of gratitude as, readying to leave, he speaks with a sudden look of business.

'I live Ramallah, but I have permit. I work in Tel Aviv. But before, I am from Imwas.' He points south. 'Between Tel Aviv and Jerusalem. My village. Now there is nothing. Village gone. In 1967 Israel destroyed it. Everything. 1967.'

Abu Bakr looks at me, eyes keen and his face urgently, politely serious, as if this is a key point of information that he must impart. He says it without anger, but as if I should know this fact, that it is important, that it is the story that produced him. Right here at the roadside, Abu Bakr, a gardener who I suspect at some point has also been a decorator, turns lobbyist and advocates for his Palestine. Somewhere in the certainty of how he says it, I get the impression that Abu Bakr has deduced that if he tells this one, simple truth to everyone he meets, then eventually, the whole world will know.

He reaches down and takes a scrap of cardboard packaging from inside the glove box. He scribbles his number and gives it to me.

'You need anything. You call me.'

He gives a last nod, then pulls away with a short fire of the horn followed by an arm waving out the window. I watch his car, small and white, as it makes for the enormous gateway of the hills that watch over this valley in Palestine. And as I pedal on, I consider how Israel arrived here with force, and then legal documents to codify that force, all of it determined to disregard the laws and the documents that people set down by word of mouth, in stories, in the lived histories before that arrival. I watch Abu Bakr disappear from sight on his own daily journey, the name of *Imwas* repeating in my ears. Not for the first time, but with a new and deeper understanding, I realise what the Jews who set about building their dream of Israel once knew so well, but in dealing with the Palestinians have since forgotten. You cannot, in any circumstances, silence a story.

Garrison Boy

The land opens out of the hills, all of it lifting in a song, a chorus that reveals olive leaf on red soil that is etched by tracks leading out to the villages. I ride beside the desire lines of new paths being created, where earth has been smoothed by livestock herded through. Here and there appear concrete slabs and razor wire laid down to stop people on the tracks completing their journeys. Occasional barbs are knotted with felt from passing animals, blowing on the breeze. Over my shoulder, a section of wall stands so high but ridiculous, like the tallest kid in class, but so sure of that rank that all you can do is laugh at its earnestness. Fig trees lean up behind it, over it, and on its concrete canvas an artist has painted the wailing figure of a body and face made from olive branches. A truck winds towards me, throwing up dust that gets trapped against the wall and, with nowhere to disperse, strikes my body and face. Further down the hill a faint track is guarded by many dogs, with a dozen kennels lining its side and a few Alsatians padding about on the end of long chains. At my side a lizard, its skin black and leathery, darts away from my rolling wheel, drags its hot belly along the concrete footing before vanishing between rocks.

Pedalling steadily on, from around a bend appears an emerging turret and rickety-looking watchtowers... all of it draped with dark black netting that offers camouflage against the world without and shade to those within. The nets hang, waving on the breeze like ghouls visiting a grave, and the garrison stands over this road with a coldness that shudders through the warm hills. Razor wire locks the site in place, but bougainvillea blossoms pink around it, as though protesting nature has placed a flower down the barrel of a tank gun. Thistles explode pure blue from the rockface, and this fortification of the land looks peculiar, and weak, because the land itself does not care for it, and sees its intimidation but chooses to ignore and decorate rather than resist. From the highest watchtower, two windows, just black holes, stare down at the road, looking simultaneously aggressive and sinister, but also afraid and in hiding. Struck by the starkness of it, I stop and take out a camera to quickly capture this presence that attempts to capture the land. As I frame it up, a shutter slides and a shout comes down in Hebrew.

'Excuse me?' I call back in English.

'No photos.'

And then I see the young face, peering down from behind stubble and sunglasses: a surly-looking Rapunzel shut in a concrete turret. He ticks his finger, wagging his orders, but for me, a foreigner and English-speaker, he seems gentle enough.

'I thought it was empty,' I call apologetically up into the wind. The words that come back down surprise me.

'I wish it was.'

In a silence that feels like a conversation we look at one another, and a new piece of the puzzle in this strange land reveals itself. He sees me and who I am: bicycle, shorts, riding through the same Mediterranean hills where he sits in military fatigues in a hot, concrete garret. What would he rather be doing? Cycling? Perhaps. Something else? Certainly. Packed in my pannier is all the life that this kid is missing, held prisoner while he holds others prisoner. His government takes the best years of his youth, but presents the Palestinians as the reason why, and so I begin to feel that if this boy already or one day comes to hate the Palestinians, it may not be as an enemy so much as in the way a disgruntled store clerk comes to hate customers, mostly because of the boss they remind him of.

'How long you been sitting there?' I ask.

'I just started.'

'No. I mean, how many months?'

He looks at me, leans out, face appearing closer through the hole.

'Enough.'

Silence settles on this strange passing friendship of mutual regret, as I regather my bicycle and retake the pedals. He keeps looking down at me.

'Careful nobody drives into you.'

I ride on and, giving a thumbs-up, look back over my shoulder at the scene where, for all intents and purposes, Palestine sparkles in a crown of bougainvillea, but all I can see is a young Israeli shut behind razor wire and concrete, so that suddenly it is hard to tell who is truly captive in this land.

Roadsides

Just once, I have to interrupt the ride and let you know of what eventually formed almost every breakfast and lunch, and at least one meal a day. I still remember the way each one looked on the tabletop, a gallery of riches is banked in my memory, where every roadside restaurant in Palestine had its own signature, some different flourish of colour in the pickle or swirl to the bowl. This moment has occurred many times already and will do so many more, and every time it was so superb it became only routine. To tell you repeatedly would grow plain, but to never speak of it would be to neglect you. At the roadside then, if you'll allow it, we must stop and eat.

With a smile and a courteous nod that instructs my enjoyment begin, the patron appears in a smart chequered shirt, over a T-shirt immaculately white, despite the dusty roadside where this restaurant waited as if a mirage in an expanse of my growing hunger. He puts down two plates, loaded with the assurance of millennia in Palestine, timeless, across which this meal was perfected by his forebears and those they shared these lands with. On one plate, beautiful, is colour... like a palate of paints pressed from the colours of the rainbow and assembled here in pickled vegetables on a white plate. The bright pink of turnips pickled in beetroot juice. The orange of carrot, green of gherkin. In a basket, now arriving, pillows of pitta are placed, plump as a freshly made bed, and torn apart with small sighs of steam, carrying in them the warmth of baked flour.

In an earthenware bowl, however, is what I am here for. The magic word. Made from a thing so humble as a boiled chickpea – bumpy and firm – and somehow reassembled into a form so damn elegant, guarded by one poorly kept secret code word that will end your hunger so blissfully at every bustling market stall or dusty road across all Palestine. Hummus. In many ways, the more unlikely the restaurant, the more broken-down cars parked out front, the more garden furniture being sold next door, the more unassuming the establishment, the more perfect and supreme the banquet.

To describe the taste, then. Sure, why not? Smooth, with the nourishing depth of the chickpea, that most soulful of pulses. The bite of citrus from the lemon, the notes of sesame from tahini. There is, probably, a little water added – as it is to separate the flavours of a fine whisky from the intensity of alcohol – to cut through the strength of the chickpea and allow the individual notes to shine. Somewhere in that giant pot in the dark kitchen must be some small cloves of garlic, added to this culinary painting. Slight, after centuries of testing and masterfully judged, as if the recipe is lodged in the muscle memory of the fingertips sprinkling it, is the cut of salt that seasons the mix like an accent on a letter seasons a word into its true pronunciation and meaning. Throw all the words you want at this bowl. *Delicious*, of course. *Sublime*, why not? *Divine*, go for it. The words themselves, though, are like rosettes at a small-town fair, paling beside the achievement of this taste and this place.

Still more than that is the way this thing looks, and if sometimes the presentation of food can be used deceivingly to disguise mediocrity, here is one of those instances where the appearance of the bowl is perfect because it represents, honest and faithful, the total harmony of its components. The perfection of flavour is mirrored in the image, where that hummus was taken from its pan, then smoothed perfectly by a gliding paddle or spoon into the swirling eye of a storm. Olive oil flooded those turning grooves, deep, a yellow that borders on the green of trees but seems to shine gold. Sprinkled red across the top, speckled there in dusty footprints, wandering in one side and out the other is a red of cayenne, flicked from a brush. A pinch of black, cracked peppercorns was scattered after it, dropped there so that others could follow the trail. And as you eat, turning it over with a spoon, there comes a warmth from deep inside the bowl, heating the olive oil just enough to smell it, but evidence most of all that this hummus is always being eaten and so it is always being cooked, and so, quite simply, it is always absolutely fresh. The crowning pieces are those curls, petals, of raw onion at the side of the bowl. White, translucent lines with the veins that once carried water into the growing bulb are still traced through them. And with those petals I scoop up that hummus, and the olive oil, and the chickpea so that they stand against that sharp, refreshing, cooling crunch of onion, followed by a flavour almost sweet and in itself evidence of a pure culinary culture, for the use of a raw onion is the mark of a cuisine that has thrown off its inhibition and is able to delight in the unaltered sense of that ingredient so playfully fierce. With a piece of bread, I plough through the blitz of green chillies that lie thick on the surface beside what is perhaps my favourite touch. For there rest a half dozen or so battered, partly collapsed chickpeas, still retaining some shape as if evidence, or a statement: a boast of just what this bowl, this masterpiece, had humbly began life as, and from which, gratefully, I eat.

Bikes and Brewing

'Taybeh?' I call to a group of men gathered at a small roundabout, where each of them points to the right-hand fork. As I go careering down the hill, all I hear are the words 'Salam Alaikum' trailing out behind me. And, slowly, I am beginning to suspect that in Palestine all that is needed by way of a map is to call out the name of the village you desire.

On a wall by a track that disappears into a steep valley, there is painted a bottle of beer that bears the name of both the village and its brewery. I roll into grounds surrounding a hangar, with picnic benches lined along one side of the site. A coach has pulled in, a few Westerners file aboard what looks like a tourist trip, and in front of me is the wide-open hatch to the hangar from which the last of the group straggles. A large cardboard cut-out displays a beer bottle, and across it a single word is written in an ornate hand, reminiscent of old Europe: *Oktoberfest*. I watch a middle-aged couple walk slowly past, both in shorts, wide sun hats, white socks pulled high up lilywhite shins. The man is in a utility waistcoat covered in pockets, the woman wearing shades. Between them they look safari-ready, prepared for so much more than just walking the ten paved metres from transport to attraction. She turns towards the sign and as I enter the brewery, over my shoulder I hear a US accent and the words.

'Look, an *Oktoberfest*… that's so very American.'

▦

Standing behind a counter, a young woman looks up from a clip-board and gives a broad smile before stepping towards me, dressed in a navy T-shirt and fitted jeans. There are the studs of two pearl earrings, her dark brown hair shines where it is pulled back into a ponytail, but all I really see is the smile as she introduces herself as Madees, and asks kindly, 'You want the tour?'

The building runs deep, has guts, and from further inside flickers the gleam of brushed steel, polished and reflecting the distant sky through the curvature of a mash tun. Up on stilts, towering over it all, in the dim light they glow without colour, the metal cylinders reduced to shadows and lines of bright white. Beside me at the entrance are wooden pallets holding hundreds of flatpack card-board boxes, a few assembled to reveal badges of gold, red, green and orange for each different brew: dark, non-alcoholic, white, pilsner, pale. On another pallet are dozens of boxes, packed and shrink-wrapped, ready for dispatch and heading from this hillside near Ramallah out into the world.

Madees and I walk the bottling line, brown glass bottles standing neatly side by side on its narrow conveyor belt, a store of empties waiting at the far end for the rollers to turn and shuffle them towards destiny. Pistons and arms hang from above. Lines, spindles and valves hover, the belt leads in and out of metal boxes that keep their processes concealed. Madees walks and talks, gestures to the machinery as proudly she lays out the story.

'When we're flat out we can make five hundred bottles an hour. We ship now to Japan, Denmark, Germany, the United States. We have an order going to the UK soon, and to Chile,' Madees sees me look amazed and clarifies, 'Chile's got the biggest Palestinian community outside the Middle East. We have our own bottle tops pressed and printed in France, we abide by the German Beer Purity

Law of 1516, so that means our only ingredients are barley, hops and water. We get our hops from Bavaria or the Czech Republic, our malt from Belgium or France.'

She pauses, but words fail me and for a moment I make do simply with 'Wow'. Together, we step through the stainless-steel hall of mirrors that is the brew room. I watch our reflections side by side, limbs gangly, bent and out of shape in the curvature of metal, our bellies spreading out before dropping off one cylinder and jumping onto the next. We move through metal wheels that hold valves shut, pass pressure gauges.

'How did you guys start out?'

'My father and uncle trained as master brewers in the US. Then after the Oslo Peace Accords between Israel and Palestine, back in the nineties, they were ready to start a brewery, either in the US or here. So they told the Palestinian Authority that if they supported them, they'd do it here.'

Madees looks around with a smile, as if the hectolitres of beer brewing all around show how that story worked out. The feat I stand inside feels so impressive that it is almost as if even the occupation itself – the watchtowers, walls and guard dogs I have ridden by – have been overcome.

'The conflict, the occupation? It's like it isn't stopping you.'

Madees shakes her head, gently suggesting I've got it wrong.

'It makes it hard. The Israelis demand so many permits for us to export, so many fees, they hold up our orders. We had empty bottles delivered from Germany in the same consignment as an Israeli brewery, but they got theirs months before us. Ours were just left waiting. They don't let us pack complete shipping containers here – they say because of security – so we miss out on big international orders because we have to load trucks that drive to ports to be loaded into containers there.'

She pauses.

'They don't want us to be successful. Sometimes we can't get orders out on time, or our orders are stopped at checkpoints, we miss shipments. Sometimes a keg of beer gets stuck at a checkpoint and goes bad in the heat. Or international customers put us on their menus and then they can't get our beer because of all of this.' Perhaps seeing my optimism deflate, Madees smiles. 'But people understand. They're really supportive, they know what we're dealing with.'

She leans on a step ladder beneath a cylinder.

'It's great that your family made a business that was part of the village.'

'They just felt it was the only way. To build it up, a community. Making your own money, jobs. Not having to rely on anyone else.'

'You mean like foreign aid money?'

'Right…' she hesitates, 'and that's good, we need some of that. But it creates a kind of employment where a local person gets five thousand shekels for an international contract, plus benefits, so when the contract ends, they're going to wait for the next one, not go out and work for two thousand shekels with the local organisation. It's unpredictable, you can't build on it.'

Madees and I pass under the towering cylinders, step back past the bottling line, towards daylight, the shadows lifting from our faces.

'What do you think the answer is, to all this?' I ask.

With bright determination, but perhaps on account of her youth also little patience, Madees has a simple answer: 'We need new leaders. Israel, Palestine too… we have old leaders. They don't care. They're comfortable. We need the young people to lead.'

⠿

Two hours and three beers later, with most of the staff departed for the day, I pack up a pannier and ready my bicycle for a return to the road, folding the black-white checkers of a Palestinian *keffiyeh* scarf under the strap that also holds down my map. A balding man comes strolling beneath the brewing tanks, surveying the brewery like a commanding officer. He wears a jacket, has a shirt tucked over a plump, happy belly, and his chest is out but with no self-importance. He has an aquiline nose, a neat rectangle of moustache and in his hands he holds two bottles of wine.

'Can I help you?' he turns to me, speaking in an English that is perfect and with an accent almost American.

'I'm just leaving. Madees showed me around.' I nod to my empties. 'I stayed for a drink.'

'That's my daughter.' He lifts his arms and the bottles in an apology that he can't shake my hand because of them. 'I'm Nadim, one of the founders of our brewery here at Taybeh. Thanks for coming!'

'It's an amazing place,' I say.

Nadim gives a nod of gratitude, as if he knows, but also as if adjectives really aren't important here, with all the work that still needs doing.

'In Palestine we have few resources, little land, no petroleum. So we made a brewery. Now we also make wine here, soap, olive oil. We have to be sustainable.' Nadim points up. 'You see the solar panels on the roof? It all has to be sustainable.'

'It sounds like things are going well.'

He sets it out like a bookkeeper, sighing before he delves into details and accounts, but you can feel his pride in the story.

'We have many obstacles. The military occupation, cultural opposition from conservatives in Palestine, difficulties with exports from Israel. When you have no port or airport, every time there is an incident in Gaza, they close the port at Ashkelon and we have to go through Haifa, which is more expensive. These bottles, you see the difference?'

I look at the labels, my vision coming to me from out of focus. Both Syrah.

'That one says "of Palestine".' A pause. 'And that one just says "Palestine"?'

'Right.' Nadim's impressed, like I'm not so slow after all. 'We had to get a whole new label made because the American FDA said we couldn't use the word "Palestine" on its own, said it was political! We ship beer to Japan and they want a third-party just to verify that it's beer, meets the standards… the Americans don't care what's inside, just the label!'

Nadim looks at me with a *can-you-believe-it?* expression. I look at the labels, tasteful, with the paper unbleached and in a matt colouring, slightly embossed with the spreading branches of a tree.

'That's crazy. They are both nice labels though,' I say, sounding tipsy.

'We have them printed in Birzeit.' Nadim points down the road. 'We used to have to import printed labels from Germany because of Israeli restrictions on ink.'

'Ink?'

'They say it can be used to make explosives, but these guys in Birzeit managed to get the permits, so it's good to give them the business.'

Nadim's eyes smile at my shock, pleased to be welcoming someone into his world, his struggle, where everything down to the labels has been made political. He points to the back of my bike, where my *keffiyeh* is attached above the pannier bag.

'*Keffiyehs*. We used to make them in Palestine, right here, it was a real industry. Now all the factories have closed down because we couldn't get the ink. There's only one left now, in Hebron. All the jobs are gone, the rest are imported from China.'

Nadim stands in front of me, almost relishing my incredulity, having somehow learned himself how to take a satisfaction from all of these obstacles he means to defy. Nadim, I realise, actually stands with the resolute confidence of a man who – on some hidden level – is actually winning, and who's willing to win slowly, but who knows he will win and so all of these adversities become only monuments to his struggle.

'Now we've got a water problem too, because of the climate, not so much rain, and the settlers here keep taking more and more. They get as much water as they want, and ours is rationed to certain hours of the day. We had an attack on our computer systems too, cyber-crime, a hacker in Turkey. Some conservative who didn't like what we were doing, brewing. I don't know. The Turkish authorities identified the attack and froze the funds they stole, so we'll get it back. But the Palestinian Authority… they don't have any powers like this.' Nadim drops his voice slightly. 'The authorities here don't stop us, but they don't help us either.'

Amidst this adversity, a thought occurs to me, 'Do you sell your beer in Israel?'

Nadim nods. 'You have to. But go to a beer festival inside Israel and people in Palestine complain about the boycott, but we've got to stay in business. A British brewer got in touch, wanted to do a partnership.'

I look expectant. Nadim pulls a face of doubt, lowers his voice.

'They wanted to brew something called *Peace Beer*. I wasn't so keen.'

There is a pause. Nadim sees my look and searches for the words to express himself with precision.

'I mean, we need peace, yes. But for peace, we need justice.'

In all of it, line by line, I realise that Nadim has not a flicker of hostility towards those who thwart him, as if doing so would be to waste the energy he needs to go on resisting them and eventually win. He straightens up, ready to continue with his last rounds of the brewery, beginning to excuse himself from this part-way drunk and curious cyclist.

'Which way are you riding?'

'Towards Jericho, I heard it's a good road.'

Nadim smiles. 'You won't have to pedal much.'

'It's all downhill?'

'Yes.' And then he adopts a thoughtful tone. 'But there is a very good patch of flat land, just outside Jericho, on the left. I always think it would make a good airport, when we get one.'

My heart aches at the thought of a concrete runway laid down on that beautiful red, desert earth, but it is a businessman's sparkle that gleams in Nadim's eye.

'You don't think the airport in Gaza could reopen?'

He shakes his head, like the less said about Gaza the better.

'So, *Jericho International?*' I offer, and he weighs it up.

'Why not *Taybeh?*' Nadim opens his arms, both joking and totally serious.

I laugh, and the beers I've finished make it somehow easier to ask again that idealist question.

'What do you think is the answer to the situation here? How will it get better?'

He looks at me like it's obvious.

'We need our own state. And one day, we will have it,' he says, and shrugs.

Bedouin

A flock of sheep swarms over the asphalt, their white fleeces reddened by desert earth. Two young boys herd the animals with their sticks tapping out a path, occasionally prodding the flank of a wayward sheep that veers off into the scrub. The boys see me, and arms and sticks rise high in greeting.

Pulling in at the roadside, I take my bottle of water from its cage and drink beside the main building where the farm meets the road. Five brown plastic chairs are arranged in a semi-circle, a man or a boy in each. The men sit with their legs and arms spread, tired from the heat, the chairs disappearing under their large, exhausted frames. The two boys are restless, upright, fidgeting. Their thin, tiny bodies lean forward as everybody watches me dismount on the other side of a short lip of wall around the small house. Their faces are warm, curious but kind, all of them with the dark skin of years of farming, the look of centuries of Bedouin who worked this land. Beside the shelter where they sit is a fenced-off enclosure with animals in pens. Sheep, a goat or two, move over the dusty earth that lifts slowly in the sunlight above each scuffing hoof. A small tractor stands in the sun, the chamber of its engine exposed with pipes and conchs. Sheet metal and corrugated iron lids the animal enclosures, casting black shade against the sheer white of the day's heat. Tyres filled with earth form a wall that stops the desert blowing it all away, and I remember a conversation in which I was told this was the most common solution to Israeli restrictions against the use of permanent building materials. The animals circle, their shepherds rest.

At the end of the crescent of men arced across the balcony, one lifts forward from his pose. He pushes up on the arms of the chair, raises his hand and with a downward wave of his fingers, beckons me closer. A word of Arabic is spoken and by its ending it has trailed into that familiar sound of 'Salam Alaikum'. I put down my bike, accept the invitation and smile as I look over at him. His hair is cut close to his head, a blue denim shirt is open across a T-shirt on his tabletop chest, like a cowboy of the Middle East, and across his upper lip waltzes a moustache wholly oblivious to the end of the Ottoman Empire. The crowning glory of his face, the moustache is surrounded by a few days of stubble and is flicked up at either end in two magnificent curls that take off and then loop all the way back in like a pair of jet black, grey-specked handles on the side of a tea cup. I wonder if he waxed it, if he prepared it for a day in his office of the desert. Or if he wakes up like this, effortless. Supreme, a pasha, lord of this land, the confidence of his place here is set in his steady gaze, and two deep brown eyes look at me with their own welcome, so that it is a pleasure just to see this man who has absorbed into him the patience of the earth he worked and now means for his sons to learn to work. Somehow you see all of that record laid out in him, as if he is the earth in a more relatable form. Olive trees, desert rock, blue sky, hot sun and all of it together in this man. He points to my bottle:

'*Ma'an?*'

Water? he asks with the eyebrow moving upwards and the moustache following, looping into a question mark. I raise a hand, decline, the bottle mostly full. To one side of him another man sits, also reclining, a straw hat tilted high on his forehead, a smile at the curious figure that I make before them. One of the young boys gets up, walks up to the wall – chest height – where I lean as if a neighbour across a fence. His eyes watch me, shining from under a straight black fringe.

'Where are you from?'

He asks it carefully, with these words from school, newly learned and as if they are fragile in his memory and on his tongue.

'Britain,' I answer to some nods, and then add 'and Turkey', which raises an extra nod from the pasha of the family, and seems more interesting.

'*Turkiya?*'

We smile.

Another man appears, newly in from the land, from the vast desert that begins at the edge of this small settlement in these small countries. He is dressed for the weather, more traditional than the rest of them, and the wind comes through and pulls at the long, flowing garment that clothes him in his own pool of local, portable shade. On his head are the black-yellow checkers of his *keffiyeh*, which crowns his high cheekbones as his eyes, piercing, give a look that sternly prohibits refusal of the next word.

'Çay.'

He says it looking right at me, but given as an instruction to one of the boys watching from the chairs. The boy gets fast to his feet, eager to fulfil this order, and leaves to return holding a grey steel kettle half the size of his torso, suspended on a large handle he uses both small hands to grip. As his shoulders slope down into the weight of the kettle, jaw clenched in concentration, he fills a small glass. The soft brown of the tea pours with black leaves floating on the current, running out of the spout in a graceful arc that splashes into the glass and then splashes into the otherwise silence of this space so empty and yet so full with the spirit of this family, these friends, these colleagues and their welcome. The boy steps uncertainly up to me, my glass of tea in both his hands so that he puts it down on top of the wall between us, like an offering at an altar, and then retreats.

The men, and the boys who will one day be men, watch me over this lone glass of tea, that beautiful drink through which people all around the world choose to meet one another. And I watch them back, and then the pasha gives a nod, direct, and a smile. He sips his own tea, the man in the hat holds his glass lazily in a hand hanging at arm's length and out of the chair. I take my glass, raise it a little to them all, and I drink, so soft and refreshing down my throat… the tea so bitter, the tea so sweet. I savour its taste as we all drink together in a peaceful silence and I try to hold this moment every bit as much as the taste, for it feels like, despite almost nothing having happened, I am learning a very tender truth about those who have always lived in this place. The son points to the small-holding and carefully says 'sheep'. I smile, repeat 'sheep', and nod. He tries another word, which I fail to understand, and then I try to say some other animal names that they too fail to understand.

And so after a while we all just sit there, silent, everyone with a small smile for the chance encounter that had come into their day, a gift received by us all from the road: their hospitality, my curiosity. Together we just drink tea, and that much we all understand. That is enough.

Down to Jericho

There are roads you always remember better than all the rest, roads you'll live your life by, roads that you come to treat like heirlooms, that you stow away in the treasure trove of your memory because the moment you first found them was so precious. Those thirty miles down from the Taklamakan desert into Uygur-Xinjiang. To Briançon down from the Col du Lautaret. From the Rockies on the highway east of Tijuana and down into the Sonora Desert of Mexico. And then that one, to Jericho, less a descent than a chasm, with the earth torn apart and inviting you in.

Out of that Bedouin camp it immediately begins to haul you down. Ahead I watch the black asphalt unfurl like the ribbon of a typewriter, where my bicycle hammers as the key that records this story. The red earth is wide open, spotted by the soft green of the last olive trees before the desert, their trunks twisting and leaning tired towards the ground. When finally I finished my journey in those two countries – or that one country, whatever history decides – it was mostly with the sense that I would never return. Still now, the regret that comes both first and last to mind is that road down to Jericho and the prospect of never again riding it. For it pulls you in, reeling you in towards the end, where waiting is the Dead Sea itself, and so it is less a road than a diving board to the bottom of the world. You crest a final small hill, bouncing up into the air as the last plants, a garrison tower and small settlement, dusty with goats being driven back to their pens, all rush by and disappear fast.

And then, with the road rippling, reverberating beneath, finally, you lift off, and in you go.

The first place you feel the speed is on your eyeballs, as the air picks up pace and presses against them. The energy with which you're moving – so bright, so fast – itself trickles into the mind with a subtly coded message that, truly, anything is possible if a mere human being can move like this. Next, the rush moves into the fingers, becomes nervous, tickling them and suggesting they reach for the brake levers in time for that fast-approaching turn that leans around the edge of a mountain like a drunk clutches for the bar as he goes toppling over. The brakes pull you towards them, but then you refuse, you remember your courage and you rush into the turn so that the speed comes for your stomach and lifts it up towards your chest. Merciless, the turns call out the order of events. You grab at the brake, too early and too hard, pulling you off balance for a moment before you get your lines and then, banking into forty-five degrees, the old feeling of descending and immortality returns, and the rhythm of how to crest a mountain makes its way back to your muscles and the posture of your body. One exit points into the next entry, and a line of delicate memory is sketched on the road for you to follow.

Leaning down, I flatten myself against the bicycle so that the two of us bore a faster hole into the air until I must lift with a gasp and brake with my chest, a hopeless parachute that catches a little drag and slows my fall into the coming hairpin. A car pulls alongside, passing me as the road straightens and sends us along a flat ledge of the mountains: a shelf before the next drop, where cracks break free in the tarmac, small fissures from a part of the road slowly slipping down under its own weight, readying to join the sea and the wrecks at the bottom of the world. The ploughed earth of farmland ends, turning to dry grasses and the final grazing animals. Bedouin boys stand at the roadside with their flails – always aloft – in a wave to me, their jeans rolled up on skinny legs. Opposite and in the near distance, for the first time I see the mountains of Jordan, cradling out of sight that ruby of the Wadi Rum. Nearer at hand the brown red of hills slides into a rocky desert landscape, so that earth grows tiger stripes where the depth of old hollows and dried rivers leave the shapes of their black shadows. The mouths of the ravines gape wide, and the land commands me call out the voiceless names of those deep contours written in the earth and into which I scream. I smile, the earth lending its lightness and its play for just a moment, dissolving the politics as a sugar cube falls into tea. I see, but just for a moment, the faces of young children, pressed to the glass as the adults drive by in a car, and a young girl gives a smile and then a wave. Below I can see Jericho, see the outlying buildings that gradually cluster together and form a town, then a city, where Jesus was baptised at the foot of the mountain I race down. As it all flattens, I see the rigid rectangles of green palm plantations, growing like a verdant patch slapped on the desert, while beyond the town a pale white haze shimmers in a sign that there waits up ahead a vastness still greater than the one I see before me. An old house stands in ruin beside the road, its walls made from dried earth, a rich yellow marked with empty holes for its missing windows and doors. It is all crumbling back to soil, but beside it, where once might have been a garden, a perfect palm lances clear out of the ground and shoots up to the sky in proof that one day all that remains of our human projects are the trees that we planted. I take a new bend leaning out from me, and in my head ask myself again how so much that is ill can come to pass in such a place as this. The same voice as always chides me, a laughing comes through on the wind as the desert answers, simple and as flat as these opening horizons.

'Because humans have not yet learned how to fall in love with the earth.'

114

Onwards we continue, one of those impossible descents, tear-jerking with the rip of wind and the sheer audacity of so much earth to suddenly fall away so fast. I give a nod of thanks to the desert for its wisdom, take its offered thought and realise that perhaps the world it is not inherently beautiful, but that it is only able to show us that beauty which we keep inside us. While we still have unconditional love for ourselves and those we meet, and for the world itself, then land inspires in us change. But where eventually that strength of feeling calms, it becomes only land. I pedal fast between the drops in the road, along the brief bits of flat snatched back from gravity, and on two wheels the mountainside itself rides like a tiny evidence of freedom, so that as I bank quick left-rights and pick up speed, it feels clear that freedom exists in this world, and that it is inviolable.

But back to the road, back to the descent. Forgive my wandering mind a moment, it is just that here is one of those places where you can forget yourself a while. You forget the limits of regular possibility and regular speech and are simply lost to the desert, where polite company and measured statements do not tread, and if they did... forgive me, but they would look so ridiculous and suburban beside a landscape so eternal, just as all this talk of a freedom so complete maybe reads loud and garish when placed inside the quiet café, the armchair, the passing footfall of the streets outside where you perhaps now read these words. As on we press, the city of Jericho opening fast around me: where children play on bicycles, a woman buys baklava and *kadayif*, and an attendant with a hose sprays an arc of water across municipal gardens at the roadside. I move on through, see a church with a few nuns and the last of a worshipping congregation outside it. Pedalling now more slowly, I look through the iron gate, where *Ethiophian Orthodox Tewahdo Church* is written above two stone columns painted in the colours of Ethiopia. Clear bands of red, yellow and green frame the entrance beneath a metal cross pointing up towards the sky. And at this moment I see only a church and have no idea of the story waiting up ahead, the tale of faith that is kept strong inside this congregation and that I shall be able to tell you more of later. I flash by as a pair of fighter jets roar overhead and out of the town as I press down, deeper down and under the sea.

Training Drills

The Dead Sea is a parking lot. At the end of the road is a stretch of gravel, then a muddy expanse with pools of brackish water that slip into the narrow canals ploughed by tyres of tourist coaches rolling in and out all day. At dusk, a few coaches still remain, lined up inside the chain-link fence, where some bushes and small, dust-covered trees are dying, and the sea retreats with each of the rains that no longer fall. There is talk of replenishing this vanishing sea with water pumped overland from the Mediterranean, but some doubt it could work at all, and Israeli corporations that mine the valuable minerals of this rare earth worry the new water could upset the precise chemical balances their business relies on. Above ground too, this sea is also a cash register, and the day's last tourists walk out through a turnstile bathed in the neon sign of a bar featuring a palm tree. Plastic products are on sale, mementos and fridge magnets, as Westerners sit and sip at glasses of beer, eat fries. I walk up to a kiosk, where under a bright light a man waits framed inside his window.

'Is it this way to the beach?' I ask, pointing.

He nods. 'It closes soon, but for the last hour it is a discount.'

'I have to pay to get to the beach?'

His eyes roll with *of course*, but he says only, 'It is a private beach.'

I look at him, then the tourist shop, the parking lot and the chain-link fence. A sign shows a woman, her face and body covered in a mud apparently bestowed with magical, youthful properties. I look down at my forearms. As a touring cyclist, the idea of paying money to be covered in dirt feels odd. Even without that, the irony is too much. A beach resort at the very easternmost edge of the West Bank, taken from Palestine and then proclaimed a private beach by Israel. Often as I cycled, the only way I could make sense of what was being normalised was to imagine such things elsewhere, where the relevant rules were still intact. Here we were, in a beach resort separated from the country claiming it, by the entirety of the country in between and to which the beach in fact belonged. The Israelis making the town of Kalya their own is, in Europe, the Italians laying claim to a French beach, only not even one adjacent to it on the border, perhaps a plot outside Cannes, but in the west, at Biarritz.

Riding back out of the tourist compound, immediately behind its perimeter I pedalled past abandoned concrete huts, brightly coloured and flanked by a battalion of young Israeli soldiers practising military drills. I watched as they moved through the makeshift buildings in army fatigues, full uniform and with rifles drawn. In formation they stood, looking down the sights of their guns, feet spread, beside empty buildings simulating a combat zone they may or may not go on to fight in, but which would enable them to live all their lives seeing those people they lived among as enemies instead of friends. With sharp strides they moved forward to the calls of a superior officer. Through the dusk I could make out that each concrete hut had large illustrations painted on it, like grim murals for war. The words *Camels and sand*, were written above one concrete building painted yellow and red. *Wow*, began another hut, altogether stranger on the other side of the road, where underneath ran the line: *By using imagination hooligans turned wall to ART!* Finally, on the blank concrete wall that faced the battalion's thirty gun-barrels, most eerie of all was a building on which a figure was painted. In white underwear the yellow body of a man with the head of a fish stood confused beneath the words, *Am I Dead?*

⁂

Night fell soon after. Beside the road was a large drift of something halfway between mud and sand, white in colour, a solid escarpment with short, tufty bushes growing from it. I waited for a break in the occasional traffic on the road, and when the last tail lights were gone and no headlamps coming into view, I pulled off the asphalt, up the gravelly bank and out of sight. Pushing my bicycle at the handlebars I moved off into the desert, my rear wheel sinking into the earth as, slowly, the surroundings became as familiar as those I've known all over the world. My favourite bedroom anywhere: a place where I can see others and no one can see me.

⁂

In silence, the moon rises over the Jordan River, almost full and coloured the soft, ruddy yellow of a russet apple, from the sides of which passing clouds take perfect black bites. Sleeping here feels different to all of those other impromptu camping spots I've found around the world, where the land is more welcoming to passers-by because disputes over who owns it are mostly settled, distant enough in history not to trouble newcomers. My bed is contested, and so the land and the night are trapped.

A car tears by on the road behind me and I shuffle in my earth bed, feeling it give generously around the shifting imprint of my body. Heavily, silently the night sits, but for the passing winds that hit my bicycle spokes and bags. Am I afraid? I ask myself that old question, and wait, and I realise that, no, I am not. The question feels somehow more relevant here, in this land seized by Israel, for eventually in life you realise that a life lived with fear is in the end always worse than the thing you feared. Perhaps a country needs to live a century to learn that lesson, just as I had to sleep at more roadsides to figure it out, but, even then, my absence of fear is not really about faith. For lying beneath the stars, I do a working-out on the possibility of something bad happening to me here. I have met many people on my travels, including many who have had unfortunate lives, but still I found humans marked mostly by their tenderness or, at worst, their indifference towards others. On this evidence, it seems that the chance of life leading a person to do harm to others must be slim. Then, sleeping behind an anonymous bank of sand on the edge of the Jordan Valley, with not a soul about, the chance that anyone will find me here at all is also slim. The chance that the person who finds me is that same rare one willing to do harm to others – it must be almost impossible. And even in those circumstances, I have a final advantage, because I know that I am here and nobody else does, so that anyone who by chance discovers me will be more startled to find a stranger hidden in the desert, than I will be to find someone walking by. And so, in all things, I am not afraid as I fall asleep. But none of this is really faith, and certainly not bravery, but more, in all honesty, just arithmetic.

▓

On the edge of a waking sleep, eyes shut but blinking behind the lids. My face twitches. Footsteps. Unmistakable. A car door shuts. Someone's coming. Awake. Shouting, more shouting. I open my eyes, the moon has moved over the sky but everything else is unchanged. I roll onto my front, pull myself up the bank with my elbows, peer over the edge.

Lights, a flashlight on the tarmac, strafing over the earth, two vehicles pulled in, an engine rolling and then a small flatbed truck appears. On its back is a giant sign lit with heavy-duty bulbs that raise a huge red cross into the night. An illuminated arrow points to the other side of the road, directs passing traffic to give space. A road crew. Another shout goes up and the truck begins to move slowly, a man sitting on the flatbed platform with a pile of small, dark pyramids beside where his legs dangle above the passing road. The driver fires the horn and the man on the back lifts a pyramid, a traffic cone rises with a fluorescent flash, and he drops it to the road where it lands with a soft, heavy thud. The engine turns over, steady. Truck drives forward. Horn fires, man drops a cone, lands with thud. Forward, horn, cone, thud. Getting quieter as they move on down the road. In time floodlights are set up and I see the dark shapes of plant machinery with their teeth low to the ground. I roll onto my back and watch the sky as the machines trundle along, hammering, eating road, stripping it of asphalt and readying for a new surface. The road screams, the machine screams back, a pitched argument and all of it collapses into white noise as new vehicles arrive, dumpers piled high with aggregate. The long shadows of workmen move under the floodlights and I roll back onto my front, peer out again, watching like a witness as Israel builds out its infrastructure into a land that isn't theirs, but with the clear purpose to one day make it so.

The Road North

Dawn colours drop from the sky as I begin riding, my head heavy from a restless, waking sleep and its visiting thoughts. At the roadside are two gateposts, standing either side of open gates and a land otherwise unfenced. Beside a plot of land, an abandoned mud house of crumbling walls falls back to earth. Outside, an old garden of trees decays, and beside the broken house, two dying palms on wilting trunks drop down, one cleft in two and looping round on itself. And it all looks so grey and so aged, like old mammoth tusks, rib cages, serpents made in stone, snaking out of the ground.

Beneath the ruin, a tiny brick hut sits above a field of neatly planted date palms. A motorised buggy is parked, a small agricultural vehicle, but the place otherwise deserted. My water bottles are empty and so I walk in to see if here there waits any human, or preferably just a tap. By an old seat, plastic fabric fraying so that its bottom is falling out, hangs a cracked wall mirror, and in it I catch sight of my reflection. I see furrows in my brow, creases in my face, and as I look back at myself, I feel certain that this place is coming to haunt my dreams. I don't remember them, I just know.

⠿

Riding north that day, the reality of the maps became clearer. The occupation appeared at the roadside, parallel to the Jordan River, and in that stretch I also saw the meaning of the 'West Bank', a name that had always seemed odd for what was the *eastern* part of Palestine and Israel, but made sense once you saw it was simply the west bank of the river. The name corresponded to a time when today's Palestine had, with the retreat of the British, fallen inside Jordan, only for Israel's wartime gains to see the land settled as its own, and the people in it placed under military occupation. Behind solid blocks of green plantation, and in front of dusty red mountains that beyond them held the Wadi Rum, the drying river meandered faithfully over my shoulder.

As I went, the truths of the frontiers were revealed in those imaginary lines I rode over. For all my life I'd seen some version of the Palestinian territories as a wedge at Gaza and then a sizable bulge that spanned the bank of the Jordan River, sweeping north as high as Jenin, south to Hebron and, including East Jerusalem, took mostly a half of that land between river and sea. On the ground that day I realised that it was not so, for nobody had thought to tell the settlers about those lines or any legal force they might have held. I saw the politics of the water scarcity Nadim described, and all along that stretch was water shut behind lock and key. Beneath razor wire and inside high metal fencing stood pipes and hydrants and valves, looping into U-bends and uprights as they moved water into plantations, monocrops of palm trees, a regimented green canopy under which nothing else lived. That the cars passing me on the road had mostly Israeli plates was nothing new, and not really surprising given that Palestinians of Israeli nationality or with travel permits might well have been among the drivers. What was more telling was the number of Hebrew signs on plastic banners advertising something – perhaps jobs, perhaps produce – outside the settlement farms, so that across those miles of Palestine the number of farms using Hebrew must have outnumbered those in Arabic by ten to one.

Gradually I began also to notice the drivers, in large pickups and often Ashkenazi. They were hillbilly to look at them, so that in their European faces you saw just how the land had been colonised. At one moment, halfway up a broad sand dune, a man sat alone in the near distance. He was cross-legged, watching the desert with his dog, its front legs and paws stretched out in front. And in that image otherwise so peaceful, I realised that the occupation, determining who was able to sit where and in what degree of tranquillity, had made even the simplest of things and scenes so complex, or put more succintly, so wrong.

As the road unwound out of desert and into scrub, the crops changed, and palm trees gave way to plastic tunnels, acres of them glowing white in the sun. The water remained under padlock, and through the occasionally open plastic sheet I saw vines and plants with tomatoes or aubergines growing in rich red spheres or small orbs shining purple. Other fields had already been harvested, and across the dry earth were snared lengths of torn plastic and mangled metal frames where it had been easier to move straight through in a tractor without concern for what was being upended. So much expensive machinery itself indicated the presence of settlers, well-funded and subsidised by the government and the Jewish diaspora outside Israel: all of it sent in the aim of making Israel, from the river to the sea, a foregone conclusion. I thought again of where I was: on a Palestinian riverbank farmed for profit, but on its furthest eastern edge and the farming done by what was, by rights, the country to its west. In my mind I placed it in Europe, imagined Spain claiming a corridor of France for agriculture, not at Perpignan, but down the distant German border on the Rhine. The distances in that fifty-mile territory I rode through might have made it seem rather more trivial, but there was no escaping the principle at work.

Naturally the appropriation was not taking place without cost or consequence, and in front of the bus stops through that settler beltway you saw concrete barriers, painted yellow-red or left a dusty white. Each one was a crude monument to the fear of roadside ramming by Palestinian drivers finally taking what action they could against the occupation being waged against them, deciding to take matters into their own hands by removing a few settlers from the equation. As the whole country went on in its permanent war footing, in the background of these fortified bus stops I looked at the fortified water infrastructure, at those well-irrigated plantations, while Nadim brewed with rationed water, and the inevitability of conflict under such injustice was matched only by Israel and the world's indifference. As I rode, I thought of laws in the European Union demanding the labelling of food produced in these illegal settlements, so that customers had the power to choose not to buy it. Israel called the labelling, rather than the illegal seizing of Palestinian lands, a racist policy, and so the feud rumbled in European courts as the water kept coursing into the plantations.

Next to all of that, it was the Palestinian villages that said most about the cartography of the country and Israel's hold over it. At roadsides I would see those villages, built from sections of concrete, loose wood, sheets of metal, and every bit of it still resembling the temporary constructions civilians had thrown up as refugees from Israel's last war with its neighbours. At the entrance to each village, turning off the road, was always that large, red sign in white lettering and stern language. Hebrew, Arabic and English all warning of the lethal danger, and illegality under Israeli law, of citizens entering the Palestinian areas behind the sign. I had seen the same signs outside Ramallah, Jericho, the villages near East Jerusalem and many other smaller places so that – just like the Israeli soldier locked up in a garrison – here was another new perspective for me to make sense of. I'd always understood that Palestine was in no way contiguous territory, but suddenly I realised that the towns made sense mostly as a series of ghettoes. The map of Palestine and Israel, complete with its traced lines, served the powerful and the proud on both sides, and gave an illusion of two distinct territories, something that allowed Israelis to wash their hands of people in reality under their control, and allowed Palestinians with a dream of nationhood to pretend they held some sort of land befitting a state. The truth was that Palestine was a Swiss cheese, had more holes than my socks, and was only a constellation of villages with the people shut inside. Save for a few cities that served as larger ghettoes, Israel controlled it all.

It was looking at those red signs and the words 'Under the Palestinian Authority', that you realised the extent of it, and it dawned on me that the Oslo Accords had been nothing but an accountancy trick. The Palestinian Authority was a second set of books, a ledger onto which Israel shoved that which they did not want on their own accounts. What had happened was no different to the fate that had befallen the Native Americans under the reservation system of the US. Whether it was the pollution of a chemical factory, or oversight of a Palestinian population, the lines that had been lent to maps gave Israel a place to put anything it did not want and simply lie that it was in someone else's jurisdiction. The same accountancy trick was being used in Palestine to corral into small areas those people Israel sought to deny the existence of, and the fraudulent charade of a Palestinian Authority – with a few of its top brass bought and paid for – was intended to obscure rather than advance the lives of the Palestinians themselves. The ruse allowed Israelis to deny their responsibilities to those who had lived more than half a century without rights under Israeli control. As always, the land refused to go along with such a lie, and down that road I watched as Palestinians tried to build lives for themselves in what space had not been claimed by settlers.

With evening drawing closer, sun sinking lower to the west and a few fighter jets moving overhead in the direction of Syria, the fences began inching towards me. The Jordan border crossed the river and pressed its fence but a few metres from my side, and Israel pressed back with its own. Up and down each hill and divot in the land those fences were awkwardly laid, with electric voltage fed through high wires as the fencing performed contrived gymnastics between each elegant contour of land. Off to one side was a modern tractor and plough arm, or rather a sort of harrow, parked beside the border, leaving me confused at what or why agriculture would exist in such a tiny, arid gully. It was as I rode on that I realised, seeing neat lines of soil in regular spacing along the fence, that just as in Arizona I had once watched tyres bounce on rattling chains as a jeep pulled them through borderland dust, here too, the Israelis were raking clear the earth so that they could detect any footprints making their way in from the other side.

It was then that I stopped, fatigued with it, frustrated. I took my bottle and felt cool water move inside me as I drank. A little beyond me a sign read *'Stop! – Border in front of you'*, and at that I leant up my bicycle, stepping down past the sign, for I saw no border and no line that I was willing to honour. I climbed down the bank, down to those neat, tiny furrows of dry, ploughed earth, and because a border exists only where nobody troubles it, where nobody ever makes for the other side, I walked down, heavy-footed, through those furrows, marking my feet on their way towards Jordan and then, heavier again, back towards Israel, so that, although nobody really crossed into Israel at that spot that evening, to the border patrol, they would have done, and so I could help by reminding them once again, that they always would.

In the final hour of light, it happened, when all the world had been given gilt edges and begun to shine. Though life on the road is always full of moments that bring a wry smile of wider symbolism to the rider, most are meaningless to those who do not sit on the saddle with the lonely cyclist, who mostly goes happily and contentedly mad in the comfort of their own mind. That one, though, that evening... let me tell you, that instant was as if ordained by higher powers sending down a message.

For as I rode on, under the shadows of fences and razor wire, towards me they flew. Just a couple of dots at first, over the brow of a hill coloured in dry yellow grasses, the birds came, framed by two proud trees against a blue horizon. That couple became a few, and then there were a dozen, and then more still. The sky filled, all of those birds with wings beating in such elegant black lines, sketched carefully and flying through that perfect sky, down through the Galilee where the dozen became a score and then a dozen more, and then perhaps a hundred all in immaculate formation.

And I smiled as I rode, for it was just as Michael had told me back in Tel Aviv, only I thought that he'd meant something small. Some tiny curiosity for enthusiasts with binoculars around their necks and books in their pockets to identify different species of migrating crane. I hadn't expected this. By the naked eye alone you could see the colour of each feather, and if you missed the detail on one bird then you saw it on the next, and the next and the next, for the sky massed as if it were a single bird pressing south, the cranes making their journey away from the coming Russian winter and on to Africa, with all this terrain – the 'Middle East' to Westerners and 'West Asia' to the emerging Chinese – all of it just land in between. Moving above in close formation, so perfectly spaced, still more cranes kept coming into view until all the sky was filled. The rustle and hum became a rhythmic purring, a *whoosh, whoosh, whoosh* as birds pressed through the atmosphere in unison, each silhouette so graceful, steadily lifting on the air currents as I went north and they south, each of us in our own migration, all around the rustling sound of a million feathers gliding through that dusk and – it may sound odd, but I promise you – those feathers filled and then cut the air with the sound of a gentle laughter, falling down across me, and upon the borders below.

Part III

THE NORTH

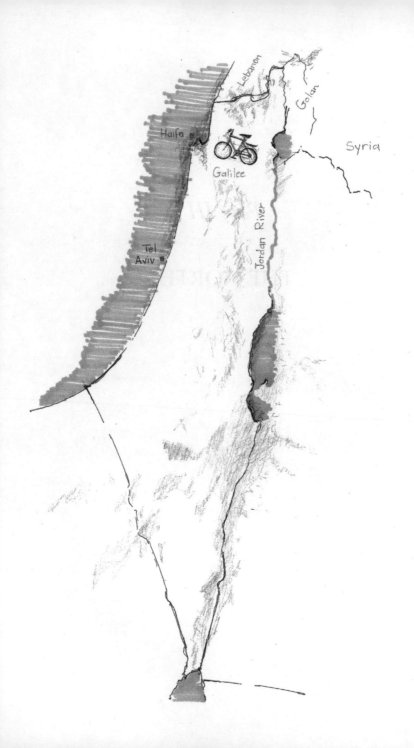

Druze

He stands over me, slides down a plate of fries, piled around and over the top of a small ceramic ramekin filled with an orange-coloured sauce. His other hand follows, sweeping down to give me a pitta wrap. Salad and a part-crushed falafel are falling out of the thing with the smell of broken cumin seeds.

'What's that?' I point at the ramekin.

'*Amba*!' he announces with wild fanfare, his bald head shining under the patio lights, eyes wide and face grinning. 'It's like…' He rubs his fingers, looking for the word on their tips.

'Spicy?'

He shakes his head, frustrated.

'A little spicy, but no. More like…' And he emits a noise of pain at the missing word. I sniff the sauce, look up.

'Smoky!'

He points right at me, smiles with satisfaction. 'Yes! That's it, *smoky*.'

I pick up a chip, begin to eat, the white light of his restaurant spilling out onto these few wooden tables beneath a shelter. Inside the restaurant two children play, pushing cars across the floor so that plastic wheels rattle and now and then a shrill siren sounds at the press of a button on top of a fire engine. We stand together, him with the look of a proud proprietor, curious at what I'm doing here, but for now more eager to find out what I think of his cooking. I give an approving smile. Laid out in front of me is my map of the region: a mess of lines, a damn mess of terrain all carved up. There are black dashes, solid purple lines, purple dashes, solid purple overlying black dashes. Each one looks like stitches, like humans attempting to clean up wounds. Some wrap around the nearby Sea of Galilee, one stakes out a nice plot on the beach while others cut out for the sparse hills of Golan where there are few villages but many rivers. The name Yarmouk, written in blue river, weaves through the mountains as the one thing that just goes where it pleases.

The picnic table at which I sit is just outside the main block of Israel, located in the corner of another territorial fillet. A few dates, years written in small font – *1948, 1976* – swarm across the lines, trying in vain to rationalise them, to make sense of them. Words also try to do their bit to calm the situation: *Regional. Frontier. Occupied. Neutral. Demilitarised. Armistice.* But none of them, try as they might, can make sense of so many human scribbles on those hills and valleys. International law says the land is Syria, reality has recast it by force as Israel, and the Yarmouk flows on, trying simply to ignore it all.

'You are cycling.' He asks his question as a statement.

I nod. 'Through Palestine, now to Haifa, then Eilat.'

'Ahaha!' He bursts out laughing. 'You cannot!'

I smile with him, go on eating and pull the map closer to the two of us.

'Can I ask where am I?' He looks confused as I ask, 'Is this Israel?'

'Of course!' His body language shifts. A quizzical smile, then a frown.

'And that way,' I point into the hills, 'to Syria?'

He raises his voice, 'You cannot go into Syria!'

'I know.' I point to a purple line. 'But is it the border there?'

He shouts again, 'You cannot leave the borders of Israel!'

I back away from the subject, sense that this guy is looking out for me, perhaps thinks I really might be crazy, smitten by some sort of conflict-wish, but his manner has overshot eccentric and feels unnerving.

'OK.' I try to calm the tension: 'But Golan? It's Israel, or Syria?'

We look at one another, he in his striped apron trying to figure out this strange provocateur with a bicycle.

'We conquered it.'

The word, so specific, settles with me in the night. His English is good, but that the word 'conquered' – which means only one very precise thing – has made its way into his vocabulary reveals something, a glimmer of language betraying culture. Briefly silent, we wait for the other to say something.

'But the people there…' he goes on, 'are good people. The Druze. They are Arab, but they are good people. They fight in our army.'

He moves on from me as I wonder how or if this loyalty is repaid, and then put away the thought to return to some other time. The man picks up trays with the discarded packaging of meals left on nearby tables. He wipes them down with a cloth, another who is just making a living behind the military curtain that shrouds this land. As I eat, the warm air and the food revive me, and it all feels so nourishing after the long road north. From inside the restaurant, the children shout at one another for their turn with a game. The smell of frying vegetable oil presses out the door and toys clatter faintly from a place far away from this talk of conflict or territory. A woman pushes a bucket across the tiles with her foot, where grey waters retreat from the cloth tassels of the mop head. Something has settled between me and the proprietor, an unspoken sense from somewhere in our evolution, our biology and our perception of threat, that this exchange can go no further without entering a condition neither of us wants, as if our brains are free to disagree but our bodies should not meet such tension lest it bring conflict. We step away from it, both of us with the luxury to get on with our lives, to leave it be because Israel's seizing of territory mostly only impacts on us in the abstract. He clears a few tables, then passes by me on his way back inside. A conciliatory smile appears in his dark, thick stubble, then a wave of invitation to the benches and rudimentary roof above as he disappears back inside with an offering that takes me by surprise.

'If you want, you can sleep here tonight. It is a good shelter.'

Across the patio, out of the corner of one eye, each of us watched the other eating. She had a sprite-like appearance, sitting bolt-upright and dressed in a loose shirt and sensible coat. The patio lights cut across her, so that half her face was darkened by a shadow.

'You're going to Haifa, by bicycle?'

She asked it almost in the concerned tones of a mother, and in perfect English. Her voice was sort of floating, dreamlike, but at the same time with that gravelly accent, passed down from the Eastern European Jews who'd first taught languages, whether Hebrew or English, in the days of Mandate Palestine, and then in Israel. They who left their rasping Yiddish and Slavic intonations to live in Israel's languages forever. I nodded as she went on eating: glasses perched on her nose, eyes soft and curious in a kind way as she ate her food slowly.

'It's a nice city.'

'Yeah?' I asked.

And she gave a nod and a happy smile. 'Different to any other city in Israel.'

'Different how?'

A laugh, a small enjoyment at keeping me guessing about that city by the sea. 'Oh, you just go, you'll find out.'

At our separate tables we went on eating, and I watched as

daintily she dabbed a paper napkin at her mouth. About her was an air of someone who is open to conversation but at the same time detached, like an artist or a dreamer, something of Neta, quietly indifferent to everything, as if the world were all just faintly ridiculous anyway.

'You live in this town?' I asked.

'Oh no, I'm just driving through.'

'Going far?'

'Not right now.' She chewed a mouthful of pitta, pressed into a pool of tahini. 'Down Highway 90, to near the Palestinian territory.'

I started at what this kind but very Israeli woman could be doing driving towards Palestine.

'I just came that way,' I said.

'And what did you think?'

'I don't know. It's hard to see.' I thought about what to say in response, and in this country you have to watch your tongue, but I resolved to trust to our common humanity. 'To see all of the settler farms in Palestinian land. It looks unfair, while the Palestinians are still in refugee camps.'

She gave a nod and went on eating, then spoke again

'There are also good things, examples of people coming together. We had one group of mothers, working together. Israeli and Arab together. And you know, I think it helped some of them to become better mothers.'

I bit my tongue, but perhaps my eyes gave away my thoughts, for in the tone of her voice was peace and warmth, but I sensed that she did not mean that both sides became better mothers, and rather that one had imparted wisdom to the other. And I consider all of the mothers that I have known across the Middle East, and in all the world there surely was no power that could match that of a mother from the Middle East caring for her child. So that in the end my tongue could not help itself.

'I don't think it's right to say it made Palestinian mothers better mothers!' I guffawed. 'I mean, that idea, it's so, so *colonial*.'

She smiled. 'Yes, yes, I suppose it is.'

Silence returned, a rustling of packaging as we went about our meals and I considered how it was that someone so seemingly thoughtful could think and openly say such a thing. I couldn't help but ask.

'Why are you going to the Palestinian territories? Isn't it illegal for Israelis to enter?'

'I don't go through, but I have to meet someone and drive them to Haifa.'

I kept looking over, confused.

'I'm in a group. We meet Palestinians to drive them to hospital appointments.'

Something in me thawed.

'Someone told me there are people who do that.'

She gave a nod. 'It is something we try to do, to help. To show that we do not accept this idea that we are so different.'

'It's a really great thing.'

She gave a half-hearted shrug, as if it mostly was not.

'It reminds us all that we are human in this conflict. That we will not be enemies.'

'It must be an interesting journey with your passenger.'

'It's always different, it is people. Sometimes a person wants to talk, sometimes not. I did go inside the checkpoint once, near Ramallah. I had an old lady with me, and it was raining and I was supposed to meet a family member who wasn't there, and there were no taxis. The soldier at the checkpoint let me in, it was no problem. I've never had any problem with any of the soldiers.'

She looked and gave a short grunt of laughter, raising a finger playfully.

'You see, we are not all such bad people. And many of the Palestinians inside the cities live quite normal lives.'

'I don't think you are bad people.'

In a distant voice she started talking again, visiting a memory.

'Last time I did it was very strange. It was the summer, and it was so hot. We were driving, me and the patient. I collected her at the hospital in Tel Aviv, and she was from Gaza. She was an old lady, she had cancer. Chemotherapy. And she was in the back seat, she was silent the whole way. It was early evening and as we got closer to Gaza, I saw these large shadows on the road, floating in the sky, all of them coming towards us.'

The woman lifted her arms and let them drift back behind her, as if swimming backstroke. She stopped talking, moving from her trance to look at me, speaking from another place as I listened, transfixed, and she giggled eerily.

'It was these, these fire balloons that Hamas send up, to attack us. That they fill with gasoline to float up and start fires when they come down. There was smoke on the horizon, and the patient and me just went on driving with the shadows on the road. I remember most of all that it was such a strange, red light, a really beautiful evening, and me and the sick woman driving together into the light, under the fire balloons.'

Towards Damascus

In the end I decided not to stay beneath the shelter at the restaurant, however kind the offer, but cycled out to sleep among the blankets of those hills folding into Golan. I camped in a field beside a stack of beehives in wooden crates. From there I could see one moonlit hillside beyond which I knew was Jordan, below me was the Sea of Galilee in Israel, and where I sat was legally part of Syria. The Druze of Golan, those the café owner had spoken of, are an ancient sect of mixed religions and secret orders, and the logic by which they survive the modern age is to make no trouble over the borders of which nation state claims their land. On the Syrian side they are Syria, on the Israeli side they are content to be Israel, but still they acknowledge themselves to be occupied, in anticipation of a day when the land will perhaps be restored to Syria, at which point they do not want their loyalty to the new claimant to be questioned. Wherever they are, they are Druze.

It grew cold on the banks of those old hills, and all across their slopes the night poured down. My temperature went with it, plummeting as cold worked into my bones until I was conscious of every bit of my rigid body. I welcomed it. There is something about the cold that presses at the soul, seeks it out, turning you to stone and in that slight discomfort it makes you forget all but the innermost parts of yourself. A wind came barrelling over the mountains, and found me, parted either side of my body, like a flooding torrent and a protruding rock. In that cold everything turned eternal, and I was so small, so timeless as a passing traveller exposed to those ancient mountains. My body searched inside itself for what warmth it could. In the backs of the legs, beneath my arms, my consciousness pulled there like people on streets gather round a fire in an oil drum, or an old man with a book covets the light in a dim room as he reads. Eventually, after I do not know how long, even that warmth was snuffed out, and the cold had all of me, made me one with the mountainside and the black sky. The rain fell gently on my tent, so light and so kind, the sound of its patter, tap-tapping, tap-tapping a song, as the wind blew still from the depths of Golan.

On the opposite shore of that sea, I watched the orange lines of street-lighted roads and the sprawl of cities. In the evening now gone, helicopters or jets had moved above, heading northeast, deeper into occupied Golan and across the Syrian frontier beyond. In the darkness, with the towns of Israel and a few holiday villages below, it was hard to imagine that Damascus was only a few dozen miles away. As the last of a civil war faded, to leave only rubble and the fears of retribution by an untoppled regime, I imagined the city that refugee friends in Istanbul had told me was famed for its fragrant jasmine on every street, and which I had tried to tell them would one day be known again for such beauty rather than sorrow.

Between that land where I slept and Damascus were the last battling fighters of Daesh, built out of the remnant of the Iraqi army once routed by invading forces commanded from Washington and London. That spent force had gone on to fuse with a disaffected rabble arriving from around the world, who had taken the symbols but not the faith of Islam and started what they had called a caliphate, the so-called Islamic State. You know all this now, but still I feel that I should state it, because one day in a land as old as this, it will all just be the history of a brief time.

In the hills behind me, so sparsely populated, two things had received less attention even during those days of a sudden, frenzied interest in the region. In the fences beyond my camp, where the Golan Heights that Israel occupied turned to Syria proper, injured jihadi fighters had crossed regularly into Israel for medical treatment, arriving to be stitched up and then returned to the battlefield. Others still had received weapons for fighting, and though it was said that none had been directly supplied to Daesh, little was known of where anything had ended up. Even as Israel's allies in the West declared Islamic extremism to be the world's greatest threat, Israeli generals were clear that they were less concerned by such terrorists than a Syrian regime receiving support from a regional power like Iran. As has always been the case with calculations in the Middle East, Israel was content to support a few religious extremists, so long as they fitted a wider strategy, and gambling that they wouldn't be made to regret it.

To Haifa

From the hills over Tiberias I look down at Galilee, trying to see beauty in the view. The land is set in uniform squares, coloured mostly with the pale, dirty white of banana plantations. The plants grow under large expanses of nets, made from mesh dense enough to hold moisture inside and save water, but open enough to let sun pass through. Beside the plantations is a jigsaw of intensive agriculture; the many slanting rectangles of cattle-shed roofs line up one after the next like the teeth of a saw. I see silos, hoppers, metal turrets of the animal feed factory, and other concrete boxes from processes kept invisible. The earth here has been capitalised, industrialised. Earth itself has been put to work, and while that might be the case across so much of the world, here, with the memory of the West Bank, and the knowledge that much of the land is technically Syria, it is hard to separate the view from the politics of who controls it and for whose benefit. Next to the industry, suburbia never looked so normal, but at the same time, I think suburbia never looked so compromised. The plantations, the dairies, the ranches, all of it pulls the water from that parched West Bank downstream on the Jordan River, which as I pedal higher, I can still make out winding sleepily south. The houses all around me are in orderly lines, like children's toy sets where the streets cut the village into grids. It is all of it so managed, so neat, but at the heart of the project *here*, I know there is a contempt for those I've seen *there*, and I cannot shake my thoughts from them.

Sweating into the long climb from the valley, upwards I move, with heavy breaths pushing out from the steam of my own engine. To travel by bicycle is always a pilgrimage, one where you work for every metre of land, based on an assumption that the sweat you spill will give you beauty, will take you someplace pure, bring you to a peaceful place and not one that is filled with this sort of unease. Perhaps normally we are able to see land without seeing politics, in a way that feels impossible here. I put my head down, watch my legs rise and fall as they turn their orbits and the chain shines, reminding me to oil it. Done well, climbing high hills is a sort of meditative act, where your mind has to take a certain leave of itself in order to shut out the distractions. Most of the time, you settle on a single thought to block out all the others. The wind on the mountains, the dots of colour from roadside flowers, the sky blurring blue... it all helps. But on this hill I have been struck down hard by thought: I try to see beauty but I can't, I try to see beauty but I can't. The sentence does laps in my mind, attached to the turning chain ring as the road stands up square in front of me, with the sun shining off its sheer face as the hills command the words:

'Try harder.'

Over the crest I motor, shift gear, pick up pace and head west. Out of the Jordan Valley the land begins to move, opens, so that I can see across hilltops yawning for the new day. At the roadside the rosemary has gone to seed, bolted blue and into flower. The city of Tiberias sprawls up a hillside, regular blocks of white concrete, as I round another bend and watch the Sea of Galilee and the Jordan River trickle finally away and out of sight. Either side of me I see tree plantations, quarrying, warehousing and then housing plain and simple. Shovel-ready, earth is being broken for new residential property. Hoardings go up offering units for sale on the legally recognised part of Israel – behind the Green Line – where the well-off or simply more conscientious families like to buy their fair-trade home on legal land but with the price premium it involves.

From on high I can see the entirety of the land, spreading over sunlit hills beneath the gaping brown ridges of Golan, where the slopes under which I slept are set with the wrinkles of long-gone glaciers. Among all the signposts I see a few illustrated with a symbol of tombstones marking cemeteries. One after the next and I can't help but consider how much territory that was of Palestine is now home to the bodies of a Jewish diaspora, sent for burial in lands they never lived in and perhaps never visited. An Irishman once told me that the national airline had stopped flying bodies back from the US to Ireland, a service that had seen four dead Irish-American bodies stowed on every flight back across the Atlantic for decades. Humans always want to believe that they belong somewhere else, somewhere different, magical, the places we never spent long enough in to lose their romance.

Up ahead the highways stream, windscreens catch pockets of sun, glinting one after the next as they press forward. Day grows, I see towns with minarets, some towns with Arabic names and others that look like they were remoulded into Hebrew forms. I see giant basins of concrete, reservoirs mostly full, sluices opening to let water gush as birds float on the surface. In roadside laybys are vast puddles, spreading into darkening earth. The water, sweet water, drains away towards lush green weeds that shoot up and indicate that this spillage from the tanker happens often. I ride through fields planted with pistachio trees, fields sea green with sunlit grass. I see the scrape of excavators quarrying, turning mountainsides to right angles. Trucks remove earth and rock, a plume of dust floats on my headwind from where a digger lifts dry soil into a dumper, rotating on its turret, a construction pirouette, breaking earth for the housing project on another billboard. And it all looks unstoppable.

East to west I shift, sun south over my shoulder and racing me for Haifa and the Mediterranean as traffic builds. The two-lane highway turns three, turns four, turns trucks, *trucks-trucks*. Thirty miles for the day comes and goes, then forty. 'Haifa' gets more frequent on every junction and then, cresting the slow peak of another hill sliced open by road, I see a city growing in a valley below. Chimney stacks are smoking, the rampart of a distant hill is lined by apartment towers in silhouette. There are a couple of skyscrapers and then a misty blue expanse behind them, thin and pale. There it is. The sea. The Mediterranean Sea. And I realise what by accident I've done. The River to the Sea. In barely a day, by bicycle and without even meaning to, I've ridden from Jordan River to Mediterranean Sea, those boundaries so natural, eternal, proclaimed by both as the land of Palestine and of Israel so that I bet that misty river and that poor, glistening sea wish they hadn't been roped into any of this. For the first time I realise in full clarity that this place is just fifty miles wide. Why not just have all live here as equals, by whatever name each person chooses to call it? I imagine a time ahead when this place is a single state, but in their heads its citizens will have software that will be set to a factory default that hears or reads either the name *Palestine* or the name *Israel,* as they prefer, while a few who believe in a world without borders switch their setting to *Palisrael* because it allows the convenience of receiving information on both frequencies.

Rolling over the hilltops, I begin to gain speed. There is work still to be done, a cold wind is coming and I must make Haifa before dark. A debris of road-building and smashed-glass, car-crash confetti is sprinkled all down the hard shoulder. Across to one side I see olive trees surrounded by conifer. A sign reads *Come plant a tree...* complete with the logo of an organisation, but something in this land makes me suspicious of everything and so *Plant your own tree* is the sentence I hear forming in my own head. I plough on into the remaining road, towards the first dusk-kissed outline of Haifa, winking at me in shades of red and purple, inviting me to come into its hills where, beyond, the sea waits so patiently.

With the cold wind growing, I scream down yet more hills cut through rock and, in the last valley, there appear great turrets of industry, smoking chimneys, flaring gases... as if a final fortress blocks my approach. In the outlying fields all around are crop sprayers on large wheels that carry a half-kilometre hose to irrigate the furrows. The soil is silt black but flecked with the smallest dotted shoots of lime green. Flashing by me is the sign for the refinery, where chemicals are processed beneath roaring torches of ragged flames. Its name rings out: *Gesher*, a factory that was one of the crowning industrial glories of Zionism. Its architecture sits in twinkling lights under the dusk. There is a scaffold of pipes for catalytic cracking, there are balloons of metal, there is smoke pushed from candy stick chimneys painted red and white beside that roaring flare of gases. On and off, on and off they blaze. Above metal chambers, hooked up to one another like organs of a body, the gases breathe in yellow flames. A train along the railroad shunts in slowly as another rolls out, gathering speed, its tankers bedded on railroad cots that move into the shadows of flyovers, and still more cold wind comes at me off the Mediterranean.

The traffic pummels beside me, forcing its way at Haifa, stoppered into bottlenecks at every junction. Suddenly it's like all of the beings are gone, shut inside their machines. All human activity has vanished, only industry survives and then I see a string of onions dropped in the concrete gutters of the roadside, fallen from a passing truck, white bulbs pushing out their brown skin and at last some sign of life, organic matter in a place otherwise so manmade. Cars, trucks and then more cars go barrelling down into the vortex. A speed gun at the roadside clocks me amidst the torrent, bright orange numbers flash against the black sky coming. *KMH*

85, 92, 86… then here I come… *37…* Not bad, Jules, not bad. A cold wind pushes again, up out of the sea and I should put on layers but really I just want to arrive. There's no stopping. The wind bites my skin and chills my chest as I see a human, taking to the aisles of traffic and trying to wash windscreens for a few shekels at a junction. Waved on, waved on. Fighter jets scream overhead as trucks roar at my side and suddenly it is all only engines, the sonic inputs fusing to form a shared audio track, ever rising in volume as I ride at the heart of the machine. Another freight train chugs, railway yard tracks gleam with flashes of lit steel and then there appear the empty cribs of a double-decker car transporter. I see the port, cranes with winches and pendulum hooks the size of small houses. At last, breaking through a light turning back to red, I lower myself into the closing straight. Flat to the bars, I keep the hammer down, bumping over a strip of solid white-painted lines as traffic swarms from one side to join me and the glare of bright headlights peels away my vision until suddenly, under my nose, on a blue-white tablecloth, a plate of hummus slides down with a well of oil and green spears of parsley at its centre. A hearty slap lands on my shoulder and a warm, welcoming face smiles and booms at me its one demand: 'Enjoy!'

The hummus is too good, disappears too quick, the bowl emptied clean. I'm still hungry. A man a few tables away is finishing something else. Soft red and wholesome, remains smeared around the edge of a bowl. I look up at the waiter, or perhaps he is just a friend of the owner, who has watched me eating with the proud, protective demeanour of someone entrusted with the wellbeing of a stranger. I nod towards the other customer.

'Can I have that?'

'*Ful?*' replies the man.

I nod first, then ask, 'What is it?'

The man orders for me in Arabic from the woman who runs this kitchen. She is wearing a purple apron, has a lilac scarf loosely over her head. In plastic sandals over socks she walks to a pot behind the counter, takes a ladle and drops it in before pouring some steaming lava into a bowl for me. With a flicker of fingers, she follows it with a scatter of green parsley.

'Beans!' booms the man, as the owner walks towards me, slides down the new bowl and I look at it, another of those meals good enough to create a home in an instant, to bring your grandmother back to life. She smiles at my obvious appreciation of her food, then turns slowly back to her counter, like a surgeon in theatre or barrister in court. She picks up the handle of a large glass jug that by rights looks like it should contain water or juice and yet here it is olive oil. Yellow, beautiful yellow. She returns to me, pours it and one *glug* and then two *glugs* fall into my beans so that a bar of yellow hits the heat of the bowl, and warms ever so gently the perfect smell that moves up to my nose.

'You like the food?' asks the man.

I nod, blowing on the spoon before putting it down, urging patience on myself. I tear at a pitta bread, pillow-soft, and it parts with that same breath of steam and baked flour.

'It's like it is in Palestine.'

He frowns, as if I have misunderstood something, then gently presses his hand at the shirt on his chest.

'I am Palestinian,' he says. 'We are Israeli citizens. But we are all Palestinian here.'

'Someone told me that Haifa was like that, more mixed.'

He smiles. His voice is kind, not eager to mould my view into his, only report this fact of the world.

'Haifa... it is an Arab city. When the Israelis came in 1948, we say there is no Christian, Jewish, Arab. And we keep it this way. Just Haifa.'

'But why is it like that?' I blurt it out, in search of this clue to the riddle I seek. But he just smiles.

'Palestine, Israel... It's Haifa! Haifa is like this. I don't know why.'

The woman who runs the restaurant moves along in a slow dance with her mop, pushing it across the floor. Her hair is tied back in its scarf and she looks round at us. With a big, life's-good sort of a smile she gives a thumbs-up.

'Israel OK!' She smiles. 'Israel no problem, Israel good.'

The man has his arms folded across the barrel of his chest, gives a chuckle at the simplicity of this verdict. The man and woman look at one another and both laugh before speaking Arabic together in playful argument.

'Many other places were like this once, like Haifa, with Arab buildings and people living together. But not now.'

'What changed?'

'Israel has very good army.' He ponders it, nodding to himself. 'They have good guns. They organised. That is why it happens. They don't like Arabs being strong, that is why they want war with Iran.'

'Iranians aren't Arabs,' I correct, though he bats my pedantry away.

'But Iran helps Arab countries.' He points north. 'Like in Lebanon. Israel don't like this.'

I listen to his words but continue eating. He gives another shrug, as if this is all obvious anyway, and then walks over to the door. He stands and takes out a cigarette and lighter, strikes a flame and then inhales deeply. I wonder how this country of Israel plans to survive, in this land of three threats. First: it is surrounded by neighbours that Israel never liked and that in turn came to dislike Israel all the more, countries where the population includes millions of refugees who had to flee the arrival of Jewish paramilitaries. Second: inside the territory Israel controls, the Palestinians are ghettoised, blockaded away, with grievances that become more justified and more bitter each year. Third: inside the land and even the citizenship of Israel's agreed borders, there is a quarter of the population who remember and know only too well what has been done to them, and what is being done to their relatives without citizenship elsewhere under Israeli control. The tension of this entire country feels like the culmination of these three fault lines, which can be met, I am starting to realise, with only two options. On the one hand, Israel can grow ever more brutal in its surveillance and punishment of the Palestinians inside both Israel and Palestine, while warmongering against the nations that surround it. On the other hand, Israel can take the path towards justice, and so peace. To do that, however, it must recognise that its starting point is one where much hate has already accumulated, and where much of what caused that hate was its own doing.

As the man smokes his cigarette in the falling drizzle, and the woman cleans the floor of her restaurant, I think of her position in it all: an Arab, Palestinian woman but with Israeli citizenship and no concern for Palestinian rights because she has her own rights in Israel. On one level I think she is betraying her fellow Palestinians, for she uncritically takes the rights they are denied, and praises the oppressor for giving them to her. On another level, what choice did she ever have, and what good could her own dissatisfaction bring for others anyway?

There was a twentieth-century economist called Hirschman, who reasoned that when the world gives us a dispute between separate parties, we are left with three options other than violence. They are *exit*, *voice* and *loyalty*. You can *exit* and disengage: you can boycott, divorce, you can divest yourself, but you should be sure that the severance of the ties achieves more than their leverage could have. You can use *voice*: you can reason and persuade, state evidence in the way that the man now smoking at the doorway did. Perhaps through *voice* you can set ultimatums for the eventual use of *exit*, or perhaps it can solve the dispute altogether, can rekindle bonds. As I watch the woman cleaning the floor of her restaurant in Haifa, I think I see in her the quiet, complex power of *loyalty*. First, she candidly professes her support of Israel. But, in her own way, the woman also performs an unwitting service to the Palestinians, because her indifference to that struggle in return for the Israeli good life demonstrates – even to Israelis – that on some level Palestinians are actually just like them. Her loyalty to the relationship, in some respects, works against Israel's total dehumanisation of Palestinians and Arabs, for it makes plain that Palestinians can be content with and even loyal to Israel's existence, if they simply receive justice. Skin colour, hair and native language really are only quirks of our identity as we all go pursuing the same thing. But whatever her disinterest in that struggle, her loyalty also makes a quiet threat on behalf of the Palestinian cause, for it reminds Israel that it has a degree of acceptance which can be lost to injustice, or that can be increased in return for rights. And so, perhaps it is the case that loyalty even has its own voice, but it is the quietest of the three and so too the one that Israel, at its own peril, risks failing to hear.

With a shout the man jolts me from my reflections. 'Have a good journey!' he calls out, finishing his cigarette with a wave as he heads into the night. I eat the rest of my bowl of *ful* and watch the woman lay her mop on the floor. She slides it under the metal kitchen counter to retrieve debris from the day's cooking. Tired but content she leaves everything spotless, and her politics are suddenly visible as no more than the completion of her own day's work. With a benign selfishness, the woman is performing her own service to the pursuit of peace.

As I pack up my pannier bag half an hour later, preparing to leave for where a friend waits at a bar, the woman mops the threshold clean of the last customer's footprints. Leaning out of the doorway, ready at last to end her day, she empties the bucket onto the pavement. Water and grey suds run down towards me, heading for the gutter, parting for a moment as they meet my feet, wash under me and away.

Darina

The venue has a fashionable crowd, is elegantly lit and is found halfway up the highest hill in the city, where outside climbing plants fall onto a terrace. 'Haifa is changing. Now it's the same as everywhere... the Ashkenazi, the rich people, live at the top of this hill, Arabs at the bottom.' With a voice of cynicism, someone in the bar will lance my cheerful impression that Haifa is maybe something of a model for Israel. Around us, the walls have been peeled back to their plaster, with a few shreds of paper and wiring as a mark of what was once there. Across from me sits Darina – nose pierced, lipstick scarlet, short curls of hair standing upwards – who makes a look of apology and takes a call, mouthing the word '*sorry*' as she answers it.

While she talks, let me introduce you. Darina was at first in fact only the friend of a friend but apparently – among Palestinians and with a bicycle involved – that was close enough. At the time of our meeting, she had just fulfilled the unfortunate first requirement of becoming an artist, and moved out of her own apartment to go and live with her parents. Life there was driving her almost but not quite as crazy as the jobs she'd previously had to work on behalf of a landlord, and she was trying to spend what she saved on rent buying art materials and promoting herself, rather than going out to preserve her sanity. Living thirty miles from Haifa, she visited the city often, her friends were there, and when I got in touch, gladly she had said she'd organise for me to spend the night at the apartment of her old flatmate.

She laughs into the phone as I watch the room, where a small crowd is forming in the corner of the bar, and a musician tightens the strings of a cello. Darina looks up apologetically from her phone call. I give a small wave of my fingers and the waiter comes by, asks in Hebrew what we're drinking. Darina looks at him and then at me, 'Two beers?' I nod as she turns to the waiter and speaks a few words of Hebrew, then returns to the handset where she speaks Arabic a few moments longer, before hanging up.

'Sorry about that.'

'It's OK. It's fun, strange, hearing you move between Hebrew and Arabic.'

'This language, you know, sometimes I really dislike it. It is a language of my oppression, against my people. But sometimes I find myself even thinking in it.'

The waiter returns, puts down two cold bottles of brown glass, *Shepherds* the name on the label.

'It's from Palestine,' she says proudly. 'Nablus.'

'I didn't know there were so many breweries in Palestine. I visited Taybeh.'

'It's growing. Some Israelis didn't want Palestinian beer sold in Israel.'

I roll my eyes.

'And I heard some people in Palestine wanted to boycott Taybeh for selling their beer to Israel.'

'I guess I understand it.'

'Really? Isn't it just good to have people drink Palestinian beer in Israel?'

'I don't know, yes. But this is not a neutral thing. Why sell to the person who is trying to ruin your business? The export controls, the checkpoints. All this is deliberate, so why sell to them?'

'I guess the people buying and drinking it don't feel that way. And at least it makes people in Israel aware that Palestine exists.'

Darina straightens slightly at my choice of word.

'This cultural *awareness* stuff, this normalisation of what is happening, we have to be suspicious. Israel are happy to claim our food, our drink, our music, our embroidery for dresses. They claim all of it as Israeli, but they deny our rights. All over the world people are talking now about Israeli falafel, but falafel is not Israeli. This is not for peace, it is stealing our culture, which is all we have.'

'How does it feel living here, inside Israel?'

She sighs, opens her arms wide. 'I am Palestinian. I am also an Israeli citizen. Arabic is my mother tongue, but I am bilingual Hebrew. There are two million like me inside Israel. There are two million Palestinians in Gaza. Four million in West Bank. My family live in their "original" home, but inside Israel are many Palestinian refugees who were moved from their homes in '48. Another four million Palestinians in Lebanon, Jordan, Syria. We cannot all just disappear.'

Darina looks at me, her dark eyes smiling, though maybe also a little tired.

'But I am afraid that all of this started with some big trauma in Europe, a catastrophe. And maybe that is how it ends here.'

We drink for a moment in the deepest silence I have felt so far, as a Palestinian confesses her fear of a final solution. Darina has a headband with flowers on it that match her blouse, and she puts down her bottle and resets the headband, her red nails bright against her black hair.

'How do you deal with it?' I ask.

She gives a shrug. 'I just want to leave. I have been two years in a long-distance relationship with my boyfriend from Ramallah. We live less than one hundred kilometres apart, but he has no permit to travel to Israel, and I cannot visit often because Israel might not let me return home.'

'Really?'

Darina nods. 'They do this sometimes. They don't let you back in if they suspect you. My aunt for years also had her life ruined because she had the guts to be in a relationship with someone in Palestine. My parents are afraid of the same situation for me.'

'What did your aunt do in the end?'

'Eventually, you have to find a way.'

I nod, still curious at the enigmatic answer. 'What was hers?'

'In the end, they got papers to move to Sweden. She and her husband are together now in Stockholm.'

'That's crazy. How do you and your boyfriend manage?'

'We see each other in Jordan, in Turkey, Istanbul. Holidays. He is studying in Amman now. I have applied to study in Japan. So we could go there. Japan is starting to make immigration easier because of the low birth rate.'

I smile at the thought of two Palestinians relocating to Japan to be together.

'Do you ever feel guilty? Having an Israeli passport and knowing it makes your life easier?'

'It's hard. I just got my Palestinian passport, last month. And it meant so much to me, even if it is just paper. This identity that I feel but in Israel I have no evidence of. It's me.'

I look at her: the pierced nose, the floral dress. Twin tails of eye liner flick up in black at the corner of each eye.

'Maybe you are how it changes here? Because you will stay in Israel as the person you are, living your values and making change. Or you leave, and you take that perspective and those values to Japan, Sweden, wherever. Then more people become aware and eventually everyone will know what is happening here.'

Darina nods, half-convinced. As if this is as good a plan as any.

'Tonight I can take you to Khalil's. But if you want a rest tomorrow, and not cycle, in the morning I can pick you up and maybe we can visit Akka. It is a nice town on the sea. I can show you my village, my parents' place?'

Darina gives the invitation with a bright smile. I think about it a moment: Brain considers the miles I need to cover, only for Soul to remind me that there's no point travelling anywhere unless you're prepared to change your schedule once in a while.

'Thank you,' I reply. 'That would be really nice.'

In the corner of the room the cello strikes up, the bow reverberating across the strings as the cellist shuffles upwards to settle the varnished wood between her thighs. She stops a moment and takes her dark hair, places it over a shoulder, looks up and gives a smile to the small crowd. Her face is Palestinian, Arab, but really, she is just a musician. Candlelight breathes up and down the walls. Her drummer is Ashkenazi, but also, again, just a musician, dressed in denim dungarees over a white T-shirt and with his head shaved against the onset of balding. He dusts his sticks lightly on a snare drum and cymbal, and I watch his feet tap out a rhythm as heads in the room turn towards the makeshift stage with the slight hush of quietening conversation.

A Big Stress

Khalil sits on his sofa, feet up on the table. Opposite us on the screen is a news reporter, talking about events in Tunisia, a deal in Qatar. Khalil looks over at me, makes eyes as he invites another toast of our wine glasses. Rain hammers down outside the window, its drops catching the lamplight as they stream from spilling gutters. Khalil wears an immaculate white shirt with a stiff collar unbuttoned to the chest, which looks like it has maybe been waxed, or at least groomed. He has a day or so of stubble on his cheeks and chin, but a perfect black moustache: a picture of handsomeness. Two wine glasses face one another: his nearly empty, mine mostly full. The wind off the sea, the chill and then sun and then chill, those miles and those hills on the road from the Jordan River – my energy is sapped.

Eager to sleep, out of politeness alone I drink more, accept his top-up. The flat is small, tasteful, has a kitchenette with a coffee machine, some art on the walls. On one wall is the framed illustration of two Arab men, face down on a bed and wearing only socks and pants, one reaching off the bed for a bottle of liquor, and out of the window the minarets of the mosque. He senses my tiredness, pats the sofa.

'You can sleep here on the sofa.' He points to the door to one side. 'Or we can share a bed if you like. It is up to you, whatever is most comfortable for you.'

I look at him, looking at me, everything about him so perfectly made up.

'I'm always good with a sofa,' I reply. 'What are your plans tomorrow?'

'I have work early. I go to the studio and prepare the afternoon programme.'

'How is it, working in news here?'

'It's OK. Our station is independent. We broadcast to EgyptSat, the Egyptian satellite, so we have more control.'

'It goes across the Middle East, not only Palestine?'

'Yes, the whole region. But it's hard being an Israeli-Palestinian in the Arab media. People do not really see us the same way. We don't get the opportunities, so it is hard to move away.'

'And do you feel you could be at home in Israel?'

'No,' Khalil smiles warmly. 'But I'm not talking to my Israeli friends about this anymore. They don't get it.'

He sips his wine, sighs the sound of a long day, a long week, a long life. He goes to the bottle, offers me more and I place my palm over the rim with a grateful smile.

'You get on with people OK though? I mean, you do have Israeli friends?'

'Of course. But Israel, here, it is different to anywhere else I have been. It's like there is a big stress on them that we cannot help them with.'

Khalil gets to his feet with a smile, leaving me with his words to consider. He takes a long drink of his wine, almost finishing it, then puts it back down on the table.

'I will get ready for bed now. Like I say, you can sleep on the sofa, but I will have to turn the light on in the morning. Or, if you want, we can share the bed?'

Darina – Akka

We walk along the end of the sea wall, Darina taking the role of my guide. The Mediterranean looks angry, ill-tempered, and yesterday's chill wind has grown up to the beginnings of a storm proper. The sea hurls itself against a sheer fortification of old brown stone wrapped in the rich blue waters.

'This is the wall of the castle. Here in Akka, in the summer, it is a big thing for a boy to jump from here into the sea, to show he is a man.'

I look over the edge, some twenty metres at least.

'It's a long way down.'

Darina nods, points through the spray at a thick cloud that sits so low.

'And when the weather is good, from here you see Lebanon.'

I follow her pointing finger, straining my eyes.

'See, past those rocks there.'

The wind blows against us, leaving some dark and distant shapes of land just visible before again disappearing into mist. On a strong wind, large and heavy cloud shifts slowly, like a herd of grey cattle making its way across the sky, their dust and haunches bulging outwards, opening and closing ranks. In the opposite direction are Haifa's docks and cranes, and again I realise how compressed this land is.

'It's all so close.'

Darina nods. 'That's why I think Israel has peace with Lebanon now. Because Hezbollah are stronger and it is more dangerous to attack. Last time Israel fought Lebanon, they said the Israeli soldiers were not prepared. They didn't know how to fight. They were afraid. Hezbollah were hiding and jumping out on them. They were stronger, better.'

We walk back through the town, passing a large group of Dutch tourists with umbrellas and plastic cagoules, raindrops spattered on see-through capes over their clothing. We walk through old arches of stone, with shops selling household oddments, herbs, spices and dried fruits. The smell of coals and a quick front of heat moves out from one of the archways, and a man wafts a piece of cardboard at a tray of embers, beside skewers waiting to be rested upon them. My legs are weary, from the riding of recent days but maybe more because I am not riding now. Footsteps so quickly become unfamiliar.

'It's a really beautiful town,' I say, meaning it, but also to make conversation as Darina moves ahead of me with an umbrella under her arm.

'It is, but because it is an Arab town, there is so much politics here. People are not allowed to do renovations on their buildings, so eventually they fall down and Israel will rebuild them in an artificial way. People worry that Akka will become an Israeli version of an Arab city, like a Disneyland by the sea.'

'Do you visit a lot?'

'I used to. I used to work with young Palestinians here. They have problems, because schools in Arab areas get less funding. There is discrimination, so jobs are hard to find. So the kids are vulnerable. Some turn to crime, of course. I know one teenager who was smuggling drugs for dealers to make some money for his family. His mother was so ashamed when she found out.'

We walk beside another store with many colours of plastic bucket and bowl piled up outside. A woman in a long coat and the uniform of a housewife out shopping stands, holding a new cheese grater in one hand and a plastic bag of vegetables hooked over her elbow. I turn to Darina, not sure what else to say but the truth feels so inescapable that not doing so seems odd.

'It feels like every part of life is difficult here, has politics in it.' She nods.

'Everything is difficult because even outside of the occupation, or the blockade, our communities get less. We have so many fights to fight. Women's rights, gay rights, the environment... for Palestinians we have these struggles but all our energy has to go fighting the occupation. Now in my village we are collecting money for Gaza. The children there. This week I wrote to some companies, asking for donations for food, this dehydrated, medical food, to send to children having chemotherapy in Gaza. They can't afford anything, not even the... I forget what this is called, this dried powder?'

'Formula?'

'Yes, they cannot afford the formula. I had to go through the village collecting. People help, of course they do, we have a small charity to get donations. Last month I went to the village account-ant... he does our taxes, as a donation. I told him about the new programme to raise money for the sick children in Gaza, how they have nothing to eat. Right away, he opened his drawer and gave me 300 shekels. Then another man walked into the office, the town chemist, and when he came into the room the accountant pointed at me and ordered him, right away: "Give this girl 300 shekels now."'

Darina laughs.

'Then we explained the money and he said he was happy to. He went to get more people to donate. The community all try to help, but what they have in Gaza is so deep. There is so much trauma there now. A friend who lived there told me that sometimes you worry if just any noise outside is the Israelis roof-knocking.'

'Roof-knocking?'

'It's when they fire a shell at a building to bounce it off the roof. It is to get people to leave before they blow it up.'

Sometimes the words are too much to believe and I have none of my own.

'The first time I met that friend – we are both Palestinian – it was in Istanbul. He had got out. He had tried for years for his visa, so many times, and he never got it. He had almost given up, but finally they let him out. We agreed to meet at a café and he was an hour late because he got lost.' Darina smiles. 'But when we met he was so happy, because in Gaza he knows every corner and there is no way out. He said that being able to get lost, it was so new, it was like freedom.'

'Istanbul is a good city for getting lost in. How long will he stay?'

'I don't know if he will go back. It's hard for people, once they leave. Because their family are in Gaza, maybe their home is. But there's no life there.'

☷

We pass under the last grand archway as the rain comes down harder. We run for Darina's car, parked outside the city walls. I watch her throw her belongings onto the back seat, her black curls rain-slicked to her pale forehead. The engine starts, she drives, and I sit with the beginnings of a rising temperature and hear her stories repeating. I listen to Darina again, sitting silent in my own mind, as she relays each injustice with such strength and feeling but also total sincerity and no seeming exhaustion. It is as if she could go on forever, tirelessly, and I wonder where she got this strength from, this need to keep on naming the wrongs and demanding the rights. I worry that I am asking too much of her, asking her to relive thoughts, to visit sorrows that it will be my luxury to leave. The highway scrolls by, buckets of water falling off the windshield, thrown aside by the wipers at full pelt. It is a good day not to ride.

'My mother said that you must come for dinner, but that is later. We can go for a walk, if you like. Inland is sometimes dry, even when it rains at Akka.'

I turn to her with a smile and nod, but I feel tired. My temperature goes tingling even as my body stays cold, as though there is a great warmth inside my body, feverish, waiting to envelop me, at once cosy but also uncomfortable. Darina moves through the traffic: the freight aboard articulated lorries, a few old, mud-spattered trucks, moving slower with tailgate and sides bolted up into position, holding cargoes of fruit trays, huge cauliflowers. Large signs above us point traffic to Tel Aviv, Haifa, Carmel. I remember the speed of my bicycle and inside the car it all feels slower and yet comes so much faster, while all I have to do is sit, passive as the world passes. The road, the traffic, all has about it a searing purpose, striking through red earth and fields lined occasionally with olive trees. Eventually Darina flicks an indicator and we take an exit, winding up into hills and out of the deluge, so that the shapes of individual clouds return and show the edge of the rains in the distance. At the roadside appears a strip of housing and buildings, a footbridge over the highway, the minarets of a mosque.

'That's my village,' said Darina with pride as it passes. 'Majd al-Krum.'

We leave the car at the end of a dirt track on the side of a mountain and set off through the wet earth, red soil pressing up around our shoes. Rainwater squeezes from the ground as we pick our way around puddles, then meet with a more recognisable path. A few rickety fences dot the land, shepherd tracks lead into the under-growth, and on the bank of an opposite hillside a few houses have been settled. Further distant, larger towns blur into the weather. Grey tails of raincloud sweep down and, for a single brightening moment, orange from a sunset trickles like egg yolk over the edge of a high stack of cumulonimbus.

'Over that hill is Majd al-Krum, where we just were,' says Darina. 'And that way is Carmel. It's one of the largest Israeli set-tlement cities in the north. When I was a child, when Israel and Lebanon last went to war, Hezbollah fired rockets at Carmel, but because Majd is in the middle, some hit us. One hit the minaret of the mosque. We had air-raid sirens, we had to shelter.'

'That must have been frightening.'

'Yes, but you know, many people didn't mind so much. Many people supported Hezbollah, not the Israelis.'

'Do you think Israel knows that is how people inside the country think?'

Darina nods. 'Yes. They know.'

We take a path above a field of olive trees bordered on both sides by pines, planted in neat, orderly rows. With a memory of my road through the Galilee, naively I try to change the subject, only to discover that in this land there is no change of subject.

'I saw a sign yesterday, with a lot of pine trees, saying *Come plant a tree.*'

'The Israelis do that a lot. Tree planting. So many of them came from Europe, they wanted to make this land look like Europe too, so they planted pine trees. People all over the world pay to plant a tree here, to support Israel.'

There is no change of subject. The subject is everything. The subject is totalitarian.

'It's funny, I saw the sign and something about it, written in English, I didn't trust. But I guess a tree isn't so bad.'

The path crunches underneath us as we walk, picking our way between red puddles.

'They plant them to change the land, to cover old Palestinian villages they destroyed. They did that a lot in this area.' Darina gestures down the hill to a line of pines. 'Sometimes they plant them to get in the way of Palestinian farming, so farmers cannot plant olive trees. The pine isn't...' She pauses. 'What's the word? When something is from here?'

'Native?'

'It isn't native, and the pine needles make the soil very acid, so other things don't grow. Lots of herbs that we used to have on the forest floor now cannot grow, herbs that my grandparents made tea from, like *farfahina* or *sinarieh*. I don't know their names in English.'

Darina looks round, with a smile for my sigh.

'It's sad, right, how this occupation can even make you hate a tree?'

As the evening light failed, we made our way back to the car and drove to the village and home in time for dinner. Outside the front door was some firewood newly split, and the sound of pans clanking and a tap running came from a kitchen window left ajar. Forgive me all this detail, this account of all of our time together and its every conversation, but I must go on... I must tell you about all of this day, for if the world obliged Darina to live it then who am I not to write it down? The fever too, sitting on my forehead, perhaps it makes me repetitious, a little dizzy, sensitive to the intensity of what I heard and saw across our time together.

Darina's father walked in, wearing slippers and a sweater with holes in the elbows. In front of a small heater I sat, my damp socks resting over the top of it as the man gave a slightly confused expression at the stranger, barefoot, in his front room. A moment later, as if the unfamiliarity was insignificant, he broke into a warm, happy smile. Darina turned to him, introduced us.

We kissed on the cheeks, a shine in his eyes as he turned from me and kept looking around confusedly before disappearing from the room again. Darina's mother greeted me with the warm smile and full embrace of a Middle Eastern mother, bound by higher law to look after those who come into their home. She handed me a bag of *fatayer* she had prepared for my onward journey, at least a dozen triangular cases of wholemeal pastry filled with spinach and onion. I pressed my hands to my chest in gratitude as I said *shukran*, before a bell sounded and she turned back to the oven. I watched her lift a chicken in a tray out on a gust of hot air, the bird roasted and steaming with the smell of home, of all the homes you've ever known. Darina's father spoke as if thinking aloud, then looked around and shuffled back out of the front door, closing with a jangle of keys left in the lock.

'He says he's lost some papers,' said Darina. 'It happens a lot. We think he might be getting early dementia.'

'That must be hard.'

'He and my mum do not get on so well. It doesn't help. Last week he thought he had lost a bag of seeds. He spent days looking. Then my brother went to buy more and we found them the next day.'

The door opened again, the same chiming of key. Her father looked in, holding the handle and shaking his head bewilderedly so that whatever it was, it was still lost. Silence met him.

▓

Together we sit around the table, *maqloubeh* in the middle, large puffs of wheat, freekeh, with hunks of chicken and roasted carrot and onion all through it. There is a tray of olives, small and puckered and shining black. Tiny purple aubergines, pickled and stuffed with peppers. A bowl is passed down the table, Darina hands it to me.

'Maybe it's strange, but we always eat yoghurt.'

'It's OK. We have yoghurt with everything in Turkey too.'

And Darina gives the same smile she always does, whatever the subject and like she's bigger than this entire place, bigger than the circumstances in which she finds herself, like she's got spirit enough to keep on undimmed, no matter what is thrown at her. The four of us eat together, quiet but for the sounds of food, that happiest of sounds. Now and then I look up at Darina's father, a gentle face, somehow a touch pale, wan, like the life in him is fading and the pace of him has slowed. He sits there, a little absent, smiling to himself as if in another place, distant, maybe slightly better. His eyes move, like he's thinking over something. Then he looks up, smiles and then frowns, then smiles to himself again. Damn, but I think I'm cracking. Life is so hard anyway... our age, our brains, our hearts, losing each of them, to love, to life, to forgetfulness. I can feel myself buckling. The hard ride to Haifa, the chill of the wind. It's in my body. My socks are back on, but damp. I feel shivers, shivers and fatigue. I sit eating the *maqloubeh*, the aubergine, eating slowly and I feel so sad. Numb. My eyes are hot, I could blub. I realise I'm on the edge, but it can't be the damn Westerner falling apart and leaving the Palestinians to pick up the pieces. I keep my head down and, together, we eat.

Back to Jaffa

A storm came in, as if all that sea's weather was trapped there at the end of the Mediterranean, so that every drop of the water in that sea's clouds gathered to fall upon the land. The rains flooded, spilled into the city and towns. Streets turned river and metro excavations choked, gagged, coughed up muddy waters from new guts being bored below. I rode on through, tired at the rainfall, tired at the wet and the slow, steady scream of the road as tyres passed me. I rode through with rain running into my eyes, dampening the sleeves beneath my raincoat as the roads went roaring and speeding car tyres unzipped vast puddles. True to custom everywhere, drivers fired impatient horn shots as if they too, dry inside their cars, were actually getting wet. I rode the roads beside a large highway, where the trucks and buses became galleons, my bicycle a kayak, and I paddled south and inland, the mudguards pouring water into my feet as if they were ladles for the road soup all around. The rain pelted the eucalyptus, every tree was stripped loose of the bark that gathered brown in heaps around each trunk, as if the poor things had shat themselves at the coming thunder. Floods hit, a ten-year storm they called it. Telegraph poles grew from puddles and fields pissed brown into the rivers and over the roads.

Weary from illness and the miles, I loitered in cafés and drank coffee, waiting for days as the worst of it moved through and the sun returned, dragging the summer back in on its rays. With bright, shimmering heat the beachfront of Tel Aviv returned to view between my forearms and above my front wheel, where waves rolled in and went crashing against the shore to rise out from the spray as skyscrapers. High-rises pointed upwards, one after the next and stuck against the landscape in steep right angles. Running down the beach and into the sea, from where I floated on the turning tide, I watched my bicycle and the city on the shore, the waves receding from me, heading for the beach where concrete warped under liquid heat.

In front of me on the beach was a makeshift line of plastic tape stuck to stakes in the sand, so that a red-white cordon was sagging into one of the less effective fences in the land. The tape fluttered pointlessly on the breeze, beneath a sign that stated clearly: *Swimming Prohibited*, and which each of a hundred bathers had strode happily past, carrying inflatables, toddlers, bats and balls and paddle boards, goggles and smiles. Authority said one thing and the people did as they pleased, so that in this respect Israelis, not disobeying authority so much as not even noticing it, for the first time to me they seemed a little like Arabs, Turks, or at least, perhaps for once truly of the Middle East.

On the sand was more of that subtly shared culture. A line of deckchairs held men with round bellies, sunk beneath parasols and looking every bit like they had sat there forever with no plan to move. Next to them the waves lapped against the shore, as if the men and the sea were sizing one another up to see who would blink first and budge. Whole carpets of hair, bona fide rugs, covered chests, shoulders and backs, just as sunglasses covered eyes. Though all this could have been perfectly Mediterranean – Italian, Spanish, French Riviera – what made it the Middle East was that, on a Saturday morning and heading for the beach, these men had also made sure, among the parasols, straw mats and towels, to pack the national flag and a flagpole.

And so there it pulled, ragged on the wind – *blue-white-star* – and next to it, another: the United States. Star-spangled it fluttered beside the Star of David, up for good measure to remind everyone not only of the country in which they bathed, in case anyone might forget, but also to remind bathers of that country's place in a wider geopolitical military axis. The outpost of US empire. Who knew when reminders like that might be useful? Disputes over a towel on a sun lounger could always escalate, and in all those flags you saw that – while Israel tried harder than ever to be seen as part of Europe – really its people had more in common than it wanted to admit with those of Turkey, Jordan, Morocco. For flags are the peculiarly potent pieces of fabric that people raise most of all where they are insecure and need to feel seen.

Pushing my bicycle along the sands, I watched as black pucks were batted back and forth by bronzed men clutching paddles, now and then grunting with competitive exertion. Four girls in bathing costumes – pinks, yellow, blue – each sat on the corner of a beach mat, holding their phones extended like the angular filament of exotic flowers, recording images of bodies held tight in Lycra to be shared with the country and the world, asserting that this – titties and ass – was what it looked like for a woman, and apparently so too a country, to be free. The skyscrapers appeared as if the future had stridden onto the shore. That mass of buildings moved up in staggers, like some concrete hulk stepping out of the sea and getting to its feet. One after the next, they stood against the sky in escalating right angles. A Chinese woman walked alone before them along the beachfront, wearing a T-shirt with an awkward English slogan and, in this place, I willed it to mean what I'd want it to mean: *One more chance*.

Inland a block I found the shorter, squat buildings of Bauhaus apartments with rounded balconies and vines flowing down into the street. Utilitarian things, they had been built by the Jewish refugee architects of 1940s Europe, who came to the Arab town of

Jaffa and placed Tel Aviv on top of it. Between the Bauhaus and the skyscrapers, it felt like you could see the two fronts of Jewish Zionism colliding. The first apartment buildings were smaller, just a few stories but built with the unmistakable confidence that comes only with humility, attuned to an environment and some sort of human scale. In those flats was a Zionism that came to the Middle East from Europe with the goal of founding a state that held and protected the meaning and poetry of Jewish values alongside those that were already in Palestine, but not a Jewish state distinct and cut off at the expense of those around it. That jump, from Bauhaus to the skyscrapers, was like an architectural metaphor for Israel as a whole, for it was a shift from shared values to values that were impenetrable and built in glass, concrete, steel. Pedalling through, a different city rose up, one where cars were scanned on their way in for bombs, and barcodes activated gates through which only the rich could enter.

That shift somehow mirrored the defeat of those early Zionists, cultural Zionists, who had believed in the sacrosanct strength of Jewish values. They lost their dream and their nation to those political Zionists, who instead emphasised a Jewish territory and who – when push came to shove – believed in the forces of borders and of guns above the strength of a spirit. That defeat was crucial in the foundation of what Israel was to become, but tell me, across fifty years in a world dictated by money and weapons, where was that same defeat not suffered?

Sperm Smuggling

All around me, people do laps of the park, walking with their thoughts, spouses, children, with their dogs. Parks in cities are the only public places you find human emotion, as if the grass were a repository for our thoughts, as if in earth we find a terrain where our feelings can finally grow, or drain away, or just feel at home, free from the concrete that otherwise makes no sense to our souls. I sit and watch the evening descend. People play football, a goal is scored and an African man in a red bib runs with arms outstretched towards the corner of a pitch without any lines marked for it. At the side of the path where I sit is a plaque, commemorating a battle waged on the spot by the Haganah militia in 1947, successfully repelling Arab forces who tried to take back Jaffa from the many settlers then arriving, their numbers swelling with the outflux of Europe's Jews, steeled and traumatised by the horrors they had fled.

A dog pads up beside me, sniffing at a pannier bag in the hope of food I must once have carried there. The owner walks over, dressed in black jeans, black trainers, a loose-fitting grey sweater. She has pale skin, short hair shaved close at the sides and a large, natural quiff at her fringe. She has thick spectacles and small eyes that look tired. She says something in the tone of an apology, I guess for the dog, to which I wave my hand but she goes on speaking, so that it becomes my turn to apologise and explain that I do not speak Hebrew.

Adi switches to English. 'She's a rescue dog, from the shelter. Normally she's cautious around strangers. She must like you.'

'They say dogs can be like that, after a bad owner.'

'Guess so.' Adi smiles as the dog turns to me, presses its head to my thigh and sniffs at the back of my hand, the dog like a chaperone creating the conditions in which humans, though strangers, are willing to talk to one another. Opposite us, in multiple games, the thud-*thud-thud* of footballs being passed and kicked keeps time, and instinctively it feels that this is more mixed than any other neighbourhood I've seen in Israel. Palestinian-Arab men play with Africans from south of the Sahara, darker-skinned Jewish men, and then the coffee-skinned and tall, slender people of the Horn of Africa. In my head I pick through their ethnicities, reminded that race is a child of racism, and it is only the human failure to treat everyone equally that gives any need or meaning to my guesses at the geographical origins of a group of humans playing football. Jewish families walk through the park, men and women with large, four-berth pushchairs, dressed conservatively and working class to look at them. The women have their hair covered, wear cardigans, stockings and simple shoes.

'It's a nice park,' I say, breaking the silence as the dog keeps on at my bag.

Adi nods. 'You're travelling here?'

'Yeah, cycling through. Israel, Palestine.'

Adi smiles at the notion. 'That must be cool.'

'Yeah. It's interesting, there's a lot to take in. This place feels different to most of Tel Aviv, or Israel. You live around here?'

'For a few years. It's a nice neighbourhood. Not the best area in some ways. I mean, it's poor. But there's some Ottoman law over the land and ownership, so it's been harder to move the communities out of their housing.'

'It seems more mixed than most places.'

I nod towards the many simultaneous games of football, allowing the different ethnic groups to say eloquently what I don't want to mouth bluntly. The games continue with shouts and pointing arms directing players to positions, openings nearer goal. Neither of us is really watching, the game just offering reason to stand with a person without saying much. The dog sidles against me again.

'Sort of. Everyone says racist things and complains about each other all the time. The Jews swear about the Arabs and the Arabs complain about the Jews, but it's more relaxed than the middle-class parts of Tel Aviv. There a black guy might get asked by the police to move on if he's sitting around somewhere. People here are not so polite, but they're more tolerant. Like everyone's poor together.'

'I always felt people I know in the Middle East were more likely to say "the Jews". You know, things about money or whatever. Westerners are more likely to control the language but...'

I trail off.

'What?' she asks, enjoying my awkwardness.

'Well, persecute Jewish people.'

'That sounds about right.'

The thud of the ball being passed fast and accurate, boot to boot, echoes in front of us and Adi points at my bicycle.

'How long have you been riding here?'

'I dunno,' I say, truthfully, for time has blurred. 'A few weeks, some in Israel, some in Palestine.'

'You must have seen a lot. Hey, if you are going to the West Bank anytime soon, there is a hip-hop festival happening in Ramallah this weekend. It will probably be pretty good.'

'Hip-hop?' I ask, surprised.

'It's big there. Palestinian youth really like it.'

'Thanks for the advice... I should be heading that way in a day or two. Maybe that'd be fun.'

Adi gives a smile, a don't-mention-it sort of a look.

I try to resist the question, but finally it comes out. 'What do you do?'

'I'm a researcher here, at a university. My work looks a lot at the conflict.'

'What sort of research?'

'Fertility rights, mostly.'

'I guess that's a big thing here, with both populations trying to be larger than the other one.'

'That's it: the "demographic war",' and Adi rolls her eyes.

'People take it seriously?'

'Very. Israel used to give a subsidy to families with more than a certain number of children, to encourage it, but then they found out most of the women getting the support were Arab, so they stopped.'

I laugh. 'It's crazy.'

'That's nothing! We have an old woman who is at the Supreme Court now, her son died in the army and she wants the right to take his sperm, which she froze, and use a surrogate to make a new son or daughter.'

'OK. *That's* crazy.'

'And the mother says it's her right to do that, so that she can send that new child back to the army.'

'Yikes. So losing a son and wanting the situation to continue.'

'Yeah, kinda a memorial, being willing to sacrifice a new life. It's been a big case here, lots of people are talking about it.'

'Reproductive technology is big in Israel, isn't it? You have big pharmaceutical companies that specialise in it?'

'Yeah, there's a big market. Gay couples use it a lot, and even the religious communities mostly support gay people having children here, because of the whole demographic thing. It's created a big demand for surrogate mothers. Filipino women were doing it a lot, there's a whole economy for carrying other people's embryos and giving birth to babies.'

Of the many occasions behind and up ahead, Adi and her dispatches from dystopia will remain one of the most unbelievable.

'Then on the Palestinian side, they have this sperm smuggling going on.'

'Sperm smuggling?'

'Israeli prisoners are allowed their wives to visit for sex, but Palestinians aren't, so some Palestinians smuggle their sperm out to start a family.'

My eyes widen. 'How?'

'In visits. In a bag or something, they pass it on and the women maybe hold it in their armpit to keep it warm. Prison guards are controlling hugging at visits quite a lot now, because the smuggling became a big thing. The Israelis say that it would not be possible, that the sperm cannot survive outside of the body that long. The Palestinians say that Palestinian sperm can.'

I laugh out loud.

'There's a fertility centre in Nablus, another in Ramallah. They offer to treat Palestinian women with the sperm for free, they say it's a humanitarian assistance to the women.'

'Does it happen a lot?'

'Maybe a few hundred inseminations, and they claim dozens of pregnancies. It started because the Jewish nationalist who killed Yitzhak Rabin, the old Israeli Prime Minister, wanted to have a family, so he sued for the right to a visit from his wife in his maximum-security unit.'

'Did he win?'

Adi nods. 'His wife was able to visit him in Ramon Prison. Now he has a family. If you're going south, you'll see the prison next to the highway. The Palestinian prisoners tried for the same rights, but nothing.'

'Have you travelled in Palestine at all?' I ask, suddenly aware that Adi speaks with an unfamiliar empathy.

'A little,' she responds. 'It's hard for us but sometimes I went, with groups. Normally as part of protests.'

'How is it being there, as an Israeli?'

'I never felt uncomfortable around Palestinians. Our culture's the same, I like to think. I went with friends to Bil'in, to a protest against the fence the army put through the middle of the village there. We went to stand together with the Palestinians. We were one with them. Not only because we were all protesting together. It just felt like everyone was OK with us, as individuals, but Israel teaches us to be afraid, teaches us that Palestinians hate us.'

'I guess that's how you create apartheid. You make people feel that another group is dangerous, or deserves less.'

'Maybe, but this is worse than apartheid now. It's worse than South Africa. All of these words, none of them work. *Occupation*… it's a bad word for it, it makes it sound temporary. This is seventy years now the Palestinians have had to live like this.'

Adi points to where men are doing pull-ups on metal apparatus next to a board of illustrated instructions for keep-fit routines. She takes off her glasses, rubs her eyes with the back of her hand.

'The board there, showing exercises, they call them *Combat Exercises*. This is a war society, it's everywhere.'

You can feel it on her… the weight of the occupation, or the apartheid, or the conflict that is no conflict at all, but more of a chokehold. She gets it, hers a soul big enough to demand fairness for all the world. With many Israelis who are interested in peace, I sense it is like a person interested in sourdough baking or a Spanish class or woodworking course. It's a nice idea, helps with their stress, they've an affection for the notion. And then they go back to work. People like Adi, Dorit, I realise they feel the venom of Israeli society cast against them almost every bit as much as the Palestinians, and differently too, because Israelis see them as an enemy within.

'We do some stuff here in the city, activism. Mostly now with the Eritreans, the African community who come here as refugees. They face so much racism. At first the authorities just left them at the border with Egypt, Sinai, in the south. Then that started causing problems, so they put them on buses and started dropping them here by the Ayalon River. The government know we need the labour, for construction and stuff. But they don't want to do anything to help the community. Most are homeless. We try to help organise things.'

'What kind of thing are you working on?'

'We had some public transport protests, because the bus routes only go from here to the rich areas where Eritrean women work as cleaners. But there are local markets and things like that, nice places that people would want to travel to, but it's too expensive without public transport. We campaigned for new bus routes. The city said no.'

'Why would anyone say no to that?'

Adi shrugs. 'Sometimes it's like we got, you know, the worst of the Middle East and the worst of the West.'

We fall silent, the light almost gone and the footballers picking up their goalposts, packing balls away. Together we stand there and, as so often, I hear again and again the words she has just spoken, like an echo, and think what they mean.

Her dog begins pulling at its leash, sniffing the ground and moving away. Adi points over her shoulder at high buildings and the pink ripples of dusk in the sky.

'There's a woman's refuge, an Eritrean centre, just a few hundred metres that way. In those warehouses. If you're interested in the community, you should go and look sometime. It's a special place.'

▓

Soon after we parted company, Adi walking on into the dusk with her dog loyally beside. In those weeks pedalling through Israel, I learned so clearly that it is not essential for anyone in an unjust society to bring injustice to an end, but it is essential for many well-meaning people to believe that they are about to, or that they one day might. Harmless in itself, the problem is that people need the *belief* more than they need real evidence for it, and soon enough it gets easier just to kid yourself.

With Adi you could sense it was different, she suffered it. Each society has its type: its malcontent, its misfit who sees how the world is wrong and believes how it could all be better. Many people like to believe that this is them, that they have these radical, visionary qualities. People of stature, broad shoulders, flowing hair and grand physique... stereotypes of a leader drawn from a history book. Yet the truth is that it is Adi, in baggy jeans with a rescue dog on a rope, short hair and spectacles, but comfortable enough in her own skin to feel, a thing so rare and pure, the truth of her own country, and the fact that she is not free until all are free.

Back on my bicycle, I cycled slowly out of the park and into the street, moving around a corner, where a Palestinian-Israeli vendor with a giant pot was selling *sahlep*, the semolina drink I knew from cold days beside the Bosphorus in Istanbul. Children gathered, and he smiled with contentment at the joy he was bringing, sprinkling generous cinnamon and pieces of crushed hazelnuts and raisins on top of the drink.

Next morning, I did as Adi had instructed, headed back to that same district and the large building she had pointed to. Following a colourful, paper sign showing African handicrafts, I made my way up some flights of stairs, saw the sunshine pouring into a long room with a window at its far end and light glinting on the metal runner across the threshold. A few faces turned to me and smiled, looking curiously at me and the bicycle –

But sorry... we have miles to make up, and this story it is not for here, it comes later in our journey.

Dorit 2

She sits down across the restaurant table from me, smiling, ready to laugh. A little amazed that this is even happening. Her eyes shine with amusement at where her idle comment in Edinburgh has led.

'So,' she begins, placing her hands down on the table, one laid over the other. 'How is it going? Do you understand it yet?'

I sigh, suddenly conscious of how far from that I am.

'No.'

Dorit is wearing a dress of burnt orange, buttoned up with dungaree straps against her brown skin. She repositions her chair, crosses her leg to reveal a foot pressed inside a pair of neat orange shoes, matching the dress perfectly. Of course, matching perfectly. She lifts her shining black hair above her head, ties it into a knot, and her smile softens.

'What have you been up to?' I ask.

'I'm planning a lecture, about how today the writer must write as if nobody is reading.'

'I like that idea.'

'Thanks. I think there are so many pressures, expectations, and readers are conservative.'

'Same back home,' I reply. 'And in the end, if you are writing for the people reading, and not yourself, it can never be true, so it's not as good.'

Dorit lifts her pouch of tobacco from the orange handbag of woven leather hanging from the back of her chair. Part of me breathes easy, this sudden conversation from another place, from back home and mostly free from politics. The intensity of the weeks lifts a little.

'Where did you come from today?' asks Dorit.

'I was in Jaffa this morning. I decided to walk here.'

'That's quite a schlep.'

I laugh. 'Your English is always great, Dorit, but I'm impressed you know the word schlep. That's so English.'

'It's an old word,' Dorit rolls her cigarette, savours. 'From Yiddish.'

I laugh again. 'Now I feel stupid.'

'You should.'

Dorit shoots me a wink and laughs kindly in my face.

'So, really, how is it?'

'It feels more oppressive than I expected. The weight of it, everywhere.'

'What did you expect?'

'I don't know. People back home talk about apartheid here, but things like the settler farms in the West Bank, the idea of just taking the land, the way people think and talk. It's all so true, it's so colonial.'

'Ah Julian! Don't use these words. It's bad enough that we do this to our neighbours, but it's not apartheid. We don't need to import these simple, Western names for it.'

'Apartheid isn't a Western name, it's a definition of a system.'

'Julian! Look at our football team, it's half Arab. Arabs sit on our supreme court.'

'OK, but in Israel. So it's an apartheid set by geography, not only race?'

'This is a new country,' Dorit pushes back.

'Sure. But you don't think certain words have the power to force change, to shock people so that they take things seriously?'

We pause a moment, both resolute. Dorit annoyed as always that I get to arrive and drop into my views, my opinions. The table we sit at is on the edge of the terrace, and bright sun casts half of us in white hot light and half of us in shade.

'Do you mind if we move the table?' Dorit asks.

I shake my head and the two of us lift a little from our seats. Dorit's chair scrapes backwards and we shuffle into the shade as a waitress appears and looks sceptically at the broken symmetry of her terrace. The two of them speak Hebrew with firm expressions, I watch their body language.

The waitress moves her hands to her hips, stands tall. Speaks, sternly.

Dorit holds her head high, points her chin straight at the waitress and then nods to the band of white heat now avoided. Not giving an inch.

The waitress nods understanding, but seems to repeat something, sternly, gesturing at the other tables clearly forming a neat line.

Dorit nods her understanding, gives a smile that looks condescending, then speaks a word of Hebrew that has in it the intonation of resolution. Without a smile, the waitress also nods and then the conversation moves to English and the order. She looks over, expectantly.

'Are you ready to order?'

'I've been a bit ill,' I say to Dorit. 'Maybe something like chicken soup would be good.'

'We call it the Jewish penicillin,' says Dorit, giving an agreeable expression. 'Here it's good, I will join you I think.'

She turns back to the waitress. 'Two chicken soups.'

'OK, and would you like a main course?'

Dorit looks at me. I shake my head. Dorit turns to the waitress, shakes her head.

'Drinks?'

Dorit looks. I shake my head again. Dorit turns to the waitress, repeats.

'And would y—'

Hard but with a mischievous smile, Dorit slams her palms to the table.

'Just hurry up and bring us the damn soup!'

And the waitress puts the cap on her pen, tucks her pad into her apron as she leaves.

Dorit turns back to me and relaxes. I laugh in disbelief.

'I still can't get over how rude you guys are to one another.'

'It's not rude. It's actually a kind of intimacy, you wouldn't do it with just anyone. It shows we trust one another to be like this and not be offended.'

'That's a way of looking at it.'

For a moment I play with my fork, pressing its prongs so that the handle lifts. Part of me holds back, but it's been on my mind too long, I have something to ask.

'Dorit, how did it get so bad? Israel doing all this?'

She pauses, rolls her eyes at how incessant I am. Then looks for whichever answer comes most readily to mind.

'The Palestinians were failed by their own leaders.'

She says it earnestly, but in her words, I hear also the voices of others before her. This is an Israeli catechism, the easiest line and one to obscure the fact that, when all was said and done, they were failed also by theirs.

Across the table, Dorit watches me, that same irritation in her look, one that is frequently present but never quite breaks to anger. The price of what they have done to Palestine, I am coming to realise, is that Israelis on some level must always know, until it stops, that they are doing something wrong, and so the criticism is valid and must be heard. *But what*, thinks Dorit, *does he expect me to do about it? And what, if he were me, would he do?* Perhaps beneath her look is a frustration that this is so easy for me, to come with my judgements and then leave with them too, rather than live a life in political sin. We sit in silence, in this friendship where for some reason, despite the disagreement, it isn't too awkward. Perhaps it is the love of writing, of words, of having met in Edinburgh… somewhere that wasn't here, somewhere I had to be more polite because then she was a guest in my country. A pigeon, red-breasted, pecks at crumbs on the path in front of us. Dorit looks at me, steadily, then lifts a finger.

'I think I know who you should meet.'

Conflict Resolution

The door opened to reveal a woman in a pink sweater and spectacles, her straight fair hair falling to her shoulders. On her face was a smile matched by a warmth in her look. Behind her, the sight and smell of a home, a perfect home, where vegetable soup bubbled and sent out its aroma from a kitchen just out of sight.

'Julian? Dorit said you would come over. Welcome, come in.'

Ruti ushered me inside, onto the tiled floor where pools of bright light fell through large windows all around a vast single room that combined a study with a kitchen and a dining area. A long sofa, bookshelves, some varnished pieces of hardwood sculpted into ornamental animals. An old grey cat wound around a chair leg, back arching and tail up. Ruti smiled again, another mother who in that process of raising her own children has unearthed a calling to take care of all the world.

'Gili will be home soon. You'll join us for dinner?'

⁝

Roast chicken, potatoes, a salad with feta and spinach, olives, stuffed aubergines, a bowl of yoghurt, a length of baked bread with steam still rising from the golden crust. Everything is spread out on the table by the time Gili walks through the door, taking his seat opposite me and among his adult children, two daughters and two sons, home for a family meal at the start of Shabbat. A tall man, olive skin and dark hair cut smart and short. He has bushy eyebrows, gentle eyes, an Iberian look that I will later learn comes from a family of Sephardic Jews, originally Spanish, who escaped the Inquisition and had lived each century since in Jerusalem. If Gili was to prove more capable than most in this land of diplomacy, I realised it was in no small part because nobody could have suggested he was not from it. More than the Jewish of the Maghreb and Middle East, and certainly more than the Ashkenazi, only the Palestinians would have lived between the River and the Sea for as long as Gili's family line.

With marked politeness he shakes my hand, then drops heavily into his seat. He takes his chair by the arms, pulls it closer to the table and, with the look of a long day at the office, picks up a large spoon and begins to serve himself, simply looking down at his plate.

'Gili, are you OK?' asks Ruti.

He stands again, steps over to the counter and fills a glass of water, returning with the jug.

'We had killings today, outside Ramallah. Two of our soldiers dead.'

He sits again, almost with a thud, as if the weight of each death was on him, as if he was supposed to have done something to avert it, as if he could have, given the chance. Gili the diplomat in a conflict left to combatants, and like he knows – and can see so clearly – how it could all be so different. He looks up at me, businesslike.

'Dorit said you were cycling around the country. After dinner I'd be interested to hear your view. And, of course, you are welcome to stay here tonight.'

'Thank you, that's very kind. Dorit told me you know the conflict better than anyone.'

He gives a humble frown, as if to suggest that it was not untrue but that he wouldn't want to be found saying so. The children talk in Hebrew as Gili eats quietly, and I sit and eat, feeling at once a stranger in this home and yet also totally welcome. Ruti gets up from the table, giving her husband's shoulder a comforting squeeze on her way to the kitchen. She stands there, beyond the counter.

'What did I get up for?' I hear her say quietly to herself. Her hair swishes as she looks straight from side to side, as if in the hope that a clue might be on the walls, the cupboard doors or stuck to the fridge. She gives a slight smile, then a shrug of resignation before coming to sit back down. I watch her across the table, eating delicately, patiently, as I try to learn that life lesson of eating slowly, but the first instant of roast chicken and roast peppers in the mouth always tastes so good that each time it has me hurrying for the next. One of her daughters turns from her siblings towards our end of the table, conscientiously opening the conversation for me as she asks her mother in English.

'...we think we'll go at the weekend. Did you find the box of books?'

Ruti gives a blank expression, then the slight grimace that comes with the return of a memory that reminds a person they have in fact forgotten.

'I'll do it after dinner.'

We all eat, crockery clatters and bowls empty. The bones of the roast chicken start to appear through the flesh, pulled off the bird in the centre of the table and placed on our plates. I can't help but think of Majd al-Krum. The chicken, the stuffed aubergines, olives, the many hands reaching to the centre of the table. Out of the corner of my eye I watch Ruti, eating slowly, and I think that the happy shine in her eye and the smile that she is always on the cusp of perhaps hides a little of her age. I wonder if the forgetfulness is just the result of a busy week, of preparing a meal for an entire family this evening, or of life in a country always half at war. But more than all of that, I can't help but think of Darina's father, going around his house not so far distant and asking where he's put his belongings. Two people with such different lives, 'sides' and experiences, but each one only a brain that comes one day to forget where it put its own belongings, what its body had got to its feet and walked to the kitchen to retrieve. Ruti looks up from her plate, suddenly struck that she should have been more attentive to me. She reaches for a metal bowl in front of her, shining with the light. She lifts it, hands it towards me.

'Here, Julian, take some more yoghurt.'

⠿

Outside, the light of the day is gone, the traffic of the busy street runs quieter. Gili sits in his study, a wide desk flanked by books in the corner of that single large room where we had eaten. He pores over a spread of paperwork, furrowing his brow. Ruti watches television with her feet up, the two of us talking occasionally about politics.

'You might think we are strong, Julian, but Israel is like the dog that barks. It tries to scare people away, but look around us. Gili lost some of his best friends, fighting the Egyptians in Sinai in 1973. We have enemies on all sides. Look at all the countries that would like us to disappear. We are vulnerable here, and we are the only democracy until India.'

I give a frown at what to say. So often was it like that, stuck in the conflict between having compassion, and then gratitude for such kindness, hospitality. Such warmth for a person, and yet.

'You are the *nearest* to a democracy until India, maybe. But not everyone here has democracy. Palestinians do not have democracy.'

'We know! It's terrible,' says Ruti, 'but we in Israel are also the only ones who care about it. A friend of mine, a journalist, she went to a peace conference on the Middle East, the whole region… and you know what? We were the only country that wanted to talk about Palestine. The Arab countries didn't want to know… it was only us!'

Ruti looks at me a while to see if she has made her point, then returns to watching the television. I consider her words, and a part of me is sad about the lack of unity in the Arab world, but then another part wonders why anyone else *should* be so invested in a problem in territories controlled by Israel and of Israeli making. What deep concern should it be to the people of another land, with their own freedom to wrest, if Israel too refused democracy to those under its control? In all the three thousand miles of the Middle East and North Africa, from Rabat in Morocco to Muscat in Oman, something in that logic itself, that the whole Arab world should care, seemed to stem again from the thinking that they were all the same. Only the world's dark-skinned people get dealt such assumptions; nuance, individuality and cultural distinction is reserved for the white people of the earth. Would the people of Bavaria be asked to care so deeply for Catalan independence because they shared a skin colour and the Catholic church? The Slovaks for the Scots? Would Italians annex southern France but think it unremarkable because the French there could simply go and live in Spain?

Ruti gets to her feet, placing them into the slippers positioned neatly in front of her. She walks back to the kitchen and fetches herself a small teapot with a wicker handle left brewing on the side. Returning, she glances at Gili.

'Oh, Gili dear,' she puts down the teapot as she passes him, 'be careful with this.'

Gili looks up from his reading, lines of thought in his brow so deep they make ravines. She gives a smile and, leaning over him, pushes her fingers over his forehead to smooth the furrows.

'There, that's better.' And Ruti picks up the teapot and returns to the sofa.

Gili lowers his reading and removes his glasses. He leans back with a sigh, places his hands behind his head.

'So, Julian. Tell me, what do you want to know?'

'Well, Dorit said you would be the best person to help me understand the occupation. She said it was your job.'

'I have some experience with it, yes. I was in the government in
the nineties. I was a lawyer, an advisor. Prime Minister Rabin asked
me to go as a negotiator to the Camp David Accords, and then the
talks in Oslo, when Arafat and Rabin were brought together for
the peace process. I led the negotiations for the last agreement we
signed with the Palestinians, at Sharm-el-Sheikh.'

'When was that?'

'September 1999.'

His tone marks the distance of the date, but there is a calm to the
way Gili speaks, a voice that is trained to impart clarity. He gives
a fond smile, quietly proud to have had such a responsibility. He
wears the credentials humbly, simultaneously as if they were no big
deal but aware that they speak for themselves, and I realise that here
I sit with a small part of the Israeli establishment and its history, the
institutional knowledge of a country.

'I'm interested what you think about it,' he said. 'From your
travels here? What stands out?'

Like a doctor he leans forward, ready to gather evidence, and I
listen to the rough softness of his Hebrew accent, so patient, always
inviting of the next question, while I sit and wonder where to begin.

'It seems like the checkpoints are the worst. The basis of where
everything is going wrong. It's like they're the heart of the sickness.'

I venture back into that odd space, the mood that settles in
talking to Israelis you don't know so well… where I am required
to criticise the essence of their nation but not them themselves. I
tread tentatively.

'It's as if… maybe if your army had a manual, some training, for
how to operate there, in those situations, to act morally, it would
help. I mean, the soldiers are so young. They don't know how to
handle the responsibility, and they are doing so much damage.'

———

Gili shakes his head. 'It is not possible.'

Instinctively, I recoil at this reluctance to accept a small concession, even such tiny dents in the occupation, but what comes next confounds my reaction.

'The checkpoints cannot be made good. They *are* the problem. To do this, to institutionalise checkpoints, would be to entrench the occupation and give it legitimacy.' Gili points at me, friendly but firm. 'If I put you in one of those checkpoints for two weeks, you too would not recognise yourself.'

I try to make sense of what I'm hearing from the mouth of an Israeli negotiator.

'So... you say, remove them all?'

'Yes. Or, if you have them, and they really are made for security, you must stop settlers too, because these guys drive right through. But no government now will make this policy.'

There is a pained expression where the politics meets the possible, and I can sense his life's work being frustrated.

'I remember once, during peace talks, one of our Palestinian negotiators came very late. He was red in the face, furious, because he had been stopped at a checkpoint. He had presented his pass, showing he was an important person, from the negotiations. But the soldier had just looked at it and said, "I don't recognise this pass". And that was that.'

Gili brushes his hands together with finality. 'When the negotiator arrived, he just sat down and he refused to engage. He said, "Today I won't negotiate, I don't want to".'

'Isn't that just it though?' I ask. 'The whole thing requires the Palestinians to constantly rise above the circumstances they have been put in. They are the victims of your occupation.'

He stiffens at my choice of word.

'Both of our cultures have a shared history of victimhood, unfortunately. This is now a part of the problem we have to overcome.

Theirs does not go back so far in history as ours, but the Palestinians too are learning to see themselves only as victims.'

'Is that part of why the peace deals didn't work?'

Gili weighs it up, not about to be drawn on any statement so straightforward.

'There were many reasons. Often, we got close to deals and when things were almost completely agreed, the other side would step away, would not commit. With the Oslo Agreements, the big ones, the problem was that neither side really followed it *to the letter*. Both sides violated them.' He stresses it, makes sure I know he's not making excuses. 'We did too! And in the end, nobody could see past the infringements that were piling up. Sometimes we have been really close. We have had engineering firms consulting – Germans, Japanese companies – on a bridge or a tunnel to connect the West Bank and Gaza, to make it a contiguous territory. It can be done.'

He pinches thumb and forefinger together.

'It's just that forty-seven-kilometre stretch at Hebron to Gaza.'

'But don't you think the idea of something like a tunnel joining the two is part of the problem, putting the Palestinians out of sight?'

'We looked at a bridge too. But the point is, it's symmetrical. Like this there is a divide at Gaza and the West Bank, but also Israel's north and south, and everyone can move. It is the same for both sides. The goal was always that first we have *safe* passage between the two states, and then, in time, that becomes just *passage*.'

He smiles at the simplicity of the distinction, and for a moment I consider what he says, before Gili carries on and the thought leaves me to be found again in empty miles on the road ahead.

'We have really talked about everything there is to consider. The rights of Palestinian refugees to return home to a Palestinian state from inside the West Bank and Gaza, but also to return from

Jordan or Lebanon. The rights of some to settle in Israel. We need compensation for Palestinian refugees from 1948, and a recognition *by Israel* of the harm that was done in making the state of Israel as a result of the war. Then there is also compensation for the Jewish refugees who came to Israel for safety from other Arab countries. Things like the property they left behind. And there is the right of some settlers to stay in the West Bank now, but under Palestinian sovereignty. A lot of work has been done, about all of this.'

'But from outside, it sort of feels... like nothing is happening.'

Gili slaps his hand against his thigh and gives a sarcastic laugh.

'Nothing *is* happening! The negotiation needs to change – "nothing is agreed until everything is agreed" just doesn't work – we need to agree things and then implement what is agreed. And we need the political will. On our side it is the leadership in Israel. The Palestinian side is more divided than before, between Fatah in the West Bank and Hamas in Gaza. I think Hamas is trying to change, to recognise parts of the peace process, because they would like to win more influence in the West Bank – and for this they need to be seen as more moderate. You have extreme voices in Israel who would be happy with three separate entities: Israel, Gaza, the West Bank. There are some in the US who would want to give the West Bank to Jordan, Gaza to Egypt and just forget about it. And in Israel, we too are now more divided than we were. The fundamental problems are the same, but there is more religious influence on both sides, and there is less and less trust in the other.'

I wince. Gili gives a knowing, weary look, as if this represents barely the start of the many extremes that he struggles with.

'And now there is no process going on, what do you work on?'

Gili's tone shifts, softening with faint optimism.

'We have a programme with settlers in the West Bank, something to try and bring them back inside Israel's agreed borders, which most settlements are close to anyway.'

'You think people would accept that?' I ask.

'None of this is easy. Here in Israel we have obstacles too. In parts of our own society there is a negative feeling against settlers who are illegally in the Palestinian territories. But in the right circumstances – of new jobs, compensation, housing – there are those who would like to relocate inside Israel. They don't want the anxiety of life in the West Bank. Maybe they went there just because homes are cheaper, schools are less crowded. Maybe about one-third of settlers think like this, and it is our job now to say to them, "Look, you are our brothers and sisters, we want you here, it is time to come home."'

Gili leans back in his chair as the cat sidles up to him by the foot of the bookshelf. It jumps up into his lap, gets comfortable, so that this place feels very far and yet eerily close to that world of checkpoints and garrisons on the road just beyond the city. Gili sits there, so reasonable and articulate compared to some of those I've met, and some of those waiting up ahead. He is businesslike but gentle, unwavering and stern, but only for peace, one more who realises that peace is not a soft thing but one that must be built, earned, willed. Brought screaming into this world.

'You think that can work? That they'll come back?'

'It's part of a process. We need to learn the lessons from pulling settlers out of Gaza. There, when we withdrew, you had just eight thousand and we nearly had a civil war because of it. In the West Bank are half a million. After Gaza we had people unemployed, in temporary accommodation, for months. It can't be like this again, but it doesn't have to be. And Israel needs it, too. We need legitimacy and the occupation makes it hard for us, because people will continue to use it as an excuse not to recognise Israel.'

'But you don't think you're safe now, under the protection of the US?'

'We don't see ourselves that way, Israel always had to protect itself. Administrations come and go, and all it takes is one new president and everything changes.'

'So the solution then, overall, what do you think needs to happen?'

I look at his thick, dark eyebrows, his black eyes. He breathes in deeply, unsettling the cat.

'You cannot have a state that denies others their freedom. You can't, whatever the reason. It just won't work, it's not sustainable.'

I look at his dark eyes with a shine in them, born of some hope found far from here and that you suspect will not be put out. No matter the difficulties in the subjects we will discuss, his face will remain only as kind as it looks at this moment. In the gentle expression are so many lines of thought, as if every variable that could ever occur has been accounted for, tallied, and is now up there in his mind, but weighs heavy on his brow.

'We need to get the extremists on board too, from both sides. *Everyone.*' And he opens his arms to them from where he sits with the cat in his lap. 'Everyone must be at the table, because in conflict resolution, when you have both sets of extremists on board, it allows the moderates to flow.'

I smile at the musicality of the method. 'And after that?'

'After that... we need two states.'

Simply he says it.

'You still believe in it?'

'I still believe that it can be built, yes, I believe in it passionately. That was always the idea, and that is still what most people want. Two states for two people between the Jordan River and the Mediterranean Sea. It's the only way.'

I hear the reassurance of his words and his methods, his confident address, but also, and even though I try to resist it, I cannot stop myself from fearing, with a small and nagging voice in the corner of my brain, that here with me is the sculptor explaining to me his own statue. These ideas are his life's work, and – with a sadness – I realise that this is a thing in which a man might lose faith only long after the rest of his country has taken a course of action that renders it untenable.

The Hospital

There were a few of us, gathered around the bed, though I recognised nobody and saw no faces. Under a pale blue sheet that contoured the shape of her body, there was an old woman. A voice that I knew belonged to a doctor I could not see explained that the old woman was sick, weak, but that she had to pretend to be strong. With that announcement, I remember there came a loud crash, yet despite the apparent chaos, I walked slowly out of the hospital ward and into the corridor. I saw old, twentieth-century fighter planes with machine guns on their nose cones in dogfights above the hospital courtyard. An explosion went up with a column of smoke, and out of it a soldier in army fatigues and a grey trench coat came running, moving frantically towards the door where I watched him grow larger through the pane of glass. Standing now at close quarters, still through the glass, he looked me straight in the eye and said nothing, but at the same time I knew he was ordering that I let him in out of the firing. And so I reached for the large, round handle which rattled as it turned the lock, and in barged the man with a wild look in his eyes as he pushed past and from his trench coat pulled a can of petrol. I watched as he ran off down the corridor, pouring petrol everywhere, striking matches, lighting fires and still pouring petrol everywhere until finally thick smoke had filled all the corridor and came barrelling towards my face where it woke me with a start. Heaving for air I sat up, safe in bed in Tel Aviv. It was the first but not the only such dream that visited me there in that country, or those countries.

Part IV

―――――――

WEST BANK

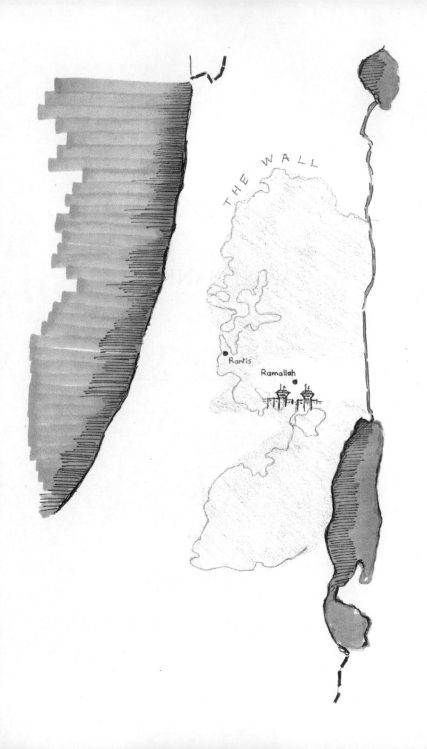

Depart

Into my pannier bag I pushed down my clothes, my notepad, fastening it and moving towards the door. Ruti appeared from upstairs, stood in the hallway with a concerned expression.

'You have everything you need?'

'Yeah, all packed up. I should get going, it's a long ride and there's a festival I was hoping I might make.'

'Clean clothes? We have a machine here, it's fast.'

'I'm OK, but thank you, it's so nice of you.'

'I can wash them in the machine and dry them, it will only take ten minutes.'

'I'm fine, but thank you, that's very kind.'

'But you must need some clean things?' Ruti softened her already very gentle tone of voice. 'Are you sure?'

I smiled. 'No! It's very kind, I do have some washing, but I have spare things too.'

She laughed at herself. 'I'm just like a Yiddish mother...'

'What's that mean?' I ask.

'It is just a Jewish stereotype. I suppose it means that I always worry! You never realise how true it is until a time like this! Come, let me do the washing now, you have some breakfast.'

And with that, Ruti gave a satisfied smile and I opened my bag and, with thanks, handed her a few T-shirts and a vest.

'You go and eat something.' She gestured to the table, where Gili was getting to his feet and gathering up his briefcase.

'Morning!' Gili boomed happily. 'Which way will you go today?'

'I think towards Rantis... into the hills. You know it?'

He sighs. 'Rantis, Talmon, Dolev... I know all about that area. There's a row of settlements, and a lot of tension.'

And Gili shook his head at it all, his brain like a map of the West Bank. He stuck out his hand for me to shake as he headed to the door with the words:

'Be careful there, especially after dark. Don't ride too late.'

Cardiogram

Deeper into hills I headed, the terrain rising from sea level and climbing higher. The urban landscape first thinned away and then left me altogether, so that red rock began to trickle in torn flashes of earth where the concrete finally stopped. As I pedalled inland, out of Tel Aviv and east, I saw it stretch, again that primary line in this land of lines – Armistice – a concrete swathe cut through the middle between River and Sea. East I continued, watching that strip of broken road and concrete barrier, beyond which the Palestinians had been removed n 1948. The line scarred over my shoulder, through the pine forest and bush, and a signpost stood instructing trucks to pull over where barbed wire and concrete blocks flanked the road ahead. I turned a few more pedal strokes and then, that was it. With a quick flash of fence, I was back in occupied Palestine.

⸭

Above an empty hillside, the familiar jury of pigeons line the electricity cables, watching as I make my way along their road. A few dozen kilometres earlier, back in Tel Aviv, city pigeons had done the exact same thing, although here perhaps half the number of power cables run across the pylon. From a ridge beyond them, higher up still more red rock, are hundreds of watching eyes, gathered in a line of sparkling black as a herd of goats clamour to see my spectacle. A wave of motion is stored in their haunches, rippling in lean muscles waiting to flex and then descend. A shepherd jumps down the ledge and begins to lead them on, hitting the rock with his flail as the herd impatiently begins to break ranks. Barely a teenager, the shepherd calls over to me in Arabic, then turns away and strikes his flail again, shouting orders at his goats to hold still. I call something back in English, and he repeats the same words, but raises his index and middle fingers to a V and points them at his eyes, and then at me, and then down the road, calling anew in Arabic so that now I understand what he is saying: *Watch for cars.* The road slopes in a blind bend around the hip of the hill, where he moves out into the tarmac to face his flock... a poorly disciplined army massed along the precipice. Then, with a different shout, waving his flail forward-march, he turns hard on his heels and strides across the road, his animals seeing this familiar purpose in their master and so surging after him in clouds of brown, white, black. Like brackish water poured from a terracotta jug, they find the gaps in the red rockface, and hooves on thin legs individually scramble but collectively stream onto the dusty grass verge, over the tarmac and traffic lines, back to grass again and finally after their young shepherd, flail above his head as he strides through an olive grove and down to the holding pens of a small farm.

Moving after him, again the animals watch me watching them. Those on the edge of the flock look fearfully at me, this possible predator, standing beside another possible predator, less familiar and with two wheels. I see eyes, shining black as jet, set on each side of the head so that a goat can see in panorama and detect threats approaching as it grazes. And I wonder if the goats detect that my eyes are in the very front of my head, targeted and precise in their vision, inadvertently revealing my distant history as a carnivore, a hunter who once had to track his prey and strike. One intrepid goat moves a little towards me, pushes out of the herd of shining eyes. The animal waits, watching me, then startles at the sound of a falling rock behind and runs on thin legs back to that stream of goats flowing over the road and away.

Picking up my bicycle, returning to its wheels, finally momentum comes to my pedalling, and I begin to move. The land at last gives me its rhythm, puts patience in my head and cadence in my legs, offering the small magic of the world that is all it ever takes to remind you: take your time, enjoy. I look down between my forearms and handlebars and at my turning feet. Here is the desk where I get most of my work done. Here is where I feel thoughts most keenly and so here is where I write, where sentences form as regular as the wheels turn.

In the deep blue sky above, as I round a high hillside, there is a silver flash and tethered to that sky the plump body of a blimp comes into view. Floating there, above a small military building, it gathers surveillance images of the goats and the shepherds going about their lives. Closer round the bend comes the throb of engines and I see soldiers packed into a sand-coloured jeep, wearing shades, the beat of the V8 engine leaping from under them as the boys have a whale of a time. For a split second I see them before the jeep passes by, each smiling face like a boy scout with hardware, kids sent to earn that 'battle-tested' badge for which Israeli military products – having already been trialled on Palestinians – command a price premium. There were times, riding through the West Bank, when I would consider how the Arabs of Palestine, for all that they had it bad, at least were lucky in that they didn't have to worry about being invaded by the United States. And then I'd pass a military jeep with its smiling teenage soldiers in their sunglasses, and I'd realise that they perhaps felt they already had been.

As I ride, a frustration weighs me down, pulls me backwards, for often it feels like the occupation is designed in such a way that it will kill all hope. With the guns in the jeep, the military eyeball lurking above the olive trees and watching everything, the totalitarian presence leaves me, more than once, asking what use there is in even writing any of it. And then I pedal forward, that motion by definition optimistic, and again I realise that there is nothing for it but to keep on trying.

Left I bank, down into the next turn, around the terraced hillside and into wan sunshine. And I see the chain turn over again, reminding me quietly that I know no other way than this. Up and over the crests of hills I rise on the air currents and then blow back down, carefree for a while, and every child shouts *Hello!* and each old man calls out *Welcome!* Sweat runs in my eyes, vision blurring, sun and mist pour down over a countryside where recent rains evaporate towards the sky. Far into the distance, I see the land like a milky white sea, the backs of many hills rising at the surface just barely, as if whales lifting out above and then slouching back beneath the waves.

That was a sight to behold, that late afternoon, where one after another and endlessly repeated, I saw for the first time the magic of those hills of Palestine. Immersed in them, I rode upon their rising and falling heartbeat, until it was not a landscape that I rode through but a cardiogram, where up and down my emotions they sank and soared. That afternoon, I think I understood how it could be that those Palestinians I met, none of whom had ever lived in their own independent country, could still feel with such strength the freedom that was in their spirit. Because to sense freedom is like seeing a person you love out of the corner of your eye and for only a moment in a crowded room. You still recognise them.

Riding through and along the hillsides, I passed a babbling spring near the village of Nabi Saleh. I passed an open window to a kitchen that let out the smell of sautéing onions, invoking impossibly strong the sense of home. In another small town came the sound of notes practised on a recorder or flute in a room above, dropping down to the street below. Such things were evidence – no matter the official status that an occupying force claims for itself – that somewhere in this world there is a great beauty, and that a part of it belongs to us all. That is how freedom forms, I realised it there in Palestine, and pure as my wheels turning under me, the idea only grew in me as I rode. It was all part of the same immutable law. Anyone who ever saw such sunlight at an afternoon's end, the long rays of light refracting in red earth to illuminate the gently burning sky, will know innately and forever what freedom is because at root, freedom is only the insistence of a soul to be left in peace to enjoy the sunset.

Hours up and hours down I laboured, coming slowly to realise that there is no holy site in Jerusalem or anywhere else that could hold a candle to those hills of Palestine, for they were the most precious of all sights. Among them that afternoon, eventually I found a moment of peace, my legs turning regular circles that accelerated even as the landscape slowed and, finally, speed returned to my wheels as I shot fast out of the frame and into the next.

Gunpoint

As the miles passed, the hills began to turn in the dusk, shifting from clear beauty to something more uncertain. There was something different about that space, too, for ordinarily borderlands are the grey areas that come to feel neglected between two other places. They are unclaimed. The roads that connect two different peoples are normally those that fall first to ruin, overgrowth, because people have more business and travel within their own state, back towards its centre, than in the direction of their neighbours. Everything turns sleepy.

Beyond Rantis it was not so, for there the space between two peoples was not neglected but coveted, and the land loaded with the competing claims upon it. That same twilight as had settled on me outside Jerusalem came down fast, and though I tried hard not to, I kept remembering the moment of that rock flying at me. I saw passengers in the Palestinian cars that drove by me, staring hard, their eyes fixed, and quickly a fear rose in me of what might happen here if someone thought me an Israeli. The barefaced front that it would constitute for me to ride straight through Palestinian lands where settler gangs had been known to beat and kill Palestinians, where soldiers and fences stopped Palestinian farmers reaching their farmland or waterways, and where new settlers arrived constantly to take still more land. For all that to be happening and a presumed Israeli to be so brash and comfortable that he would ride a bicycle into the gathering dusk without fear of reprisal. The cheek. The barefaced cheek of it. I'd have deserved my hiding, every last bit of it. But still, that's not how it played out.

░

In the nape of two hills, as the road loops around itself, there rises a spring. One man kneels by it and another stoops beneath a silver arc of water falling from a stone face. Beside them is a large plastic bottle, maybe a gallon in size and full, and one man steadies a second bottle as they place it to catch the *slap-slap-slap* of water falling into it. The afternoon behind me was hot, Ramallah is still some way distant and, nervous though this whole situation makes me, my own water bottles have run empty and I must refill them. One man, positioned on a step down to the spring, wears jogging bottoms that, as he kneels, push the tops of his buttocks out in the universal image of a man at work.

The two men look round as I appear, the *click-clack* of my cleated shoes coming towards them. The man with the bottle sees me first, looks up – a bit serious, a bit afraid – and the other, seeing his friend's face, turns and gets to his feet, pulling up his jogging bottoms. I hold up my water bottles hopefully.

'You mind? I need water.'

They both look at me, silent. The man with the bottle waits, speaks slow.

'Where are you from?'

And those words, so plain, were suddenly so sad to hear. 'Where are you from?', as any travelling cyclist will tell you, is a sentence shouted at you in delight from the world's roadsides, but despite being a question, often it sounds as though it is being *said* even more than it is being *asked*. In most of the world it is the one line of English people have learned, or at least remembered, and they sound delighted at finally getting to use it. Here though, I can feel those words are loaded, and they form a question all right. *Where are you from?* hangs ominous in the air. The man's eyes are steady on me, for he knows the things the settlers did to him, to his olive trees, to his younger cousin, the humiliation of his grandmother at the checkpoint. *Where are you from?* Here it is a civilian ID check, for I sense that if I am from Israel then our engagement can go no further. Sadder still, I sense that – where here I am only asking for water – that outcome would still sadden him, but he knows and I know that it could be no other way.

'Britain,' I eventually answer, then upgrade. 'Well, Turkey.'

The man nods, his face still wary. In his hesitancy, I feel that in these hills there is such trauma and suffering that all have been condemned to live under it at all times, but most potently in the meeting of a stranger. His friend takes the bottles from me, passes them down and the water echoes as it drops into our silence, the echo quietening as the vessels fill and then are handed back. Still sad, still slow, the man watches as I turn to walk away, as I say *shukran* and give my nod of thanks. He looks in the memory of another place for what to say, a place past but that will one day return, and that therefore a human spirit knows it must stay connected to, however stretched it might feel at the time. In order to make that better time one day rise again, the man nods back and slowly speaks the words. 'Welcome to Palestine.'

⁙

The road forks. Left is open, right a checkpoint. Three army boys stand in olive green fatigues, guns pointing downwards beside the red-white barricades that form their roadblock. I stop, mostly out of politeness, also because I am already near a standstill from the unrelenting steepness of the hill. A little awkward, disappointed I've stopped, the boys move towards me. In the minutiae of our reactions to one another, their hesitation, I realise that most of the occupation is in fact just a role-play that helps drum nationalism into the citizens of Israel. Before I came, they were just three young men, towards the end of a shift and standing at a roadside in the hills. I was just a cyclist cycling. But because I lazily decided to stop, we must now all play at occupation and conform to norms that there is a situation to secure.

'The road to Ramallah?' I ask, out of breath, pointing by their roadblock.

The boys step towards me, curious, one to the fore. The boy at the front is Ashkenazi: olive-skinned, dark stubble, handsome, just a few spots from the end of puberty. His manner is gentle, and I feel his soul's embarrassment at performing the functions of opacity and misinformation that I have begun to suspect is the training that he and all the occupiers have been put through and instructed to implement. When in the Occupied Territories, you do not help people find their way, because you do not want them there.

'The road to Ramallah? I am not sure.'

And then his inner soldier challenges me, where I feel that his own nature would prefer to be friendlier.

'What are you doing here?'

'Travelling,' I answer. 'In Palestine and Israel.'

I notice the *keffiyeh* on the back of my pannier, see him see it out of the corner of his eye. We both know there is nothing incriminating about it: only a cloth of black-white squares, harmless, legal. But we also know what it means, an affiliation that now colours both of our filters. For just a moment, two humans at a roadside try to undo their instant political judgements and return to being only two humans at a roadside. Over his shoulder, another boy steps forward. Mizrahi, with pale skin but his hair and eyebrows dark, his stature dumpy, uniform unbuttoned like he's too hot in the humidity.

'You're cycling?'

I tap the bicycle.

'How is it?'

He blurts it out, a bit clumsy, overeager. He forgets to play at occupation. He isn't supposed to be asking casual questions about my journey, not while we all know they should be pretending not to know the road to Ramallah and that we are in a security situation. Because of all this obstruction, we are not exactly friends; a review of my travels is not really required military intelligence, and he has no business asking it.

'It's good,' I reply. 'But I have to go, if you don't know the way.'

The Ashkenazi gives a nod, himself looks ready to ask something about camping in Palestine, but before he can, his compatriot puts in, can't help himself, stumbling forward.

'Are you pro-Israel or pro-Palestinian?'

I don't have time even to compute the question before the Ashkenazi has rolled his eyes so high he looks like he might fall backwards, looking over his shoulder with a glare of – *you idiot… what a dumb thing to say* – shot at the immediately embarrassed colleague, the kid in the playground who never says quite the right thing and just wants to be cool. I clip my shoe back to my pedal, gather my thoughts and leave with the words, 'I'm pro-people.'

⁝

The hill shoves me down a new valley. Speed falls immediately into my wheels, pulling me in as if they were a reel and the line of the road were winding towards its end. Up ahead, coming quick, I see more red-white barricades: two shapes in olive uniform, one seated on a chair and both bored-looking, like they'd rather be riding the jeep. I'm gathering speed, don't want to stop, gathering speed, refuse to stop, and so breeze between them, lifting fingers from the handlebars in an acknowledgment-cum-apology. Behind me shrinks the first checkpoint I'll ever pass with entitlement alone, evidence that there is a military rule here, but then there is also the rule of a human on a bicycle, half-flying down a hillside, and it is this law I realise with light relief – as the two conscripts stay seated – that is the greater of the two.

The descent rears up quickly into climb, my speed is taken from me and halfway up the next slope I see a gate, houses. Purple sky. It looks like a settlement but the three teenagers outside it look so Palestinian that I'm not sure. I am yet to learn the rule of thumb that if it looks like a settlement, it's always a settlement. The Jews and the Palestinians will forever look alike, meanwhile, because both groups are ethnically Semites, two peoples forced apart primarily by politics and, secondly, and mostly as a veil for the politics, by religion. In front of the teenagers, looking at me intently, I pull to a halt and wave a greeting.

'Is this the road to Ramallah?'

The truth is that by now I am quite sure it is the road to Ramallah, but the hills are rising with the concern inside of me, and so I'm asking in case there is a magic valley, straight and flat through the mountains, that will take me there direct. Making a hip-hop festival would be nice, but truly, I just want the safety of people around me, away from a terrain that feels so beset with recriminations and the memory of my own last dusk in contested territory. This road, this shortcut, is now a thing I want so badly to exist that I feel it must, or at least it might. The teenagers – a girl, two boys – look at me, a little stupefied. With them is a dog, a black Alsatian, who pads over to sit at the foot of the girl, dangling from the concrete block that works as both a barricade to the settlement and also a chair for the three of them. She kicks her heels in the air, legs swinging. Beside her is an older boy, curly-haired, wearing a sort of beat-up utility jacket, looking like he might be taking a turn as guard. A second boy, shaved head, stubble, a round belly pressing a sweater, jumps down and stands beside me.

'To Ramallah?' And he whispers, 'They will kill you in Ramallah.'

Which clears up the question of ethnicity.

He says it slow, dangerous. It is a tone that is incongruous: full of the softness of his years, but with a hardness he has been taught in this land.

'In Ramallah… they cut your throat.'

In Hebrew, the boy in the utility waistcoat, a little older, calls to his friend, chiding. *Too much* says his tone, calm it.

The performer smiles, dancing on his tiptoes, enjoying himself.

'But why, why you want to go to Ramallah?'

'I'm travelling, through Palestine and Israel.'

My voice must betray my haste, and the girl smiles a sweet smile. She has thick black hair, falling in waves down her back and tied under a red bandanna. At the end of her jeans are a pair of soft leather ankle boots, laces loose, bohemian to a tee.

'Come,' she says kindly, patting the concrete. 'Come sit with us and talk.'

And she says it so softly, her voice so kind, placing a hand beside her on the concrete.

'I'm sorry, I think I have to get to Ramallah before dark.'

And she smiles again. Such a nice smile, as the boy beside me, the joker, points back up the hill I just descended.

'That way. Then go right,' he says, points the way I've come. 'Then left.'

I ignore him, look to the boy in the utility waistcoat, who slips me a human look and in it we establish a brief trust outside of our political roles and the required misinformation.

'Is it this way?' I point down the road I'm heading along, and he gives a nod, the kid with a better eye contact than I've felt in a while. The two of us look at one another, momentarily without that veil of forgivable lies that shroud most communication here.

'You pass Talmon. When you get to Dolev, go left.'

※

Twilight passes. Darkness is coming. The anatomy of concern at running out of daylight goes as follows, and the truth is that at about 14mph it all happens in slow motion anyway. Hours out, the whole time through, you know you won't make it. I've experienced it before, of course, but in the past the only threats were thirst and hunger, maybe missing a train, camping before the desired destination… all of them discomforts more than dangers. In a conflict zone, the stakes move higher, yet still with some recognisable features.

Between the afternoon hours of two and four you are uneasy, but you are worrying for the future, which is never a true worry, because something may yet occur to make it OK before the future happens. The miracle of the flat road, tailwind or your own oddly marvellous fitness levels may materialise. An unknown-unknown may grant you reprieve. During the hours between four and six, you know the game is up, your goose is cooked, but the light is coming through the cloud just so, splitting to a pearl white so that all the world is shut inside some glorious lamp, and the silhouettes of the hills cut across it so elegantly that, in a spectacle such as this, no harm shall or could ever come to pass.

After six, you are done for, and this is where you find me now. Normally I would not be concerned, could ride after dark, but in a land where every Palestinian knows or loves someone killed or wounded by Israeli soldiers or settler gangs, and where those gangs are content to kill and to wound, then I am not safe. I have removed my *keffiyeh* from my back wheel, stuffed it in a pannier. I want no affiliations. Any affiliation, other than common human-ity, represents a risk from the other side. My only safety is that all should see me as just a human on a bicycle, and for them to have been sufficiently unharmed by life that they have no wish to do injury to such a traveller on the chance that he belongs to the group they reject.

In my mind, I keep seeing so clearly the rock from Jerusalem... its quick black shadow now lives more powerfully than any impact it managed that night. The light conditions are the same, identi-cal. I berate myself repeatedly. I'm an idiot for not leaving sooner. I promised myself I'd be sensible, not get caught short again. Where do I lay blame? It doesn't matter, it is all immaterial in the dusk. How will the rock feel this time, I wonder? I think the car will come more slowly alongside me as I crawl uphill, it will not just flash by fast on a highway. They will have time to aim. I will look right into the slingshot as it smiles out the window at me. Where will the stone hit? In the leg, ribs? They wouldn't do my face, would they, not at such close quarters? Damn, but it's gonna fucking hurt. You should know that none of these things are appearing as questions in my mind any longer, it's all certainty, and I can scarcely pedal even half as hard as I need to because fear has taken my head and all of my forward motion is fizzing in useless adrenaline that bursts in my kidneys. The cardiogram has altered beyond recognition... *b-bum, b-bum, b-bum* is a thing of the past and this, this haywire is all that I have for company. Come, pick up my wheel... ride with me a while.

⠿

Headlights up ahead. Headlights parked up. The air is getting chill, the hillside is heavy work. I've seen a pickup sitting there for a while now, black and large. The driver gets bored of waiting for me, my slow progress, releases the handbrake and rolls down, pulls to a stop in front of me. I see his face: lean, long, pinched. His glasses catching the light behind the windscreen. Door opens. He steps out. A suede work boot plants to asphalt. Another. Long legs in shapeless jeans, a *kippah* on the back of his head, fair hair, a dusty fleece, a flak jacket and from under it the white cotton tassels of his religious tabard hang down to his thighs. Shit. A semi-automatic rifle. Battered black gunmetal runs the length of his torso, but at least it is pointing down.

'What are you doing here?' he asks as I get off my bike.

'Cycling to Ramallah.'

The answer sounds stranger with each hour passing. As he steps up to me, I see his face, dotted with a tiny sty, a knot of bubbling, hardened skin where each lower eyelid rises towards the nose. I see cold blue eyes and my heart sinks. For his eyes have God in them, which is to say they are glazed, have turned to glass. I know this look from evangelicals with loudspeakers, speaking of sin and brimstone as they preach to gamblers on the Strip in Las Vegas. I know it from the differently acquired but exact same result that is methamphetamine. This man with his semi-automatic is from a different place to me, he lives on a different planet. His voice is flat, comes from far away.

'Where are you from?'

'Britain. England.'

'You have passport?'

I nod, go into a bag as he walks forward with the gun. I hand it over.

'You Muslim?'

Brain speaks to me. 'Don't you dare. Don't you fucking dare.'

Because Soul has been doing this for a while now, decided a few years back to now and then offer a sort of random act of religious education and help people re-evaluate the prejudice of their stereotypes by meeting me, a sort-of-Muslim.

'Well. Yes, I am a bit Muslim.'

Held at gunpoint by a settler, in the deserted and most contested hills of the West Bank, Brain drops his jaw. *Really? Here? I can't believe you just did that.* The glass God-eyes lift up from the passport. *Look at me.* His face twitches with the spasm of a madman.

'You Muslim?'

Shit. Brain has a point, even Soul agrees this time. I'm an idiot. I back up.

'No, I'm from England.'

'England is Muslim.'

Damn. But if the guy hasn't swallowed some hard-right conspiracies too.

'No. England is everything. Muslim, Christian, Jewish. Everything.'

And then I renounce Mohammed for a moment, consider going all spiritual, gesturing at the hillsides and invoking nature as my god, but I think better of it, opt against setting myself up for idolatry.

He's on his phone, punching a number in.

'I'm an atheist really.'

And glass eyes look at me, a special case right here in the near darkness. He hits upon an emotion, and the eye sockets seem to widen to gape a little more. Stupefied by me, he repeats it back.

'Atheist!?'

The one thing more godless than a Muslim. He speaks into his phone, Hebrew and then recognisable words. *Musliman.* Something that sounds like *atheist* but might not be. He stands there in his flak jacket with my passport, turns his phone on my photo and takes my identity.

'Wait!' I reach for it and he pulls it away. 'You can't do that!'

'For us,' he says, such terrifying words as I look at him with his rifle and my passport, me momentarily stateless and a small dose of how it feels to be Palestinian. He takes more photos, talks more on the phone. Ten minutes I kick my heels, beginning to think laterally. If I can just get a ride out of this valley in the pickup, I'd take that for an outcome. That way he can clear me as a security threat and just maybe lend a hand, help a stranger out and in so doing perhaps get a little closer to God.

'OK. You take it.' Finally, he hands me back my passport.

I point to the back of the truck, opportunism as good a strategy as any. Be a chancer, brazen repels suspicion. I'm happy for this guy to think me an idiot. He looks straight through me. I point again. He shakes his head. Points up the road.

'You go,' he says. 'I follow you.'

'But I'm slow up the hill.'

'I follow you.'

This guy, by only living on this land right here, feels he is already as close to God as he ever needs to get. Here's one man Gili won't ever get back inside no 1967 border, he wants these hills, isn't here for the small class sizes. There will be no ride out of here. I clip back into my pedals, I trudge up the hill. I spin with his pickup and headlamps over my shoulder, his face long in the windscreen, knuckles on the top of the wheel. We pass a turning, a road forking into a settlement. I continue, see him stop. I look over my shoulder and turn into the only sight more sinister than a settler: an armoured personnel carrier appears and rolls down towards where he's pulled over. That sand-coloured coffin comes to a halt and I sigh at how any of this even happened. Where do I lay blame? Stopping with the shepherd, writing those last few pages, the presumed wrong turn near Nabi Saleh, the laundry, the protracted and worried goodbyes on leaving Tel Aviv? Who knows. We wound up here. The engine growls, the vehicle set on wheels the size of my bike. The windscreen is only a black slot, like an arcade game. In drops my coin. I get one play. Let's see how this goes.

Door opens. Not a hiss of cushion or click of spring, it is just hinges and iron panels bolted shut, like a metal shed that rolls. Olive uniform gets out, Ashkenazi, clean shaven, young, possibly no need to shave. Fair hair, all set two years from now for a graduate scheme at an accountancy firm. Big Four for this one, he'll make partner in Tel Aviv. I quickly size him up. There is a little sparkle in his eye too, but of this world. Charmed life, wishes it wasn't here.

The vigilante talks to him in Hebrew a moment before the kid turns to me.

'What are you doing here?'

I almost groan my reply. 'Cycling to Ramallah.'

He turns back to the vigilante, who speaks in the tone of a concerned grandfather with a semi-automatic and who thinks he might be on to something big, protecting the nation, from me. I hear the word *Musliman*. I see the kid manage him, rosy cheeks, a little embarrassed about it, ending up – on the face of it – on the same side as the zealot settler, who leans in to make his point. The kid turns back to me.

'What will you do in Ramallah?'

'I'm travelling.'

And now I prepare to go on the offensive, now that there are more people around and not just one madman with a gun and only God to judge him. These boys understand schedules, secular ones, beyond the getting to paradise eventually and sunset and sunrise for Shabbat in between.

'I took a wrong turn. I needed to get to Ramallah before dark and this guy has kept me here in this valley. It doesn't feel safe.'

'It isn't.'

The soldier returns to Hebrew with the settler. Another olive uniform gets out, adjusts his spectacles. I point to the pickup.

'There's a bigger road, I think, to Ein 'Arik. If he could take me there, to make up the time, I'd be fine.'

The officer acknowledges and they go on talking in Hebrew. Minutes pass with me on the margins of what seems like a dispute, or impasse. The settler is either anxious about something or simply living his regular heightened state.

'He can't take you.' The soldier points west at where the sun used to be. 'It's Shabbat. He says there is a gate through the settlement, but he cannot unlock it, because it is Shabbat.'

Inside I laugh, the guy not so holy he can't drive around toting a one-metre rifle on Shabbat, but give him a gate to unlock… They talk more, a slight friction between them, before a nodding goes back and forth and I sense ground given.

'He says go to the settlement, he will unlock the gate. It makes it shorter.'

I look at the settler, his life lived no further from this hill and valley and certainly nowhere near Ramallah. I know that there can be no route over this hill that spares me either time or gradient in any great amount. After all the others I have met, I do not trust him not to lie. Not one bone in my body has any faith in him. But it is more than that, too, for I suspect him to see lying to me and obstructing my getting to Ramallah as a service to God, a divine obstruction so that – unlike the conscripts and the upstart kids who play the game but know it's a game – this guy perhaps thinks it more moral to lie to me than to tell any truth that will set me on my way to Ramallah and the Muslims, where a third of them are actually Christians but you won't find him troubling with that sort of detail. Something about it scares me, scares me deep and new and sinister, and in such a way that I just want to put distance between me and this place and this strange man of God.

I shake my head, point up the road. 'I'll go that way. But he wasted my time, and now it's dark.'

They speak Hebrew, settler body language suggests agreement is nearing.

Soldier turns back to me. 'OK, you get in.'

My eyes light up, the words *but Shabbat* go through my mind and then I put the thought away. Maybe settler man is more reasonable than I'd guessed. I take my bike off its stand and wheel round to the pickup. Soldier shakes his head.

'No, you're coming with us.'

The words land like a patter of gunfire next to the military vehicle. This can't be good. Suddenly cycling out of the valley in the darkness feels fine after all. These guys and military prison, detaining me, when I didn't do anything wrong. The iron coffin gives a slow creak, a rod that bolts it shut drops, turned by a handle on the inside of the back door.

'What do you mean?' I ask, afraid.

'We take you.'

Arms reach out from within, jackboots plant to tarmac and they haul me up. Eight of them. Back there in the darkness. A flood of hands and arms in jumpsuits reach out and the bicycle practically floats into the rear as I follow in my shorts and pull the heavy door shut behind me. Metal hits metal as the front doors are shut and with a deep throb the engines fire up to unfurl the highway. I look around me at a complete battalion of the Israeli army, a dozen of them all stare at me. Either side are two black guys, Ethiopian Jews, I guess. There are the Ashkenazi, Mizrahi, some Orthodox kids with their long hair uncut and curling down their cheeks. And the back of this vehicle is, I realise, a dual-purpose machine. First, most obvious, it carries troops. But second, it is a machine for moulding the Israeli nation. The engine turns a mincer pushing out Kosher sausages. They will spend three years in the back of this carrier, all their assorted backgrounds pressed together in the canner before out they emerge the other side, Israeli.

'Why you go to Ramallah?'

A voice comes from one set of the many eyes fixed on me. The question sounding more stupid each time I'm asked it.

'It seemed a good idea at the time.'

Some laughter.

A hand holding an aluminium tray reaches back to me. 'You want cake?'

Embarrassment fills me. Those Palestinians shot for target practice, their homes demolished, even accused in death of having somehow deserved it because of one association or another they might have kept. And here am I, with my white skin, English tongue and British passport, shepherded out by the army with offers of baking. The self-consciousness, my own privilege of skin colour and language are too much to bear in the injustice of the world.

'What sort?' I ask.

'Carrot.'

I take a slice. Together we all eat cake, as the engine hammers under us, propelling us into another rise and I eat cake with a battalion of the Israeli army. Ahead, through the slot of the windscreen, headlights strafe back and forth across the hillsides. The road snakes this way and that above a line of lit dials, its grey and shadowy shape winding ahead through the growing blackness.

'But really,' someone pauses between a mouthful of cake, 'why are you going to Ramallah?'

'There's a music festival there.'

The faces of the battalion give a collective and curious expression that seems to say many things at once.

'What sort of music?'

'Hip-hop.'

Nobody speaks. First, they seem a little hurt, as if to visit Palestine is to have the Palestinians chosen over them. But second, more endearing, is a look of muted surprise, as if such a festival sounds fun, exactly the sort of thing they might have considered for this Friday night, were they not headed back to the barracks, and were they not Israelis but instead Palestinians, or were that distinction unimportant. The carrot cake goes around again, slices are levered out.

'It feels tense here,' I say. 'With all the settlers.'

A scoffed laughter comes from the driver. 'You don't need to be afraid of the settlers. Only if they take you home and feed you. You'll get fat.'

'I still don't understand why you'd come here,' says another voice. 'Why don't you go straight to Ramallah, take a bus?'

He passes on the cake with one hand, the other holds his rifle to his hip as I meet young eyes under the lid of a military helmet.

'It's a beautiful country.'

I say it simply, and he shakes his head, so that I feel sad to consider that anyone would be disappointed to meet an outsider who wanted to come to the place he lived.

'It is. But not here. You shouldn't come here. Stay inside the borders.'

⁘

They dropped me outside the barracks, tried to force the rest of the carrot cake on me, wished me good luck with the rest of my journey and then shut the iron doors a final time. In the darkness across the valley the road flattened, revealing an irregular but fairly constant stream of headlights. Joining with the traffic, cars passed by me often enough to provide some company and I felt the eyes of strangers watching over me with curiosity rather than suspicion. The homes and shops of Palestine grew into a full imprint of daily life, slowing for evening, and along with the military and the settlements, my concerns fell away.

Seeing Ramallah grow larger in front of me, at a roadside grocer's I pulled in to catch my breath, gather my thoughts and eat a little before the city rose up around me. 'Salam Alaikum,' said the owner with a smile and a lazy wave, sitting in the corner – feet up – and watching as I made my way along his shelves of fruits and vegetables, where wooden slats separated the purple of the aubergine from the red and green of peppers, the curling crooks of cucumbers. I picked a paper bag, took an apple and a banana, and for the immediate energy, two single fresh dates, shining in their sticky brown cases. I walked to the counter with my small bag of fruit, the man tired at the end of the day, leaning back against the wall next to an old, beat-up till with the numbers worn from its buttons, some scales and brass weights. I offered my bag. The man gave another smile, tilted his head backwards in a gesture of *no* and also of a kindly *go*, tapping his hand to his heart before lifting it a little into a parting wave.

Yafa Street

That first night in Ramallah... ah, but it was something else. Let me remember it closely, for there was a spirit in the air that seems important to capture, that you must know about. Rolling in down Yafa Street that night was like entering into an embrace of a city, for the street opened before me and it is no exaggeration to say that after the tension of those hills, the calm joy of everyday life was beautiful to behold. Families walked together holding hands, men stood at carts and some sold coffee while others sold sweet-corn, scooping butter to melt over the yellow kernels on which the vendor sprinkled chilli flakes and cracked peppercorns. At a bar, forearms tensed, a line of men pressed pomegranates, one after the next and the ruby red juice ran into cups as a waiting group of teenage girls talked and laughed. A man with a propane canister on wheels stirred a stick around the heated metal drum above its flame, where a warm, sugary dust took shape and then formed a cloud of bright pink candy floss that was handed down to a young girl holding her father's hand with excitement in her eyes.

In the centre of town, the street closed to traffic, a trolley had been pulled out with a large speaker on it. In the heart of the music was a circle of linked hands. Men and a few women danced *dabka*, their partner occasionally let go so that all could clap hands loudly above their heads, a rhythmic applause let free for the young boy or an old man who took to the centre of the group with his own dance, legs strutting, thumbs and fingers pinched above his head as the rhythm of this life spread out through the crowds. Faces smiled so brightly and each young man stood tall, with his jet back hair swept slick into a cliff face of hair waxed up from a steep side-parting.

In and out of streets I ventured, watching a grocer playfully throw hazelnuts – fresh in their shells, with a green leaf still attached – at his neighbour in the store beside him. The man sat there, feet up on an upended crate, and his belly jumped with laughter at his neighbour's confusion at the mysterious impacts to his shoulder. I rolled on, rolled slowly past a shop of pastry-makers, where cakes encrusted with a jewellery of almond and walnut waited under an urn of tea, and I looked at the baker standing over them, whose girth rested full and round, like a testament to his own talents. His hands were planted on the counter above metal trays of sweets: *helva*, *knafeh*, baked semolina treats, each inside a grid of perfect metal rectangles, then cut into slices waiting to be prised out. I watched as the man grabbed a fistful of crushed pistachios, vibrant green, scattering them with his fingertips as if they were rose petals on to cakes. I scanned the two men beside him in the shop window and smiled at their likeness but for age, the same nose and down-turned mouth a mark that – though I couldn't read the Arabic sign above the door – here with certainty was three generations of *Father & Son*, all standing proudly behind the counter. The youngest of them had the smallest belly, seeming to grow with each generation as a quiet warning of what fate befalls the baker.

Along the street came the smoke of charcoal and the sweet scent of lamb grilling. Above it all, at the centre of a roundabout, was a sculpture of a giant key, elevated to mark the Right of Return that all Palestinians plan one day to claim, back to homes from which they were driven by the Jewish paramilitaries of young Israel. From a space between two stalls selling household goods, a drum studded with knuckles rolled, kneading flatbreads that dropped into a basket while streets filled with the smell of baked flour and its irrefutable sense of home. The baker smiled, seeing the wide and happy eyes that must have revealed me clearly as a newcomer. He hit a pillow with a cloud of flour pluming up from it, smiling at my gesture of *what's it for?*... before putting the pillow near to his head and pretending to fall asleep, then taking the dough of a new bread, resting it over the pillow and teasing it into shape.

A few doors away, finally I sat down, ordering a slice of *knafeh*, its melted cheese warm, the syrup in its golden semolina sweet, the surface dotted with green shards of pistachio. In a room nearby, someone was practising piano, spilling careful notes – one at a time and the occasional mistake crouched among them – but all of the notes climbed out of the window and down into the street. With a cup of tea, mint leaf floating on its surface, I ate and drank, and as I did a man in a smart hat and blazer, with a broom of a moustache, strode purposefully past. He walked right by, then turned on his heel and returned. He reached into his breast pocket and, leaning forward, placed something on my open notepad. He looked me right in the eye, spoke simply the word 'welcome', and was gone.

Looking down, I smiled, for there, winking up from my page in the light of the streetlamp, was a pin badge of gold with the interlocked red, green, white and black of the Palestinian flag. Dumbstruck, I laughed, and I thought of all the smears that the Palestinians were made to endure in their struggle for freedom, the accusations of violence and of terror, and yet here they were, upping the ante with pin badges. There and then I knew that one day the Palestinians would be free, for once a movement has grown committed and serious enough to start making pin badges, there is only one way things will unfold.

At the shop next to me, a cobbler was still working and the *tuk-tuk-tuk* of a sewing machine stitched the upper of a shoe back together, while his wife hammered a new sole onto another. Outside a café sat a young woman and man, smiling intently at one another, leaning on elbows across the tabletop between them. She said something, lifting the wing of a floppy fringe out of his eyes. I watched as she teased him and they laughed together, glowing like lanterns in the evening street. And in that instant it was all so beautifully normal, so defiant. From up the hill, I heard the clapping of the circle dance resume. I saw men with bright smiles, arms linked as they made their way down this joyous street. And I thought of the outskirts of Tel Aviv behind me, of the concrete and the car parks, the shopping malls, the bar codes, the streets that were walked in silence, telephone in hand, and where the highways roared with traffic. And after seeing that, and then seeing this, was it so crazy to believe that, perhaps, even after everything, it was the Palestinians who were in fact free?

Sa'aleek

Beats heave from behind the doorman, they thump the air and a sprung floor moves like troops marching. Here is the energy of a battleground but with only one army upon it, where some vast and positive force stands beyond the doors, in the tribe that waits to pass the stout frame of the man checking newcomers. A sock hat is perched high on his head, his ears poke out either side. The guy is here just off Rafat Street, Ramallah, but looks dressed for Brooklyn.

'Where you from?' he asks, slapping at my shoulder eagerly, all enthusiasm, delighted simply to stand where he stands, doorman at a hip-hop event just like he saw in all those videos. LA, West Side, Miami, Ramallah... one world all dressed in bomber jackets, where that and this music is all that this guy needs to belong.

'Turkey!' I answer, the altercation of the road still fresh, and I'm happy to be all things to all people for a while, to be as Middle East as they come.

'Turkey!' He slaps me harder, embraces me. 'You can come in for free! Your guy Erdoğan... he's the only one who talks for us!'

I hesitate, torn between breaking the news to him that Erdoğan is a gangster and a thug, or simply enjoying the brotherly moment. I go for the second option, take the communion. A month later I'll be home again and a Turkish grocer in London, Kurdish heritage, will say it better than I ever could as I report this story: 'They think Erdoğan's their friend, that's why these guys are fucked and that's why they'll always be fucked. He just says what they want to hear and then does his business with Israel, with whoever. He ain't their friend.'

But back here in the Middle East, for now principles are a luxury. Everything in this place is pragmatics and the hope that mightier powers choose to show you favour, shine on you with a little of their might. That's the game. The Middle East is the logic of the hard, hip-hop street taken to international relations.

Heading towards the music, I'm handed my ticket, look down at the design and laugh, for in a world of people made stateless, it makes some sense that these hip-hop radicals have chosen to present their ticket in the style of something so conventional as a passport.

Up in front waits the main dance hall. Lights rotate. Blue and yellow, green: a crowd of dark outlines, of shoulders and heads, they watch the stage, occupied by shadows prowling through white smoke. Off to one side is a smaller room, properly lit. I step inside, fill a glass of water from a jug on a table, ice cubes clink down, rocks that chime. I walk over to a nearby table, pull up a spare seat where four men sit. All of them look so young but full of intensity, serious. One is in the hoodie of Wu-Tang Clan, another in a hoodie and baseball cap, both in baggy jeans. Another is in pressed trousers and black top, the last of them noticeably smarter in a black leather jacket, three-quarter length, over a white T-shirt, his hair combed back slick. The guy in the baseball cap looks up at me, an excellent beard, immaculate. Truly perfect.

'Can I help you?' he inquires, direct but polite.

I try to be cooler than my thirties permit. I shake my head. 'Jus' sitting.'

'Who are you?' he asks.

'I just came in, cycling through Palestine.'

He smiles, like maybe I passed the test.

'Who are you?' I return.

Four sets of eyes look hard at me, put out, like maybe I should know that I accidentally walked backstage.

'We're Sa'aleek,' says Wu-Tang as I look on, none the wiser.

'The band,' explains the hat.

⁂

Thin sandwiches are placed before them by a waiter, received with looks that suggest they could be taken care of better than this. They introduce themselves, the biggest personalities go first. Tayseer has an unkempt, fair beard growing wispy on his face: he wears the Wu-Tang hoodie and by default seems to be frontman because he talks first. Maem is in the leather jacket and white T-shirt, tucked in smart to a belt. He tells me he's the producer and I smile and note that he dressed the part, there is a scholarly flourish to him, cultivating the look of a scientist of sound, a tiny throwback to the 1980s. The guy in black, Selwadi, slight of build and slouched in his chair, dark-skinned and with straight black hair, the most nervous-looking of the three, waits for the stage with an anticipation building in him. His legs are spread and his feet tapping, knees rising up and down like there's a pulse in them, like the shifting frequencies on a recording deck. Before long he stands, leaves his food, pushes a plate of crisps away and turns to me.

'I'm sorry, my English isn't so good, and I need to talk to another band.' He points, walks away, over to another table, giving Tayseer a solid parting grip to the shoulder as he passes. The last man looks at me, the perfect beard and the baseball cap. He has fast eyes that are keen, quick, full of determination but somehow manage to be gentle with it.

'I'm D'Keideck. Like *De-kay-deck*.' He repeats it for me. 'I'm the manager.'

I wonder if there was ever a genre of music where the manager, the boss, was so central a part of the act as in hip-hop, like he's the guy who can lead them off the street and into the clubs, the studio, the bank.

'How long have you guys been making music?' I ask.

Maem speaks up, the producer nervously proud.

'I started listening to it at my brother's house... that was six years ago now. He had records like Eminem. Snoop Dog. I didn't recognise that it was hip-hop, but I liked it. So I thought... I'm gonna try to write it.'

'What's popular here? What do you listen to?'

'We got lots of influences. Stromae from Belgium. ODZ. Chris Brown. Lowkey.' A ripple of serious nods goes between them. 'Lowkey, he's good. They're all popular here.' Diplomatically, he gestures to his colleagues. 'We all have different visions of music and sound, but we make it work. Hip-hop in Palestine... it's not everywhere. The farmers don't listen to it, but the cities do.'

Tayseer spreads his arms, expansive, takes a breath and launches in, as if his fellow bandmember has not been sufficiently broad in explanation.

'We take all the sounds and we put 'em together. The East Coast is different. West Coast is different. Dre has something in the beat, the flow.'

I must smile, that here in Ramallah this young man talks with such feeling about a place so far from him. About New York, about Los Angeles, both cities brought down right here in Ramallah. Tayseer, the performer, can tell he's being enjoyed, performs, puts his fingers together and cradles his thought.

'In that rhythm, Dre, he invented the shape of hip-hop. He builds the sound. He took hip-hop from the club to the streets. He put it on the charts. You got me?'

The table nods serious agreement, I join the nodding as Tayseer proceeds.

'With Dre you feel the swagger. With Dre, you feel like he's your friend… like he's walking with you. That West Coast sound, here, I think it speaks to us more. He has a darkness, maybe from the gang culture. Nothing was more hardcore for us than Wu-Tang. It's so grimy. So hardcore. You don't like them, they're not nice guys. Snoop, he started rapping about the problems of gun life, of gangs. But now he changes, and these new kids in hip-hop, they're singing about bullshit. New guys try to glorify the gangs, but they don't know about it… The Bloods, the Crips, gang culture. They don't get it.' Tayseer gestures at himself, at his band, 'The village at Qalandiya… You know it?'

I nod, remember its wall, razor wire, checkpoint. 'Yeah, I cycled through.'

'Right. Well, that's where we all came from. And there's violence, there's some drugs, it's hard. So the music it took us out of there. You got me?'

I nod.

'So we took the sounds of the West Coast. We took the funk, but the Arab world doesn't know funk. So we had to figure out how to bring that sound here, without stealing it. We analysed it. You got me? We became nerds before we became rappers. It was science.'

Maem interjects, like we're about to move back to his territory of expertise. He leans forward, puts his hands on his knees.

'We started with Arab world music. We played. We started to think about the way we felt the first time we heard it. We didn't have any money. "What was that life?" We asked ourselves these questions. Hip-hop culture, the lyrics, rap, you see, it works here.'

'In the Middle East?'

'Yes.' They all nod earnestly. 'Here, at a wedding we have two artists from outside the family. They sing, back and forth. Two bars, two bars – four bars, four bars. You can't repeat the word or change the rhyme. You have the rhythm section, drums, free-styling. It's rap. You have things like *ataaba*, which is singing and using the same word in three different meanings. If you find out you rhymed it once already, at a wedding or something, you're fucked. It's the biggest dishonour, getting it wrong. So it's like, as Arabs, we are trained in hip-hop.'

I try not to look too impressed, but these guys are amazing.

'How about the landscape? You talk about the cities in the US, on the West Coast. Is the land you live in your music? Is Palestine in your sound?'

Tayseer takes the question.

'You know, a music video director one time, he put one of our songs together with footage of a checkpoint. The soldiers, fences, wire. And then I realised that's where our music came from. It was the checkpoints, the occupation. We're not just repping Qalandiya in our music, we're repping everybody who's had something taken from them. We got a friend from Chechnya, he doesn't understand Arabic, but he saw the song and said, "In this song, you're talking about me." *Sa'aleek...* that's what it means. We're trying to reach your mind through the heart, you got me? Not in a wicked way. You're waging some war, God forbid, you lost your family. We try to deal with that loss. It's not sentimental, it's not bitter, but it's our struggle... *you got me?*'

Tayseer says it, and every time... *you got me...* he leans into the words, to the person he's speaking to, like he's offering a hand, pulling you up into his world.

'Of course, we don't want to talk about politics. But if a civil war comes to your country? What can you do? We want to live in a country that is ours. We didn't want to live the things we lived, but we had to.'

And again he says it, slowly with that fixed look, *'You got me?'*

'I mean, we are Palestinian, yes. But really, we're here for the people without money, for the refugees, the depressed. We're here for the underdogs. We want to make the music for all of the people of the third world.'

I feel like I just saw the occupation blown open, like no hot iron can resist that kind of heart. *You got me?* I could've listened to Tayseer ask that all day, asked with soul, as if he dug the words up and out, prised them up from somewhere deep and then put them in front of you to consider, like articles of evidence in this, the trial. In all of them there was a force, a calm passion, some knowledge of rights and no time for hate or anything but dignity, that urgency of dignity. Tayseer looks at me with a smile, like I get it, I *got* him.

Maem sees someone at the far corner of the room, points across and puts his hand to Tayseer's leg and speaks Arabic. Tayseer nods as Maem, precise and mild-mannered, apologises.

'Excuse us, we should go talk to that person. But it was good to meet you.'

'You too. Good luck for the show.'

And they get up from their chairs, leaving their food half-finished, moving to the far side of the hall where they clasp hands and embrace another act. D'Keideck and I sit quietly beside one another a moment. He plays with his beard, gives a smile and I see the guy analysing, his eyes like he's recording everything. You sense that his friends perform, while he's the vigilant one. He pays attention, keeps tabs on it all. He'll make sure they go far. He smiles.

'They get like that, before performances.'

'It's good.' I say. 'You perform a lot?'

'We got a lot of offers now. We played Switzerland last year. And we were offered to perform at Arab University in Israel, but there would be Israelis. We don't deal with that. None of that normalisation stuff. We work with Israelis all the time, our jobs, but not to perform.'

For a moment I get a glimpse of the lives they live the rest of the time, when they're not the big deal, the main event.

'You work in Israel?'

He nods. 'We're part of their society. We speak their language. If you don't speak Hebrew, you're fucked. We're bilingual, we're from here. And they just speak Hebrew. We've been living with this for so long now.'

'It must be hard,' I platitude.

'My father was born before it, he knows different, a different life. For us though, we only know this. At work, the Israelis pat us on the back, they say they disagree with the checkpoints but then they joke about it, they say, "Yeah, but we need them to protect us from you guys."'

Tired of expressing dismay, eventually I simply say something obvious.

'And you guys just want your rights.'

'Sure, but you want me to cry for them? These rights?'

And D'Keideck spits it.

'I don't want my rights. That doesn't make it better. Some Ukrainian guy, I don't blame him, he's in Ukraine and wants a better life so he says he's Jewish. The Israelis take our land and give it to him. I don't have a problem with Jews. I have a problem that some old German couple live in the house my grandparents worked thirty years to build. What about the Jews that live in Nablus, the Palestinian Jews? Why doesn't anyone want to talk about Palestinian Jews?'

D'Keideck lays out each argument, gently but with the firm purpose and certainty of someone who knows his rights despite having never lived in them.

'So if it's more than just rights... you want... reparations?'

'No.'

D'Keideck moves a spread hand to one side of the table, picks up a fist of air and moves it.

'African Americans. They were taken there, enslaved, they

worked. *They* need reparations. But the Israelis… they came here. They took our land.' And D'Keideck's eyes go wide a moment, his lips purse and he blows the words, he casts them at me. 'You want reparations? *You leave.* That's your reparation.'

There's a silence for a moment and then D'Keideck puts in.

'We work with these guys, all day. At the office, the shop, the hotel, where they need someone to speak Arabic. We're all two-faced. Me, the Israelis… we're all hypocrites. We're not saying anything. We're smiling together, but we don't mean it. It's a mental conflict,' he taps his baseball cap, 'this conflict it is now so much inside our heads. I work at a hotel in Jerusalem. All day. I see Israelis more than I see my family. But out of work. Nothing. I don't hate these people, of course I don't. But the whole thing is so messed up. It gets inside your brain.'

D'Keideck points, for the first time a little anguished, at his cranium.

'One day I'm going to work, through the checkpoint, and I get held up. I call the hotel, really nice girl who works there, Israeli. And I call her and I ask her to cover for me because I'm going to be late. And she says "sure thing" and I think she's so nice and, man, I'm really gonna treat her today, I'm gonna buy us all chocolate bars to share. And then at the checkpoint, I see some eighteen-year-old soldier screaming at an old lady from my village, and she doesn't speak any language he does. And I know I'm gonna get hit but I can't watch it, so I go in shouting at him and that's just how it goes. He keeps me there. I get to work even later and I see her and she's just part of it again, and I don't want to do anything nice for anyone any more.'

We sit in silence.

'What do you think the answer is? Is there one?'

D'Keideck takes a breath. 'I don't know, man, but hip-hop isn't the solution. Some people say music is good in times of conflict, but for me, art is for free people. We got six thousand people to a show in Geneva. Here, we can't get two. The Swiss guy... disposable income... sure he's got conflict, but it's romantic. Maybe he's struggling in life, so he comes to our show. He might think he has problems, and he does, his struggle is legitimate too. You have to feel for other people. But he's comfortable, he's going to be OK.'

Perhaps more than anything said before it, these words strike me. I think of all of the apparently intractable feuds that exist between different groups in my world back home, the idea that one kind of suffering outweighs another, and then here is a Palestinian who lives under military occupation and yet still is generous enough of spirit to express forcefully that Swiss – the damn Swiss! As if the Swiss ever needed someone to look out for them – hardship is legitimate because the struggle is the struggle is the struggle, and it is only a true victim who loses the ability to show compassion to those who also know suffering. And D'Keideck, he is no victim.

'When we were there, performing in Geneva, we talked about it. I thought "why not just dump my Palestinian passport, stay in Switzerland?" I can get asylum. But fuck it. That's what they want me to do. They want us to leave. That's too easy.'

'Are there places in Palestine where it's easier to be than Qalandiya?'

D'Keideck shrugs. 'It's a hierarchy, man. Gaza. Nobody can live there. West Bank. Some people in the West Bank, they've got it OK, some people in the West Bank they've got so much money, they're rich – maybe they still live in their home village, and it's under occupation but they didn't have to be moved when the Israelis came. Other people in the West Bank, they're refugees from Haifa, Jaffa, the places the Israelis took – and so they just got put in Palestine. My life, in Jerusalem, is a struggle.'

He points to Maem, sitting at the far side of the room.

'He struggles. Because he's inside the West Bank, in a village near Qalandiya. He has to live under this client government, this Palestinian Authority, who work for the Israelis. It's totally corrupt. We all share the same struggle but we share it so differently. And the killings? You can't even talk about all the killings. That's just normal now. Stop killing people. That's all they have to do first. How hard is it to stop killing people? And every time there are negotiations, the Israelis tear up everything that came before and start again, and they never stop building. They *never* stop building.'

D'Keideck removes his hat, pushes his hand through thick curls pressed tight against his head.

'Man, in the end, Israel is just one example of what happens in a world where capitalism is on steroids. Palestinians in Israel are like Mexicans in America. They need us, they need us to work. We keep their economy going, so they don't want to fix the problem.'

He shakes his head, mutters it almost to himself.

'But, you know, this capitalism… it'll never work, not with humans. Maybe it'll work with angels, but not humans.'

⁝

Up on stage I watch them. D'Keideck is leaning on a metal hand-rail at the foot of the steps to the stage, waiting down there with a gaggle of media and hangers-on. I see him and it makes sense, the guy is calmer, the guy truly gets it, has no ego by which to get carried away. A cool head. He turns, sees me, gives a thumbs-up as I watch. And I see the three of them, up on stage, each one transformed, each one five metres high, so much taller than any damn wall. Tayseer stalks from side to side of the stage, baggy jeans shuffling back and forth as he cradles the mic under his chin. Maem is the consummate professional still, deliberative, arms folded, nodding the beat, while his white top reflects the yellow lights swirling into blue. Selwadi bounces, non-stop energy and his heels lifting each line up off the ground. At the front of the crowd is a core of fans, leaning into and over the barrier to get closer, arms up and joyous, dancing, jumping. The guys stand together, voices rising, the words shoot out

'*It's hard for you to go to war... was lies...*'

صعب عليك تدخل حرب، صعب اخدك معاي، كل شي قالوه عني كذب

Tayseer calls out a line, louder, more force

'*...all you have to do is see through my eyes...*'

كل اللي لازم تسويه تشوف من عيني

He thrusts the mic out as the crowd calls back, raging but joyful and imploring, they repeat and up it leaps, louder still

'*...see through my eyes!*'

تشوف من عيني

And as I watch I think of D'Keideck's words that music and art is for free people, that it isn't the thing that can end a repression. And I think D'Keideck is right, but in the music even if not outside of it, I see that here they are free people. They made it this far because they were free people, they perform it as free people, their thoughts are the thoughts of free people. And I see Tayseer stalk the stage, I see Maem, businesslike, momentarily silent as still he nods his head to the beat he perfected in the studio. Their energy pulses from them, each one a hero, and if that energy hadn't been put into this music, then it would have gone somewhere else, somewhere less creative, somewhere perhaps destructive. It wouldn't have risen as the force of life I'm witnessing, and that one day, I know so sure, everyone is going to hear.

Part V

THE SOUTH

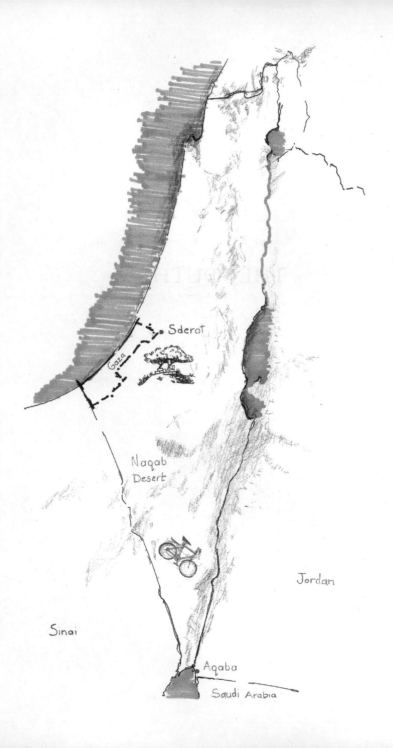

Dreamlands

One more then, another that visited me. We have to train our brain to remember dreams, and the rest I either lost or they are still in me and waiting to be found. This one, the edge of a desert and there was a young boy. African, black skin with wounds weeping upon it. I think he had been killed and so perhaps it was a ghost I spoke to. Still he smiled, though there had been violence, but he was not afraid. He smiled as he said things to me that I cannot remember, words that went into my head as only a feeling, as only a spirit, a cause for fear.

Gunships

From out of the hills of Palestine I continued south back into Israel, always heading for the shining sun that each day made its way – left to right – over the horizon. The earth dried and cracked with fissures. Large rusty drill bits, like statues placed in memorial to past extraction industries, appeared leaning against one another at the roadside. The road pointed downwards again, into gently sloping valleys and away from the half dozen clustered skyscrapers of Be'er Sheva in the distance. Shopping malls and factories stretched from the outskirts, and a helicopter gunship moved above the large blue-yellow sign of a department store selling Swedish furniture. The machine's nose tipped down, as if it sniffed a scent that set the helicopter leaning in the direction of the nearby West Bank.

The differences between the places travelled with me. I thought of the injury and losses that D'Keideck and Sa'aleek had talked of, then considered them against the landscape now moving by. Suburbia was all around in its same old attempt at normalcy. I considered it in the context of the outside world, considered it alongside racism, where Israelis and the Jewishness their government always invoked were afforded such protection against offence, while the Palestinians received protection against neither offence nor physical harm nor loss of life. In the double standards, racism nestled, so that the stark differences I saw so close together, between a military checkpoint and a shopping centre, was as if racism in Israel and occupied Palestine had here been given geographic and architectural form.

Beyond the horizon I felt a presence, growing in the near distance, and the thought stayed with me that up ahead was waiting
the most important road in my journey. The orbits of my pedal
strokes and wheels, spinning with no beginning or end, meanwhile
seemed as always to turn in tiny resistance to the idea that any
meaningful division should exist anywhere in the world. I looked
at the shadow of the turning spokes, unfurled into a fan. I saw the
butterfly kick up invisibly as it hit the air current of the turning
wheel. A little timid, through the bicycle, I asked the land why it
might have been so, from where the racism came. As my wheels
led me silently into the opening landscape, it answered that what I
could see was taking place because racism poisons all brains differently, but that it poisons all brains.

The colonial, supremacist brain – whether it is white, non-white,
Jewish, gentile, or simply Western – is poisoned by an illusion of
superiority, which then eats away at people whose lives turn out
more difficult or banal than they had hoped. It leads them to see
enmity and threat in places where they aren't, and ignore enmity
and threat in places where they are. The colonised brain, meanwhile, when it accepts the logic of racism, is poisoned by insecurity,
doubt, a sense that the world is not their world and that the rights
their soul desires are not theirs to expect.

The smell of sap pressed out from a line of trees along the road,
and my wheels rustled over a thin drift of pine needles, sending up
a whispering sound that gently asked as I rolled through:

Do you understand?

I nodded, and the hills, the opening land and the wheels of my
bicycle went on:

Where it does gaze outwards, the colonial, supremacist brain
simplifies other cultures into quick stereotypes as reference points,

but it does so differently in different places. The projection on the black people of the world, on 'Africa', is one of backwardness, laziness, aggression. Of East Asians, the stereotype is sometimes condescending but positive, with ideas of hard work and orderliness, even innovation, but it is dehumanising on the same terms, for it removes the idea of emotion, feelings or – lost in all racisms – the fact that everyone everywhere always deviates from any stereotype more than they conform to it.

At the roadside as I rode, a small flock of birds swept low over a field and then stamped their silhouette on the sky, again in the question:

Do you understand?

I nodded, and the hills, rolling down into the earth, continued:

There are shared features in these racisms, they borrow from one another. The racism that colours the white gaze of the Middle East, of the Arab, of the Muslim, is unique in that it is dominated by ideas that the people here are actively sinister, angry, even evil, and that their redeeming feature, on the basis of which they should be given any credit as humans at all, is that they have a sort of cunning. The Middle East's Muslims and its Arabs are all coloured by the colonial mind with a racism that settles not really on backwardness or helplessness – not at all, they are even seen as threatening – but on an idea that these people are hostile, are bad. From this racism there flows a particularly aggressive, warfaring racism out of the white and colonial world into this region.

From the field beside me, a quill of dust followed an old car along a rutted trail, floating skywards and disappearing to leave the question:

Do you understand?

———

And I nodded a final time as the land went on to finish:

So follows the idea that you can lock them up, that you must do so. You must protect your own humanity by denying them theirs. The cruelty you dispense comes to serve as testament to the racist's own humanity, the racist's love of life. In such a logic as this it became necessary, even essential, that around the strip of Gaza which grows in front of you, you must build a high wall, and that you must shoot dead those who try to escape.

Do you understand?

▦

Scrubland opened and from it grew Bedouin settlements made of sheet metal and canvas walls, the dwellings huddled together in and across the gullies of the hills. I watched children throwing a ball, gathering wood, chasing one another in play. Along the skyline moved silhouettes on horseback, cantering across the land with tiny explosions of dust lifting from each hoof. In Tel Aviv I had heard Israelis joke about the Bedouin, the frequency of petty crimes by them, the likelihood that they would – given the chance – steal my bicycle. And whatever truth was in it, still it seemed unkind, stark, when looking out at the entire way of life the Bedouin had seen stolen from them, as they were left to live inside whatever scraps of freedom Israel allotted.

As the day wore on, Gaza neared, and the nearness of that territory joined with all I'd ever heard of it, so that it was as if you could feel an intensity, shut there behind the blockade and growing fast. Out of sight to my left, the same direction as I'd watched the helicopter gunship disappear into the sky, lay the city of Hebron, and this meant that all around was the swathe of land described by Gili as the corridor that could one day link the two Palestinian territories of Gaza and the West Bank. Riding through, I thought again about his claim of symmetry, that the impact on both sets of people would be equal: north and south Israel would be separated by this cut, just as would be the West Bank and Gaza. Equals.

And I looked around me, at the sloping fields with their few wildflowers, at the prickly pear cactuses growing inside plant pots made from disused car tyres that held down the dry earth. I imagined it, recast with Gili's idea of a bridge joining the two territories of Palestine, or a tunnel for them, kept out of sight. I imagined it. I wondered if this bridge or tunnel would have a footpath, if it would have a bicycle lane, if only cars and trucks would have space made for them in a stretch of a country that would be no more than this road. Gili's idea inverted in my mind, and I wondered if Israelis would ever accept that corridor of land, the *terra firma* and its wildflowers, as a stretch of Palestine, while Israel's own north and south could be connected by a tunnel. Whatever the diplomatic definition of fairness, I thought, the side that is placed underground will always have lost. And the side that places the other underground will always have won. For all that Gili was wise, and determined to forge peace, I wondered what hope there was if even someone as fair-minded as he had failed to see the asymmetry of not just the conflict and its stalemate, but also its few remaining, battered ideas of a just peace.

Next morning I pedalled out into the dawn, watching the Bedouin ride their horses as the wind moved in the fabric of canvas tents and the orange light of a new day washed through the sky. The land told me then that if each nation desired this corridor beneath my wheels as its own, and if neither would share it, then it was only fair that none should have it. What if we place both countries inside tunnels, I thought, and leave the land be? Or maybe, let both have a bridge, so that instead the quarrel can become whose bridge runs above or below the other. Perhaps they could simply run side-by-side, so that both look down at a land denied to all and held instead by nature, kept in trust with olive trees and rosemary, bougainvillea and wildflowers all joining together in this orange light. Let it be a reminder of what this earth was destined to be, and that none can claim it as theirs, that we are permitted only to gaze upon it until we have relinquished the idea that any of us own any of it, and agree to share it together.

Engineering

Across from me I watched him negotiate change at the café bar, walk over to our table and draw up a chair. Allow me to explain. Tim was a man known to Michael, who mentioned him in passing in a conversation back in Tel Aviv. I'd asked if anyone in Israel really knew what happened beyond those fortified walls of Gaza. 'He's there, sometimes for months at a time. If you're lucky, maybe you can catch him on his way in or out. He can tell you about it.'

We'd sent messages back and forth, trying to see if our plans could be made to fit. Tim was on his way out at the end of a stint in the blockaded territory, suggested a café where we could meet and talk, not for long, he hadn't much time, but he would tell me what he could.

⠿

Outside there are palm trees, leaves swaying, the city of Ashkelon not far from where we sit. As the wind moves through the palms, they emit a dull roar above a street that looks from afar like one large, strange resort. Inside, from through the glass and the chill, conditioned air, the trees move with a slowness of motion, as if I am watching waves on the sea, endlessly churning. He gestures towards my bicycle outside.

'Are you travelling far with that?'

I start at the British accent. 'Towards Eilat, for now.'

A look of recognition comes into his face, the same as mine, a bit of home.

'You're British?'

I nod and give a smile, enjoy the familiarity. 'Where are you from?'

'Hampshire.'

The word itself lands, foreign as a tourist, into the Mediterranean heat.

'Michael told me you work in Gaza, but what do you do there?'

'I'm an engineer.'

He wears a stiff white collar, smart trousers with a pleat pressed straight as a plumb line down their fronts. His hair is neat, his entire look neat: a lean, angular face laid out as regular as a technical drawing.

'I guess they need that there. There must be a lot of rebuilding.'

He nods, glad to share, as though he's missed conversation.

'I work with a development agency. There are a lot of big projects that need to be done, but mostly we can only work on smaller construction, so it's frustrating.'

'What are the bigger projects?'

'Sewage treatment, power station, hospitals. Whenever there is a strike by Israel, they always take out the infrastructure first. The logic is that it will make Gazans unhappy with Hamas.'

'Does it?'

'It only creates support for Hamas, or at least, opposition to Israel.'

I consider Dorit's disdain at the makeshift explosives, sent up and over the wall to raze farmland.

'What about the attacks by Hamas, the fire balloons, are they popular?'

He shakes his head, agitated, as if my question has hovered towards him like a fly.

'The thing is, Israel pushes further and further. And when you push something further and further, eventually it pushes back. But the attention is always on the pushback, not on how far people have been pushed. And even then, I think some of the attacks, and the rocket attacks, are coming from splinter groups now. Hamas don't have complete control, even though they would like people to think they do. And Hamas know now that these attacks do not work for them... they always get hit back harder by the Israelis.'

'And the infrastructure that's been destroyed... it can't be repaired because of lack of funds?'

'To an extent. It's impossible to build anything in there because every material, every bag of cement, has to go through such an intense bureaucracy to be allowed in. Everything needs its own permit.'

'Does some stuff still get in illegally? I heard a lot of tunnels for smuggling things were found and closed down.'

'Partly, but there's always a tunnel somewhere. People are inventive, they find a way. The Israelis closed a lot, but you can never find them all. The old joke is that you can always get a hot McDonald's in there.'

'How do you mean?'

'Someone in Egypt goes to a drive-thru, makes the order, takes it to a tunnel into Gaza, it's smuggled in and then someone delivers it on a scooter.' He smiles. 'They say they can do it before the ice cream melts.'

'What's it like for you, getting in the official way?'

He seems happy at my questions, just as I'll one day realise that every outsider who's spent any length of time in this place, in either country, in any territory, is left with stuff on their chest, grievances to relieve themselves of, stresses held as a result of what they have witnessed.

'There are three borders. You go through the Israeli one, which

256

is the normal sort of interrogation of what you are doing, but straightforward if you have all the papers. Then you get to the Palestinian Authority one, because they don't really control Gaza but it is Palestinian territory, so they want to be there. Then finally you get to the Hamas checkpoint, which is the same but with some more Islamist stuff.'

'And inside? What's it like? Sorry if I keep asking questions, I've just no idea.'

'Three miles by thirty miles. Two million people.' He scoffs. 'It's a prison.'

A weight hangs in the air.

'People want to leave. Especially young people, they want jobs. It's intense in there, everyone knows everybody, everybody's business. They can't grow food, because there's no space. It's small anyway, but then there are the buffer zones around the perimeter where people could farm but they're not allowed access. So people have to pay for Israeli imports. It's an irony, where you have to buy food from the people that took the land you'd otherwise grow it on.'

'Can people fish?'

'Gaza was supposed to have a fishing territory of sixty nautical miles, but, in reality, the boats that go out more than about five miles get shot at by the Israeli navy. You don't get many fish closer to the shore. Sometimes you wake up in the night, you hear the shelling. In the morning you'll see a fishing boat being tugged back in by five others.' He drops his hands below an imaginary waterline. 'Half beneath the surface, lying low from the holes in its hull.'

A familiar song on the café radio starts up, and a teenager clenches his fists, gyrates his hips and begins a little dance in this parallel world.

'And electricity? What do people do for power?'

'Candles for light. Sometimes solar lamps. Generally, as soon as the power comes on people start charging their home batteries, so they can run appliances when the power next goes out. The Dutch government have been OK in giving support, Scandinavia too. They put in solar generators in Gaza and the West Bank. In the West Bank, Israel came in and removed them. Britain has been useless. The support varies really, country to country.'

'And what do they do about stuff that uses more energy, like refrigeration and things?'

'There isn't a lot of it. People will have a fridge, but they take out what they need for the next meal while there is power available, so that the fridge's motor can run and get back down to temperature. If you open the door when there is no power, you lose all the cold air and you don't get it back until the power comes back. So food goes off in the heat. The bigger problem really is drinking water and sanitation, because the aquifers are depleted by Israeli farms inland, diverting rivers for crops.'

I lean forward, a little embarrassed. 'You might have to explain to me how the aquifer works.'

He lays his palms flat on the table and places one partly over the other. 'As the underground freshwater gets used up, there's less pressure in the aquifer pushing up.' He slides one hand over the other. 'So the sea level begins to come in over the top of it, and the freshwater becomes saline. Gaza is poor, so people often still see having more children as a security, which leaves a growing population to support, and less water for it. It's a disaster.'

'So where do people get their water?'

'Some of the corner stores have big water purification tanks, and they have reverse osmosis systems, which push all of the salt and impurities out of the water. People buy their litre of water for a shekel, which is an expense when you've no money to start with, and you get these ponds of brine accumulating around where the water is purified.'

'Does that cause problems?'

'Not big volumes. But then I suppose that also leaks down through the ground and into the aquifers and makes them more saline again.'

'So it's a vicious cycle?'

He nods. 'And reverse osmosis takes out everything else, as well as the bacteria, so the water isn't exactly good for you. It's only water, just liquid. It stops you dehydrating but there aren't any minerals because the process also strips them from the water. That's another cause of the malnutrition people suffer from, the sicknesses children are contracting.'

'Someone told me there's a problem with growing any food too, with contamination from uranium-tipped shells, bombs, that sort of thing.'

'I heard the same, but I'm not sure of the accuracy of it. It might be the case, you hear a lot of things.'

He gives an apologetic shrug at this inability to offer confirmation, but the refusal to commit to the full story somehow consolidates the reliability of all that came before it.

'The whole place is covered in explosive dust, that's for sure.'

He chuckles, the sound of his cheer suddenly out of place.

'I bought a carpet there once as a gift. It was soon after Israel's last major war against Gaza, and when I flew home, I kept on setting off all of the sensors at the airport, the sniffer tests they do for explosive materials. The thing must have been covered in residues. They made me unpack again and again, and it came back to the rug. I found it quite funny when they asked if the explosive stuff had something to do with Hamas.' He points to the imaginary rug on the table before us and laughs. "It's all yours," I said, "I'm bringing it back to you."'

Around us the café is quiet, mostly empty, just an old man and perhaps his grandson in the far corner. Outside, the palm leaves continue to move with a calm force on the tops of their long, leaning trunks. The engineer's smile dims, suggests he enjoyed the company but now needs to head off. He looks at me, remorseful, as if he too is sorry that he can't do more amid this futility, is saddened that this conversation, for now, leads nowhere. For a moment an awkwardness settles, the two of us sitting alone with the world's most entrenched impasse for company. Once again, I have to ask, even if each time doing so feels more futile.

'What's the answer?'

He laughs, unwilling to make a fool of himself by even hazarding a guess.

'I'm not sure I'd ever want to say.'

Such a British statement, and then he finds his tongue.

'It's fucked.'

And in his long, rounded vowels of the home counties, the word 'fucked' never sounded more out of place and yet perfect. I can feel that he does not swear lightly, but he sees no real hope and so no real alternative. The street outside moves, silent, sterile beyond the glass, and we look back and forth for a way out. The silence hangs again and then, with an intake of breath, the sound of a soul unable to accept such misery as lasting or inevitable, from somewhere deep down, he says, 'But the solution, whatever it is, is political. It's not about engineering. People talk about spending billions on a desalination plant for seawater in Gaza. There's plenty of water in the area, one of the biggest desalination plants in the world is just ten miles from this place. You could spend that money on schools, on creating jobs. It's like an engineer's solution, where you use technology to build something new instead of doing what makes sense. And it's not sustainable.'

He pauses a moment, then clarifies.

'I don't even mean sustainable in moral terms. As a pure engineering equation, it's not sustainable. The Gazans are being pushed, more and more, and then there's this surprise when they have to push back.'

Looking across the table at him, somehow I think I just glimpsed again the inevitability of the end of occupation, the eventual freedom of the Palestinians. For I have now heard such things as this said by Palestinians themselves, but so too by Israelis. I have heard it said by long-haired backpackers who wear around their wrists the beads and bracelets of their travels. And now, here in this man, I have heard it said by one in a stiff white collar, his accent rounded with the elocution of a good upbringing and expensive education, his hair cut neatly into a side parting. I look at him, wearing a few days of stubble. His eyes are a cool blue, his face with a handsome calm to it, the features set with the peace of a life going well, the profession mastered, the career in hand. In him there is no trace of a radical or a revolutionary, so that I realise that right here in Ashkelon I'm talking to the middle ground, the centre, and still he's every bit as sure of the injustice being meted out by Israel to the Palestinians, because the evidence of it, all around, has accrued such weight that, like a law of gravity, it has become undeniable.

At Sderot

A car was parked at the kerbside, and behind the bus shelter a son took a piss while his father waited, looking impatient at the wheel, engine running. I stopped as the boy returned, got in, and with an angry burst of revs the car drove away. The bus shelter was a step up, even from those in the settler stretches of the West Bank, where blocks of concrete shielded passengers from hit-and-run attacks. This one truly put the *shelter* back into it, for in front of me was the colourful, painted metal of a bus shelter with its bench just like any other in the world. And at its side, cast in rigid and angular concrete, was a bomb shelter. I looked in, met with the darkness and a sudden cloud of ammonia from those unlike the boy who had taken their toilet breaks inside. A dark stain spread, still damp on the concrete, from the last visitor. Cigarette butts were scattered in confetti, some empty bottles. I looked around the walls, and, I promise, the graffiti of bus stops will yield the same insights of storytelling that today's historians see in cave paintings.

In hard lines were a few crude drawings, bright clouds of words and bubbles tagged in spray paint. And then my eyes were drawn to messages written in English. *Peace in the Middle East* read one, beneath a ban-the-bomb symbol. With a little relief, my heart smiled that even in this place some hope for a world the right way round still existed, where peace and not conflict was the norm. Stepping out of the shelter, standing beside my bicycle, another phrase caught my eye, this one in silver marker. *Your enemies want you to believe in hope.* And then another: *The road to hell is paved with good compromises. Live Free.* I read them, and then I read them again, half-understanding the meaning, but more than anything, feeling that here before me were the thoughts of a heart unbearably hard and, to be written on a bus stop, one that had become that way while still unbearably young.

※

The spot on the hill had a look to it that I can only describe as religious. It was as if that patch of land held some higher significance, was a place for epiphanies and understanding to be imparted to those who then carry messages back to the people. This feeling waited in the air, so still, with a strength beyond any I had expected, its gravity greater than had been conveyed in any photo I had seen. The earth rose higher than all the points around it, and on that small peak was a large olive tree, its beautiful branches lifting up and out like the most forgiving of embraces. In the dunes around me, true to a few adverts I had seen along the approaching road, buggies and quad bikes shot out plumes of soft sand as their riders – middle-aged couples, young men – went bouncing over the terrain in temporary simulation of adventure. Sand flats with squat bushes sloped away beneath where I looked out, where many of the plants were charred and black. All around, branches stuck like charcoal fingers on grasping hands that reached out of the earth, burnt that way, I supposed, by the fire balloons that quickly fell to earth in that small retaliation Gaza was able to muster against the bombings and blockades.

It was a sort of pilgrimage that took me there, and, if truth be told, took me there a little guiltily. Where ordinarily my faith has been that chance encounter is the best guide to a country and its people, I sought out that hill specifically, for I wanted to know what it felt like to stand in the saddest place in Israel. This hill I knew already. I had seen it a few years earlier when Israel's warplanes dropped bombs on Gaza and I, like the rest of the world, saw it on the news. At the time of that war, people from local towns had come out to this hill overlooking the blockaded city, and had watched and applauded the bombs that dropped. They had deckchairs, a sofa, everything to make the setting more comfortable. People ate popcorn, and with each explosion that went up, a small cheer lifted from the crowd. And so that late afternoon I sat on a hill where I was sure the humanity of Israel, and so in a way a part of all of the world's humanity, had died.

Above me the sun split through the clouds, sending out two lines – point to point – which shot to either end of the horizon over the distant sea. The shafts of light spread wide like the legs on a pair of compasses and walked across the sky as the wind blew through. A couple sat at a bench nearby, young lovers beneath the tree, admiring the view from a one-sided peace. On the lands below them was a concrete fence and razor wire, guarded by snipers and artillery, with the Palestinians shut inside. And this, again I thought, must have been the future.

In truth, I did not know what to say or think or feel. I saw nothing up close, only the fortifications, some watchtowers. The towns where people tried to live their lives were out of sight, and there was no way of my getting any closer. I looked down at the building blocks of a slow brutality and thought about how it had got to be this way.

In my mind I reversed the sides of the dispute. I took the Israelis, or any wealthy, mostly white-skinned people, and locked them in an outdoor prison, guarded by a brown-skinned, mostly Muslim state that starved them of life and periodically bombed or shot them. And as I imagined it, I knew there would already have been a war to topple any regime that attempted such a thing. As much as racism is about the insults people cast, more than that, it is the ideas and policies that suggest certain people, of certain creeds and colour, deserve so much less from their life on earth.

More than any time before, looking down at Gaza I realised that religion was not the fuel for this conflict but in fact more like its cloak. The true nature of the brutalities and appropriations committed in this land are often hidden behind the new, easy lie that Jews and Muslims were always fighting. In reality, all through history, it was Christians who gave Jews most to fear. The Palestinians and their lands were formally signed over by Europeans after the Second World War, when European Christians – suddenly horrified at themselves – had to settle the guilt debt for just how close they had come towards attaining the limits of their own horrendous hate. Each Palestinian death that is excused, each life Israel is allowed to ruin, is the method by which Europe and gentiles try to atone for their own crime. Israel is envisaged as a Jewish state, but it resembles also those churches, built by the monarchs of the Middle Ages, who needed forgiveness from God for the wars they waged, the sins they committed.

If that was the history, then what would come next? Behind the blockaded territory, the sun glistened on calm sea. I liked to imagine that it shone as a gift to those shut inside, a present from the universe, reminding them that there in their souls, somewhere untouchable, they were always free. Looking down from that vantage point, everything seemed suddenly to have been laid out quite simply, and I sensed that Israel had to pick one of two paths. Either it had to realise its sickness and act to change itself, knowing that no country can live with such a hate for other humans. Or, alternatively, it had to take the other path and change not its conduct but its definition of 'human'. For when you stop seeing people as human, unspeakable evils become not just possible, but normal, and even justifiable.

If the first path required brave honesty, would the second path even be sustainable? The question, I supposed, was what breaks last: the human body or the human spirit? Can you kill or punish those who rise against you fast enough that in time they will rise no more, so that none seek to follow or emulate them, and so that tyranny can be made permanent? Or is there sometimes – always – a spirit without precedent and that cannot be planned for, one that will break free to cry freedom and make itself heard?

The last sun shone on the sea, appearing through cloud to plot a bright patchwork on the waves. Looking down at Gaza, I watched little lights coming on, fluttering at the darkness, fluttering, a heartbeat, fluttering, a murmur against the dusk, pushing it back. Looking down at Gaza, it socks you like a punch, like it shouldn't be this way, and who am I and by what right was I granted the power to just walk on?

Humans go on being born, and each one is born innocent, full of all the hopes of life, up until that point at which innocence first meets with the corruption of our moral systems. Steadily, with each life that has its innocent, rightful expectations snuffed out by this meeting – the parents left jobless, the murder or maiming of a friend by security forces, the newspaper that calls you a terrorist only for demanding freedom – steadily a wave builds, indignant and righteous. What was first just spiritual innocence transforms into physical force so that, as surely as humans will go on being born, eventually that strength of spirit can be held back no more, and it resolves that it must wash away the corruption. Looking down at Gaza, I hoped that the human spirit could not be broken.

Yona

Up ahead, the lights of the highway glisten: tail lights and head-lamps illuminate red-white trails, drawing lines on the darkness. Gaza won't shift from my mind, and I wonder from where the resolution in this place will come. I think about how these territories have changed over the years. The integrity of the West Bank eroded by settlements, Israel expanding north in taking Golan from Syria. But then I remind myself that this story runs also in other directions. Israel had to withdraw from Sinai in Egypt. It had to withdraw from its positions inside the borders of south Lebanon. It had to pull out of Gaza, and illegal settlements in the West Bank, now and then, do get demolished. Dusk comes down, deepens, and takes up the stage of this theatre in which I continue south. History recedes behind me, a constantly moving process, the future always malleable until we believe it is not. I pedal on, each pedal stroke a resolution, a determination in a world where nothing was achieved without someone making a suggestion that was at first thought stupid. How to get there? As I pedal, tiredness and dusk soften my thoughts, and in the dim light I try to see answers, can just make out that there are three responses to persecution. The first is that the persecuted seek to persecute another, any other, in revenge. The second is that the persecuted seek to persecute another in the false belief that this will bring them safety. The third – the only good outcome – is that a person persecuted is so hurt by that persecution that it becomes their resolve that nobody should ever suffer

---

such hurt again. That alone becomes their life's work. How, I asked myself as I rode, can we avoid the first outcome, how to explain that the second can never work, and how to cultivate the third, for only in the third does a persecuted person ever defeat their persecution. The biggest problem of all, however, is that most people only care about persecution until they are no longer being persecuted.

⠿

The light had gone, darkness down, the village just off the highway, nothing but an orbital road surrounded by farmland. The large, metal wheels that rolled irrigation pipes across the fields were propped up against one another in cluttered stacks illuminated by moonlight. All around were the crops the engineer had talked of, grown in Israel for export, depleting the aquifer beneath me.

At the edge of the village I met Yona. She was taking belongings from her car as I refilled a smaller bottle from my larger canteen. An old but indomitable lady, in the light of the streetlamps I could see her face etched with wrinkles smoothed by a generous coat of foundation, painted over at the eyelids. A large, slightly round woman, she wore a loose red jacket over a black blouse. On the end of strong arms and long, painted fingernails, she held shopping bags, so that she looked a mixture of age, domestic chores and some glamorous determination to defy both.

In Hebrew she spoke to me, words that I understood from the intonation to be a question. Perhaps thinking still of Gaza, I responded with bluntness to her polite enquiry.

'Sorry, I don't speak Hebrew.'

In the rough and rasping voice of a heavy smoker, she said those most human words: 'You need more water?'

'No, thank you. But is there a shop here, to buy food?'

She turned away and I saw her shake her head silently while her wide body, weighed down on either arm with shopping, waddled slowly towards the porch of her house, where a light was on.

'No shop, but come. Yona give you food.'

﹟

Opposite one another, we look across the kitchen counter that functions as a table. To one side are a salt and pepper mill, a bowl of boiled sweets in shiny wrappers that she pushes towards me and I gratefully decline. My protestations that really, I'm fine, she needn't go to any trouble, have fallen on deaf ears and Yona has pulled a small electric grill out of a cupboard and plugged it in. She places a kosher sausage on it. Takes a jar from the fridge and pulls out the crook of a pickle, a gherkin she slices up and puts on a plate. From a breadbin she takes two rolls.

'You can sit down. You want this toasted?'

I pull up a chair, shake my head, bewildered. I'm still there for the Gazans, but sometimes principles have to wait until after the next meal, and Yona doesn't seem like anybody's enemy. She is still wearing the large red rain jacket and printed on its breast is the logo of an international company she'll explain she has worked with many times, taking groups of Israeli children to high-end British summer schools.

'Yona have many good times in Britain. Nice people.'

She sits down opposite, and over her shoulder the sausage cooks and the scent of grilling meat rises. Between us is a bowl. She tears open a plastic packet and pours in crisps. I look at Yona, try to guess her age, a face so cracked it looks like the canyons of the Naqab/Negev. She looks nearly eighty but with an energy far younger. Her neck is loose, her cheeks pulled tight, like she's sun-blasted, burned by a lifetime in hot sun with skin and genes that were not made for it. Her hair is straight and dyed jet black. She taps a carton of cigarettes on the table, impatient for the next one but then decides to ration herself. She lets go of the cigarette packet, takes her coffee instead and drums solid, painted nails on a glass mug. Hard as stone, *ra-ta-tap-taps* echo up to the low ceiling. Earrings appear through her pitch-black hair, two sparkling hoops

'So Julian, tell me, where have you been with your bicycle?'

I exhale. Where to begin? 'Two weeks ago, I arrived in Tel Aviv.' I consider my words, but I just looked at Gaza and can't stomach censoring myself this evening. 'Then I went into Palestine, near Ramallah, then north.'

For a few seconds, Yona's face is unresponsive, as if it takes time to shift all the age stored there into an expression. When she has reached the necessary emotion, her head, earrings and black hair suddenly shake with disapproval. The sound of a kosher sausage hisses slowly on the electric grill.

'What is this "Palestine"?'

I aim to diffuse the tension by ignoring her and tracing my journey back into Israel. 'Up to Tiberias, Galilee, Haifa.'

'Julian, tell me. Where is this Palestine?'

It isn't working. Sometimes, in some places, avoidance just doesn't cut it. And in we go.

Across the table we look at one another. Her face is kind enough, in most ways so entirely ordinary. There is a sparkle in her eye, enjoying the provocation, but I feel guilty for the cheery inconsequence of this conflict, debating rights and wrongs that hold sway over the lives of others.

'Palestine,' I repeat. 'The Palestinians. You know, the people in Gaza. In the West Bank, where the settlers are.'

'Arabs here have best life of any Arab. Look at Syria!'

How to respond to that? 'Syria is in a civil war.'

'Arabs here have best life of any Arab,' Yona repeats. 'Look Lebanon, Iraq. Look Jordan! They have nothing. Here Arabs have better life.'

———

That she won't use the word *Palestine, Palestinian,* is the most noticeable thing about it, and as she erases their existence, as she suggests that the Lebanese would in fact rather be Israeli, I try and figure out where to latch on to this, where to find an opening for logic in her total racism.

'Gaza is like a prison. They have no water or power. They cannot leave because of the blockade.'

'If we end the blockade, then tomorrow Yona is dead. Julian, tell me please, what do you say if Yona is dead?'

There is something oddly cheerful about it all, blasé, as if she is serious but altogether not, and on some level just an old lady enjoying some company.

'Arabs, they have everything here. And,' she points in the air, 'Arabs have advantage, because they know Hebrew… but we, we do not understand what they are saying! You hear them, everywhere, speaking their Arabic.' Yona almost spits again. 'And for this, listen, Julian, I know… we have only one solution.'

I brace myself for Yona's final solution. This won't be pretty.

'What's that?'

'I start Arabic lessons! Yona learn Arabic, so I know what they are saying.'

Pleased as punch, Yona straightens in her chair, proud to have figured out how to outfox the Arabs. My jaw falls at this fantastic ploy of abject racist suspicion meeting respectful cultural integration.

'Six years now I learn, Julian. I very enjoy.'

She gets to her feet, smiling at my stunned reaction, that she has silenced me for a moment, is winning. She picks up her phone, a large screen held in her painted nails. She searches its contents, finds a video and presses play. She slides the phone across the table towards me and gets up, moves over to the counter and the cooking sausage. I watch the shaky video recording, the audio picking up the sounds of neighbours. I watch a blue-pink sky, dusk, upon which tiny puffs of white smoke emerge sporadically. Yona on the far side of the kitchen tends to her portable grill, takes off the sausage with a spatula, slides it on to a plate.

'What is this?' I ask.

'Rocket attacks. From Gaza, outside. This two weeks ago.' She looks over her shoulder. 'You want me to cut up sausage?'

I shrug in response and Yona returns with the whole sausage, smiling, a knife and fork side by side next to it on the plate with some coleslaw.

'They fire rockets. Lucky for us we have Iron Dome. It fires iron balls to shoot rockets out of sky. Ketchup?'

I shake my head, begin to cut up the sausage.

'Direct hit and rocket explodes in sky. Or it knocks rocket off course. My son is angry that I go outside and take video, when I share it on internet he say "stay inside".'

Yona shrugs, as if rockets were nothing more than rainfall. 'But rockets happen a lot. No blockade, Yona is dead in 48 hours.' She thinks a moment. 'No. More like 30 hours.'

I eat the sausage, point towards my plate and Yona's absence of plate.

'You aren't eating?'

'I used to be very fat, Julian. Twenty kilos I lost. Swimming. Every day.'

I make an impressed sort of face, the woman as determined to defy age as she is Palestinians.

'The swimming is good for my sleeping too.'

'I heard that.' I eat, Yona looking at me, picking up the cigarettes.

'Here life is very difficult.'

'I understand.' I scoop up coleslaw in bread. 'But you have your technology, your Iron Dome, and the Palestinians have only rockets, or only rocks. When you strike Gaza, it's with fighter jets and bombs. It's uneven. People in Gaza are having their lives destroyed. You are all human.'

Yona taps the cigarette carton, looks at me steadily. Little do I know it, but right now her weapon system is arming, the payload is coming in, and – *boom* – Yona says it.

'All are human… but we are more human than they.'

And if they aren't the most dispiriting words you'll ever hear in Israel.

'That's an evil thing to say. That's how the Holocaust happened.'

She bursts out laughing. 'I joke! I joke!'

If this is what passes for humour round here then I'd hate to know what abuse looks like, but actually I already know, the whole world already knows. In my mind I can still see the walls of Gaza, taking the edge off the joke so that my face must be serious, dimming her enjoyment. She gives the carton of cigarettes a firm knock, withdraws one expertly.

'You mind if I smoke?'

Which seems like a considerable courtesy to ask in her own house. I gesture her to be my guest. The lighter sparks into only a whiff of smoke. Sparks a second time, into flame.

'My family, from Romania. They came after World War Two, escaping Europe.'

'I cycled through Romania… a couple of times.'

Yona looks on. Blank. Israeli through and through. As Romanian as Dorit is Iranian, scarcely a footnote. She drags on her cigarette. 'I never went.'

'You live here on your own?'

'My granddaughter comes sometimes. My husband, he died two years ago.'

'I'm sorry. You lived here together?'

'Yes. He was from Iraq. He ran construction business in Gaza. It was better then. All his workers,' she blows smoke, 'they were Arab.'

'He was Jewish?'

Yona lowers her brow sternly, 'Of course! There were many Iraqi Jews.'

I watch her smoking, taking a long, satisfied drag on the cigarette. Over her shoulder I see some sort of stained-glass picture of a deckchair and parasol on a beach, the ornaments of a simple life. I look at her, at the old face of a Slavic Jew who met here in the Middle East with an Iraqi Jew and in a place their families had felt could at last be theirs. Every time I am taken by the tenderness of that idea, a moment later I think of the Palestinians and ask myself if the Israelis deserved such tenderness if it was built by denying others the same right to a home, even in their own land.

'I will say one thing,' she announces. 'These Arabs, Muslims. They know how to welcome. Hospitality.' She shakes her head a little, with a happy but grudging respect, then gestures at my plate. 'It is very nice, how they do this. My husband... it was he who taught me all this. Before he, people come to my house and I did not offer anything. I just did not think.'

Yona draws on her cigarette, blows out. 'It is very nice.'

'You don't think it would be easier if everyone could just live together?'

'It would be nice, yes.' Yona smokes, points at the street. 'When our daughter was born, ten taxis, all from Khan Yunis, from Gaza. All my husband's workers and their families, outside, parked in cars, ten taxis! They bring so many presents, this room,' she waves large arms around, 'it was full with flowers.'

'So... you think it could work, living together?'

'I have good friend. Arab woman. From near Haifa. First time we met, at airport. She also working with the international school. She says to me, like this,' and Yona pulls a face like a gargoyle, '*I no speak Hebrew*. She says it like this. She angry.'

She scowls again to make her point.

'But now,' Yona crosses her fingers, 'we are like *this*. When my husband dies, she calls straight away, she calls, and we cry together. She Muslim, she wears burka. She wears burka and I dress fashion… But we like *this*.'

I smile, move quickly on from Yona's ideas of fashion.

'If you have Arab and Muslim friends in Israel, why don't you think it is possible with Palestinians? You wouldn't rather have peace, to not have to be afraid of rockets?'

'Peace.' Yona, she mulls the word. 'It would be nice.'

'I'm not sure saying "we are more human than they" is a good way to get peace. People are being killed… all the time.'

Yona softens, sucks hard on the thought.

'Yes,' she sucks at it some more, 'it is always a shame when people are killed.'

I eat the last of a crust of bread. Silence comes between us, and here is one more of those people in this world whose views are often vile but whose heart is not.

'But they no want peace. Suitcases of cash, yesterday, just yesterday. Into Gaza. From Kuwait. Cash, for Hamas. What do they spend it on, tell me please, Julian?'

I pause. 'I heard salaries. For officials, civil servants.'

'Missiles! Tunnels! Israel are the biggest idiots in the world. They not spend on schools, on jobs. Missiles! To fire! At us!'

Yona leans backwards to the countertop, brings out another large packet covered by an image of what looks like chocolate cases with a marshmallow inside.

'You want cream pie?' Yona thrusts the packet at me.

My face must look as blank as I feel, searching for a response to these words so soon after the concerns before it.

'You know cream pie?'

My face still blank.

'Perhaps you don't have cream pie in England. But listen, Julian,

I tell you. We are biggest idiots in the world. Hamas leader has illness… what we do? Tell me please, Julian?'

Blank.

'We let him come to Israel… for treatment!'

And in this you feel the indignation, from ordinary Israelis who know that Israel works together with Hamas where necessary: to prevent something more extreme taking its place in Gaza, but so too to control the local population. Palestinians know it, Israelis know it. The gangsters of the Israeli state and the gangsters of an Islamist militant movement, neither of whom have an incentive to solve a problem that enriches and empowers a select few on each side.

'What do you think the answer is then?' I ask.

Yona looks back, for once bereft of answers. Finally, quietly she says, 'Leaders are problem. Always the leaders.'

'You're an anarchist then?' I ask playfully.

'I don't know what I am, Julian,' she mutters, shaking her head. 'Yona doesn't know what she is.'

⁣

Packing my belongings into a pannier on the porch, I pull on my jacket for the night now cooling. Yona comes to me with a plastic bag, held open to show its contents.

'For you.'

She says it as I look in at foil-wrapped bags of cheese-flavoured crisps. The plastic packaging is brightly coloured, with a cartoon tiger printed beside an exploded image of the parading snack: some piece of mass-produced wheat batter, light as air and fried by the million, flavoured with hard cheese and then sealed inside this bag. I give a grateful nod as I look at Yona's face in its heavy make-up, concealing behind it the warmth of an old lady with so many contradictions of love and hate, and who maybe just wishes she wasn't so alone, who maybe wishes she was still a little younger. She just stands there, holding her offering of crisps for a passer-by, her cracked features heavy with age but inside of it just smiling.

War Machine

Beneath a willow tree beside a running stream I had slept, awaking in the morning to a cool mist lifting off the plains. A gravel track forked nearby, where a couple of times in the night a car had swung into its turn, with the rasping of stones that rumbled and popped as tyres dragged through the bend. I packed my sleeping bag back into its sack, took from a pannier one of the last *fatayer* that Darina's mother had made for me, and as I ate, I savoured the steamed leaf inside the pastry, green and bitter against the sweetness of the sautéed onion. From the bag I shook out the thick dust of crumbs that had fallen from the crust of the dozen *fatayer* there had been, tossed them into the stream, watching them float away on the water. I smiled at the sight, this accidental *Tashlikh,* that casting off of sins that the Jewish perform at Rosh Hashanah, a ritual borrowed from the ancient Zoroastrians of Iran, in a land where faiths have always borrowed, blindly but freely, one from the other.

At the top of the pannier, the last *fatayer* were stacked together in their bag, resting next to the packet of crisps from Yona. Eating my way through the *fatayer,* tasting its raw flavour of the earth and growing plants, I looked at the baked cases of those remaining, beside the bright, shining foil packaging of the crisps. And there was a version of progress and of tradition, but both given to a passing traveller as gifts, side-by-side in my pannier.

▦

All day I rode. The grasslands ended and the scrub thinned out, the soil turning to desert and rock. I reached the town of Sde Boker, where the land was pulled apart by canyon, a cavern that looked vast but was only a shadow of the riven earth waiting up ahead. Highway 40 moved me south along the shifting contours, taking me away from the settlements and habitation of Israel and the West Bank, deeper and down into desert. Now and then I saw hikers, some of them on well-organised camping trips with pickup trucks to pull trailers full of their belongings to ease the journey. It was quaint to think of how Israel obstructed the lives of those Bedouin who had always lived mobile and as nomads, only to begin bussing in tourists to live in tents for a weekend at a time.

At a longer stretch of highway in the late afternoon, a man moved slowly towards me, his skin dark brown from walking the desert, and over his shoulder a torn bin bag containing many rolls of bread that he carried back to a Bedouin village. Far in the distance, some miles after him, a great and blinding light shone from the top of a giant tower that loomed over the horizon. Pipes and chambers snaked up the sides of it, with sunlight trapped in the head of the turret, so that I guessed that it was a solar-thermal power station, catching the rays of desert sun and then reflecting them at water, forcing steam to drive the turbines that powered Israel. Those same forces of engineering were also being put to more destructive purposes: from out of sight, I heard the roar of jet planes' war games in the sky above. Now and then a small flock of pale, distant triangles would go barrel-rolling together, before receding from sight. Once as I rode there came the thumping, impossibly loud sound of a helicopter larger than any I'd ever seen, its rotor smashing the sky to pieces, with the spike of a gun turret protruding so far in front that it doubled its length and made it resemble some sinister, pollinating bug, patrolling the sky in search of some evil flower. Trucks, transporters carrying tanks all thundered by me with chains swinging from their flanks. Armoured jeeps and personnel carriers throbbed close as they passed, and the war machine of Israel had never felt so close. As afternoon drew towards evening, at the roadside I saw a gathering of concrete huts, and I felt a smile in defiance of the militarism, a joy, for one hut had a Palestinian flag painted on it. Someone had stolen in to claim a small victory here in the heart of this military range. And then I came closer to the huts and sadly saw I was wrong, for another had on it the flag of Egypt, another of Jordan. These were just the props of still more war games; each hut represented one of Israel's neighbours, where the youth of the country practised what it would be to invade them.

On the wind, flagpoles bent and their banners fluttered as more jet planes roared overhead. Dusk came forward and with it, around a high, sloping bend, the silhouetted fortifications of Ramon Prison, just as Adi had said it would. High walls of concrete, wire and watchtowers all stamped black shapes against a sky moving pink. Red lights marked out the perimeters and high-points to any passing surveillance, or low-flying aircraft, and inside I knew there lived the killer of Yitzak Rabin, he who had assassinated his president for fear that he might make peace with the Palestinians. Jewish law has in it the idea of the *rodef,* a 'pursuer' who can legitimately be killed if they risk the lives of Jewish people. The killer had viewed Rabin thus for engaging in peace talks, and though inside those walls leaning over me he was to be locked up until death, outside he was revered as a hero by Jewish nationalists, who campaigned for his freedom and felt he saved Israel by killing with Rabin the chance of a free Palestine. Through the shadows of the prison, moving into the next high, desert bend, a military transporter carrying large truck tyres passed me by in great haste. Two puddles of headlamps waited at the dark roadside, and as I neared, I saw that there were perhaps a hundred conscripts gathered, holding their guns and preparing to drill in the darkness. *Blue-red-blue-red,* the lights of the silent siren on a distant highway patrol climbed upwards along a desert ridge, and again, the landscape refused to lie to me. Again, it whispered that same advice as it had in the desert outside of Jericho, told me anew that to live a life in fear is in the end always worse than the thing you lived in fear of.

The road markings went on in front of me, pulling me towards them, white as ice caps that rose and disappeared to a dark sea. I kept pedalling and they kept on rising, the back of a white whale lifting from black waters, lifting and then sinking and then lifting, then gone, so that I wondered if that had been a whale at all that I had seen, or some other creature that foretold of troubles lurking closer, deeper still within my mind. And all the time I considered how to write this feeling, to seize some understanding of freedom powerful enough that Israel would come to feel it too, would begin to buckle under the realisation of how they used that strength they had acquired. Some I had met already felt it, and I knew that some were always bound to feel it sooner than others. The artists, the dreamers, the glorious misfits, those who say already 'not in my name'. In time though, this feeling, at first just niggling, would overcome harder hearts too, and those who believed in justice above all would realise they had come to have more in common with Palestine than with Israel. The occupation would not finally end with tirades and polemics, it never does, but instead with the hushed silence that befalls dinner tables when someone denies the Palestinian right to exist in their own land and realises that, at last, such a view has become unacceptable. One day, all this will be done with, Palestine will be liberated, but before then, I sensed that for a time the Israelis would hate the Palestinians not for what they do or who they are, but because in the mirror of Palestinian suffering, Israel has to see its own face and how ugly it has become. Then, only then will it change.

⁝

Time shifts forwards, the hands of the clock press on as I eat a simple meal in a small café, a falafel wrap and a salad. I take my time, draw warmth from the food, knowing that this night will be a long one, that I have distance to cover and ominous spirits wait up ahead. From this moment, coming once from the evil in Ramon and a second time from somewhere unbeknown to me, the air chills. On the distant bank is a Bedouin village, with the orange glow of a fire sputtering beneath a larger town, where floodlights roar bright white and drown the valley in their glow. The sun vanishes with its final touches of pink, a crack in the cloud bank where last light gets in. I see it. I see a darkness coming, but the firelight of the Bedouin camp keeps flickering, flickering, lights all around and flickering. The week is Hanukkah, and the Mizrahi who runs the café brings out a tray of doughnuts for those dining in his small, humble restaurant. Candles are lit, a few are placed in the doughnuts, and I watch the kind, handsome face of the owner, his curly hair and broad smile, his face illuminated in the candlelight as he cups the new flame between a palm and the match. Other diners join in the song, so hopeful, so spirited for their homeland, for a harmed people who just wanted to feel safe, and yet all down the highway outside, it is the military hardware that seems to have stolen their dream. Next to my table, a moth flutters behind the blinds, seeking the light which reflects on the dark window but repeatedly bouncing off the glass. I watch as the creature comes, again and again, ricocheting back towards me into a place from which there is no escape.

⁝

Back on my bicycle I move along the ledge, along the ridge. Way below, other vehicles crawl so slowly into the vacuum of the desert, the ravine. There is a chill rising from it, a mist, a blackness thicker than any I've seen, a darkening with the cold out of the canyon. I consider other night rides beneath moon and stars and the black canvas on which to dream. Here it is not like that. The space for imagination, where a mind can play, is snuffed out by military and threat, by a promise of conflict from which I feel myself rushing: for the next mile, the next town, the next stop. The sound of the Hanukkah song from the restaurant follows me with its warmth as I go, its verse lifting from out of the restaurant, on the wind, in the candlelight.

Oh, Hanukkah, Oh, Hanukkah
Come light the menorah
Let's have a party
We'll all dance the hora
Gather round the table, we'll give you a treat
Sevivonim to play with and latkes to eat
And while we are playing
The candles are burning low
One for each night, they shed a sweet light
To remind us of days long ago
One for each night, they shed a sweet light
To remind us of days long ago

Grand Inquisitor

From a long way out, the roaring comes, gathering closer, and then I can hear the strings of an oud, a breath blown over the thin wood of a clarinet reed. I know that finally the desert proper is coming, and I know what that means, for it is the eternal law of deserts everywhere that they contain only the necessary emptiness by which you can see your own soul and that which you carried into the desert with you. Yona's words play in my mind as the sands rear up, and I know that to hold such an evil thought when encountering the desert is dangerous. Again, her words echo at me.

'They are human, but we are more human than they.'

A ball of dried grasses presses forward with me, the silhouette of a dying tree twists into surreal contortions, stuck like a withered trident in bare earth. A few clouds break apart around the moon, leaving the shape of jasmine petals and its pointed, climbing leaves. The temperature drops, a cloud takes the shape of a horse, mounted with its rider behind a mask through which only eyes glow. The voice speaks and I realise that once again, as always, stalking the night sky, at last he has arrived. The Grand Inquisitor waits to talk with me, and I know I must swallow my every inhibition and speak plain and true.

'Why did you come here?' he asks.

'To write. To write and to ride.'

'To write what?'

The silhouette of the jasmine, with the spears of its leaves and the soft scent of its flowers floats above and wards off all harm or ridicule, allowing even the grand terms of the truth to find their way into my voice.

'I must write, write something so beautiful that none can disagree with it. And something so clear as to make it irrefutable. And I must write something so vast that inside of it is space and room and love enough for everyone to live. A world big enough to hold everyone.'

'Is that all?'

The desert asks it and its tone is sarcastic, but I know that the desert knows no sarcasm and so all I hear is the sarcasm of my own heart. Sand whips up on night air, dashed against the wheels of my bicycle. I know that the desert is testing me and that its force is almighty strong, that it could wipe me away. But I know also that the force of it is indifferent, because the desert will only banish or inflict suffering on those that bring evil thoughts into it. I know that I must open myself to these gathering wastelands, so that they can test me and see if I mean harm. From nowhere, there comes a spike in the night sky. A roll of thunder hammers between stars and a single bolt of lightning pierces down.

'What do you hope to achieve by this?'

I gulp, for I feel my answer is suddenly small and vain. Bicycle and me and the vastness of both the Naqab and the Negev, wide open and ready to devour me. Thunder cracks anew, a roar louder than the largest jet pushes back up the highway. How does any one person ever voice such a thing? All the words that I can find are each the most invisible grains of sand against all that I've seen and been told.

'I… I don't know,' I stammer, and darkness bears down at me, thick pitch. The desert lifts up to throw sand against my skin.

'Then why,' the Inquisitor roars, 'would you come here to waste my time?'

I feel myself losing, uncertainty is coming, and sometimes in life if you have doubt, you have nothing. The world really is too big after all, optimism is just red meat to the teeth of reality but then, again, in the roaring wind I see the cloud pulling into the leaves of the jasmine. The shape of them like spires and minarets, and despite the dryness of the air, the scent of it falls to me, fresh and bright, holding an invisible strength that lets me speak.

'Go on.' Softly I say the words to myself as the desert roars, so loud.

The roar comes again as I begin to speak, the roar demands of me anew: 'What do you want?'

'It seems to me,' I begin, 'that the greatest service any one of us can ever perform is to take the trauma we suffer and make sure that no other ever need suffer it. We make sure it dies with us, we try to dissolve it, and even if we cannot neutralise it in our own hearts then, one way or another, we still refuse to transmit it to any other.'

Desert screams, unimpressed. Its voice shouts its question from inside my own head, so that the wind blasts between my ears.

'But these are no answers. Tell me, what do you want?'

'I want one country,' I say. 'I want one country and one people, just as this is already one land. And in that country, every Palestinian and every Jew shall have one vote to decide the affairs of their life. And you can call this country neither Palestine nor Israel, but some harmony of the two names, just as this land will become a place of harmony for every last person that lives in it.'

The desert booms, thunders furious at my impertinence. The stars rattle in the sky.

'Nothing changes until it is ready to change,' the desert roars, ignoring me. 'Tell me, who are you to say otherwise?'

I go on, for it is sometimes important to state a truth even when it is ignored.

'And I want the Palestinian of Gaza to be able to walk free and unimpeded to meet with the Palestinian of Ramallah, in a country she feels is her own. And I want Jerusalem to be a city that belongs to no faith but to only all the people who set foot there, the capital of one shared country, or the joint capital of two. This new nation shall be governed by an ambition of one land for many people. And, having endured so much, the people of this new land will find no need to govern in the name of a God, and they will together create something so beautiful that such a need is passed. Having suffered so, the peace that builds here will glisten in proportion to all the pain and tears and sadness that came before it, and all the world will look to its example.'

I continue talking as I ride, but I am talking from my brain. Brain is making a speech. The words fall, one after the next from my mouth, but I cannot hear myself speak, for the words fail to reach my ears through the desert's howl. Then I hear a word, a word in my own voice, and another, and finally I think that I can hear myself talking, for the desert has stopped, has ceased a while, has calmed and I think I did it... I made my case, and surely now it will let me pass.

A silence drops, the pitch black continues all around and I hear the breathing wind of the Inquisitor, hear an unimpressed sigh give out, so that I realise that it was not enough. Brain stutters and then stops, falling away behind me on the retreating road. I watch it fall to the ground, slip through the bicycle and the triangles of its frame, cut by the light of a half moon. The desert whips back up in what sounds like fury, but I know is really its indifference. Exhausted, spent, I weep, I have to. I said it, did all I could as Brain falls away, so well-meaning but the poor thing entirely out of its depth beside this, this eternity of stored human malevolence.

Looking around the roadside, I see Body, lying slumped and broken out of shape. Brain bubbles, falls down, collapses and trickles across the asphalt. Brain turns to *jus*, to jam, like a pan of damsons bubbling under, quivering, quivering. So this is where it ends, I think. And in the end, it was too difficult after all. I can have no hope. A bat cuts an arc on the night. A wind pushes over the moonlit pool in the dark, pushes over the jasmine leaves in the cloud, curling with spears and clubs. Another wind pushes, and on it, faint, I hear from somewhere else a sound, a sound pure as dawn, as it comes down...

'Dance then, wherever you may be... I am the Lord of the Dance said he, and I'll live in you if you live in me.'

Through the song, the scent once more tumbles down, and with Body and Brain all gone, I feel Soul as he gives the slightest twitch. His boot draws back in, at the end of an outstretched leg, as he lifts up onto an elbow. He brushes the sand and twigs from his hair, then with three fingers presses a massage hard upon the heart of Body, above the breastplate, right on the chest cavity, just enough to regain feeling even as Brain slurps and coagulates into only useless thoughts. The voice comes again.

'Dance then, wherever you may be... I am the Lord of the Dance said he, and I'll live in you if you live in me.'

And I lick dry lips, so cracked that my tongue gets stuck on each parched ridge, plays them like the grooves in the rolling drum of a musical box. How heavy the silence falls, but in the failure there is at least and at last a sanctuary from expectations. In a peculiar, broken ease, with all else wrecked, the Inquisitor rests in the desert, motionless, and Soul speaks.

'All things considered, there's very little left here for me to say.'

I hear the clarinet play from somewhere, the oud picks notes in the firmament. Soul nods at the roadside wreckage of Body and Brain.

'I remember an old tramp we met once, the three of us riding the desert of New Mexico. I remember he told us that when he could see the stars he felt safe, like God could see him and would take care of him. But that seems funny to me here, because you've got no shortage of stars.'

The desert screams at this new offence but Soul just looks on, nonchalant.

'You can howl at me, but it won't work, 'cos I'm like you. I'm scarcely even here. A collection of feelings just as you are of earth, and I'm as indestructible as yourself, if you don't mind my saying so.'

Above shines Venus, pale and soft.

Desert, relentless, presses in, moving in. Pitch black, hard, Inquisitor states again:

'Nothing changes until it is ready to change.'

Soul smiles a sad smile, and looks at the sky, at Venus, pale and soft.

'It is ready.'

Desert howls, but it howls differently this time. The earth splits anew, breaking under the weight of dawn, and in a deep and sonorous voice, the Inquisitor speaks a final word, a desert wind blowing large through the centre of its letters.

'Go.'

Soul gets from the bicycle and steps back over to Body, then kneels, lies gently beside him, and disappears. Body's cheeks give a twitch of sleep. The jasmine and the stars above watch, fading as light pours in, bleeds down over the night, drawing the silhouettes of the land in such clear lines. Sun shines, shines Dome-of-the-Rock gold. The rocks, the trees, the scrub, the bicycle frame, even the stupid wall nearby. The sunlight pours in over us all, at first leaving its shadows but then so strong that everything collapses into white light and, in a flash, a new day bursts and in all life glowing, it rolls out over the land.

Naqab/Negev

Sunlight pierced the cloud of the previous night, and as daytime lifted and morning drew on, the military manoeuvres and hardware looked less serious than ridiculous. It was the spectre of the gathering desert that did it, for even if the equipment remained every bit as deadly, there was something pathetic about it all, once darkness was gone and it was set against a space so enormous and indifferent. From above, perched on the edge of a gaping canyon, I looked down into desert, which barely thirty miles to the east would join with the ruby sands of Jordan's Wadi Rum, and then with still more desert beyond that. Neither natural marvel before me was concerned by the human lines drawn between them, or by the quirk of distinction that would have placed them in different books, or on adjacent shelves, of the tourist guides. The two places were not neighbours: they were one.

It was just after Mitzpe Ramon, the town perched like teetering crockery on the rim of a crater, that I dropped into it. The road down must have descended almost twenty miles, but went at such speed that it felt a fraction of that, and picked its way along each precarious shelf of the crater with a vast, orange drop below. At regular intervals the asphalt reared up in front of me, hitting me with the sort of turn, looming, that always dares you to brake later and bank lower, to get your knee down and inhale as you dive in. Over the crash barriers you could see not just the road's next hairpin but the one below it, the two of them cupped together in everlasting embrace. For all that the road ahead led deeper into desert, most of the view from up there, plummeting downwards, was not solid earth but blue sky, atmosphere, as if the Naqab/Negev had been added as a hurried afterthought: a single stroke of red with the artist's brush beneath the wide blue band.

Once at the bottom of the crater, fate had determined that as always – like a cycling Sisyphus – you must simply climb back out. And so, from the base of the world, I began to pedal back up. From below the landscape shifted, and with no cloud in the sky or wrinkle in the earth, you saw your road ahead for whole hours into the distance, so that to gaze in front was almost an act of time travel, where the only thing that had changed between the moment of seeing and later arriving at the point I had seen would be my own position on it. The rest of the world remained entirely unaltered in the elapsed hours. The remoteness of the landscape began to bear down on me, shaping my every thought, so that I watched the black highway scream die-straight and unwavering towards the horizon, striking out a trajectory with that same purpose and perfection of a ball struck in a game of snooker, where you know on impact that it is headed only for the pocket. From the end of the cue a puff of blue chalk dust would wind upwards, settling overhead and returning again to the sky.

Moving slowly on, I made my peace with the distance, the gradient, and then also the squalls of a headwind that were coming for me. I lowered my head as flat as was comfortable over the handlebars, resting my fingers on the cables that ran across and between the brake levers and gear shifters. Head down I thought of this refinement in my position: of how, by lying flatter and shrinking my imprint through the air, I could move a little faster, a little easier. I remembered an old friend who had once boasted of a new cycling helmet that, shaped like a tadpole, was 'faster than a human head'. Another, a bicycle engineer, had once explained that he was experimenting with shortening his cranks, the metal lengths that hold the pedals, because with shorter cranks the process of pedalling created a smaller pool of churned and turning air, which caused an invisible imprint in the atmosphere that slowed the cyclist, who should ideally be shaped like a tapered arrow.

Onwards I laboured, considering how, in the sport of cycling, all this had been taken to even greater extremes. In that professional, micro-managed world, much of my love for the sport had been eroded by a theory known as 'marginal gains', so that each highly refined engineering process, training programme or nutritional regime had been optimised so identically towards perfection that riders were able to eke out only the narrowest of victories over others. Radio contact with a team director, via an earpiece, meant that a rider had accurate time information by which to decide their strategy, in coordination with others, rather than arriving at it within the limits and guesswork of their own mind. The result was that stages and races that had once been won by ten minutes, by fantastic daring or ability, or lost to great recklessness or mistakes, were forever more going to be decided by a matter of seconds.

Pedalling through the patience of the desert, its calm seeping back into me, that same process of controlled, consolidated time and emotion seemed to have altered the opportunity for change in all our world. Were people's views already so made up that the potential for changing a mind had shrunk beyond hope? Against those trying to protest for a better world, the troops could now be dispatched too fast, and their bullets would be too accurate. Too complete was the acceptance by others that a state could use violence to put down protest, and – I shuddered to say it – too complete was the unspoken acceptance that those who were not white, or who were of the world's poor, should be grateful for what they got and could not be trusted with true freedom.

And so it was that in that desert world through which I rode, I wondered what hope there was for the vulnerable or the malcontent to demand change. What happened once all the cracks through which the light gets in had been made so small, when all time and thought were so colonised that there remained no further room for the accidents of history or moments of heroism by which the world had once clumsily been improved? Lowered to the handle-bars, endeavouring patiently to evade the growing headwind, with my head down and thoughts circling, gradually I moved onwards, up towards the sky.

░

It was in that sky alone that the military presence still troubled me. I could hear them, so often could I hear them… the fighter jets roaring as they would barrel roll and dog fight above, way above and always in earshot but seldom in sight. For half a century it must have been so, ever since Sinai was restored to Egypt in 1980, when Israel had been obliged to withdraw its air combat training from that sparse peninsula back to their own smaller skies. The invisibility of that jet engine roar made the sound all the more unsettling. With that strange acoustic pressure bearing down on me, and to the mundane sound of industrial murder being prac-tised above, eventually I realised that the perfect solitude I'd known in every desert I'd previously cycled had here been plucked away. Now and then I'd look up and, straining my eyes towards the noise, eventually see a few dark shapes: the collected triangles of wings and a nose cone moving fast above. At one point there appeared, lower to the earth, one of the same thundering helicopters that had passed me on recent horizons, and again, led by the length of its gun turret, it pounded down the sky like a fist hammering at a vast blue tabletop.

On the ground it was tanks that kept me company. Dust storms were thrown up by caterpillar tracks as gun turrets turned, the tanks ramping up mounds of earth and then hiding from sight behind sand banks. It was all the same war-readiness but oddly small, slow-moving and unimposing. Around one encampment of tents and tanks stood a line of flagpoles, bending on the wind and each bearing the standard of the division: a flag of red and green stuck there like some crusading army, eight centuries since the days when Richard III and Saladin had here done battle. I recalled the old story of Saladin seeing Richard pulled from his horse, and so admiring the fallen king's soldiery that he sent a new steed to him in the fray, rather than see a worthy opponent come to an end in such unworthy circumstances. I thought again of Yona's dark words – 'we are more human than they' – and I thought of how even in enmity there is supposed to be a code of honour, for we have a strange bond with our foes, which ensures that if we see and treat them as less than human, then in time it also becomes our own destiny to become just that.

As the sun moved over me, it was the Naqab/Negev that brought everything into clear focus and held it there, tight. In the desert's expanse I saw a landscape that – even if each tank and warplane had fired on it till their barrels burst and wires tripped – still would have done nothing but laugh with clouds of dust, perhaps breaking into a few black pocks on the surface under shellfire. But that was all. The landscape was all but unalterable by even the fiercest of war machines that Israel or its neighbours could muster, and by that reckoning, in the clear light of day, it showed their manoeuvres and hardware in a human scale. To the last vehicle or aircraft, all of it looked slow, trivial, hulking and encumbered… a product of that human failing whereby disputes inspire us to arm ourselves in a reaction that is born of paranoia and fear, but so often gets mistaken for strength. The desert was having none of it.

When the midday sun had passed its peak, at the side of the road appeared two temporary canopies: black marquees that resembled small spider webs with clusters of infantry hanging around beneath them. As I pedalled on, a shout rose up, and then another, so that first I just raised a hand in acknowledgment, and as the calls kept coming and arms waved, I came to a stop in case these were orders rather than greetings. Unclipping my canteen to drink, I walked over towards the soldiers, standing waving enthusiastically.

The distance between their camp and the road was entirely unob-structed and looked close, but involved a few minutes of walking, long enough to leave each party awkward. What will we say? What do I want? Who is he? I gave a lazy wave, lifting a hand but not an arm, and looked about at assault rifles, submachine guns and rounds of bullets held close by a battalion of teenagers in uniform.

It is a strange reversal of expectations to be called over by the army, a force bestowed with the right to kill on behalf of a nation, and yet to arrive feeling you are the one left in charge. An Orthodox teen soldier, with bangs of curls at his cheeks, steps forward to break the silence. The last of his acne and the first of his beard is on his chin, and he sticks his hand my way as he says hello. A little goofy, he looks guiltily aware that there was no real reason besides collec-tive boredom to call me over.

More hands come my way, some greeting me in American accents, others with mumbles, the battalion a mix of white, Arab, some African Jews. Others rise from where they knelt securing munitions cases, they too shaking my hand like I'm on some sort of presidential visit: inspecting the troops by bicycle, a boost to morale, '*Mission Accomplished!*' The whole battalion comes up, eager to have a pump on my arm and my handshake in such demand it starts to feel like I should say something, some words of encourage-ment, inspire them to keep their spirits up: the war is going well (it isn't), soon it will all be over (doubtful) and they'll be home to their families and wives before next Hanukkah. I look around, a circle of guns and innocent eyes looking back at me... and I realise anew, that some look scarcely old enough to have even been kissed.

'Would you like water?' asks the Orthodox boy once all the hands have been shaken. He gestures to a black metal vessel with a tap on it.

'I'll just take a little, thanks.' I move to fill my canteen. 'You guys will need it out here.'

'Fill it,' he insists. 'We can get more dropped off. The next town is 15 kilometres.'

'I saw on the map. It's just a dot though... as if there's nothing there.'

The boy smirks in a way that intrigues me, before he responds.

'It's not nothing, it's something. But I think fill the bottle.'

The tank must hold a couple of gallons, and the trail of precious liquid splashes into my canteen as the troops and I look at one another. One boy is standing there, what looks like a full Gatling gun around his middle, the thing so long it has a tripod for the barrel: a rotary drum full of ammo, all of it hanging round the back of his neck by a canvas strap. But he rests his hands on it as leisurely as if he'd simply picked up a stick on a hike. I drink water, oddly comfortable with my total absence of anything to say.

'You want some tuna, beans?' The Orthodox boy gestures at tins stacked in a crate beside the water. 'Bread?'

I shake my head.

'I'll continue to the next town, but thanks.' I nod at a nearby gun, plenty to choose from. 'You guys just practising something here?'

A few heads nod, the Orthodox kid perhaps most enthusiastically... finally glad at some interest from me in their purpose.

'We're just waiting to go out again.'

'Firing guns at the desert or something?'

'Oh yes,' he beams. 'Just firing the guns.'

And we all look at one another. Me and all these uniforms, the young eyes of these teenage soldiers, somehow like children anywhere. Just trying to be cool.

Kibbutzim

After another forty minutes, another tank battalion with engines rumbling appears up ahead. The brow of a hill comes into view behind it, has the look of human habitation, some trees and a radio mast. Slowly it gets closer, Body ready for food. Seventy kilometres passed since the last town and lunchtime overdue. Impatience rises as the settlement gets clearer, lifts out of its outline so that I see: a fence with beach mats and other fabrics strapped to it, as if to stop sandstorms blowing in. I ride up alongside, the place looks ragtag. A few palm trees press their leaves at the wire fence. Some gardens and allotment beds appear, empty. Chickens peck the earth. I see the front gate, heavy metal rolled across the road, the place as unwelcoming and guarded in appearance as every settlement in Israel. Fenced in. There is an ornamental stone wall, and here my perception starts to shift, for on it, in cut-metal stencils, is some cross-legged figure in a yoga pose above the words *Desert Ashram*. I look back down the road, can still see the dust of the tank battalion as it rises, the tanks barely out of sight as I peer in and see a group in a corner. They wear pink leggings, neon trainers, men in vests, everyone with mats rolled out and their hands rotating, downward dog, lips soft. But it's a… yoga retreat?

Beneath a canopy sits a group of friends: Lycra gym wear is everywhere, a woman in leggings, a sports bra salmon pink, flip-flops. Another woman is dressed like a high-performance athlete and sits smoking a cigarette. Sunglasses turn the eyes of a man next to her into two panes of sheer blue. I walk up to where one woman, like a queen bee, sits with a huddle of friends and a blanket over her shoulders. One leg up, she hugs her knee. Tanks fade from memory. The woman in the blanket is eating a plate of food, notices me but doesn't trouble to notice me, as if her brain has been set to disregard the possible stress of any unnecessary information. The setting feels edged with an air of self-satisfaction that makes the reaction all the more smug. My presence in front of her is welcome, but only in so much as the appearance of a mere mortal allows her to reflect a minute on the sort of person she was before she became who she is now: resplendent in the higher realm in which I've found her and of which I can only dream.

'Excuse me? Is it possible to buy food here? A shop? Or a café?'

Queen bee looks up from her plate, throws long curls over her shoulder. She picks the bra strap that's fallen down to her arm and replaces it on her collarbone. She shoots the look of one who is both annoyed to be interrupted but glad to get the chance to register that annoyance. I see her plate as she turns: bean sprouts, lettuce, a mess of lasagne spreading over it like some Italian tapeworm. More beansprouts. But I'm hungry, it'll do.

'I guess... you could have a plate.'

She says it slowly, getting to her feet, and immediately I sense the sort of place this is, that she works here but also *doesn't*. They've not formalised this into a work environment of trade or roles, because doing so could never capture the purity of who they are and what they do. She pauses.

'It's 35 shekels.'

They've got the hang of that much.

'Sure,' I reply. 'But don't get up, if you're eating, just tell me where to go.'

'No, I take you.'

She lifts out of the chair, pulling loose pyjama bottoms up over the tops of her hips. Barefoot. We walk through the other tables, pass a counter.

'So, what is this place, Shittim?'

'Shittim it's just the map point. We are Desert Ashram, a spiritual retreat.'

She looks at me, fair hair and rosy cheeks, chubby. Unsmiling. She points through a hatch: a room with a large fridge, hobs.

'The plate is some salad. Lasagne. Other things.'

Not the most enthusiastic service, but I nod agreeably.

'You have to pay first.'

That's more direct than I expected.

'Very spiritual,' I mutter, by accident.

'*What?!*' she caught it, snaps.

'Nothing,' I retreat. 'My money is with my bicycle. You mind if I wash my hands and face first?' I gesture to a bathroom.

She rolls her eyes. 'I got up for you, and now you ask this. Do you want food or not?'

My eyes turn speechless. Damn, but by Dorit's reckoning, if rudeness in Israel is in fact fondness, this girl must be running hot for me, positively wild. Indignant, she goes on looking at me like I'm the worst thing in all Palestine or Israel. I wonder, surely this must now be in the realm of actual rudeness rather than cultural quirkiness.

'In there,' she points, warden-like.

And I keep my dumbfounded eyes on her as I follow her pointing arm.

'I just want to wash my hands and face before I eat.'

In the dim light of the bathroom I turn on the tap, take the water and press it to my hot, dusty face so that it squeezes out between skin and palm and slaps back to the basin. I am tired, hungry, only the desert up ahead, but the cool of the water revives me with a clear thought: I can't give this person or any like her even a shekel that is mine. This thought is superseded by a second question, stark and serious: How does this society truly plan to work within the Middle East? Because the Middle East, for all those things its countries and its people get wrong, excel in nothing so clearly as welcoming a stranger. Whatever other rights are flouted in these lands, that one is sacred and ensures that a traveller, fresh from the desert, must wash upon arriving and, still more, do so before a meal. From Istanbul to Kashgar and down to Isfahan... in each truck stop, impoverished rural hovel or sprawling city, nobody has or would ever treat me in this way, subject me to their crude European *toilets-are-for-customers-only* poison. The white man and woman have had their hearts eaten away by love of money and right here, I realise again, is how the Palestinians, but in fact all of what D'Keideck called the third world, will be needed to teach the financially rich but spiritually bankrupt nations of this earth how to live again as humans, how to treat a stranger in off the road. I leave the bathroom. See her hovering near the fridge with food that I could eat instead of returning to the empty road and distant, hungry horizon. But I can't.

'Sorry, thanks, but I think I'll continue.'

As I roll back out into the desert, I see a line of arms and legs in Lycra pivoting and tilting in their own manoeuvres, as the tanks nearby go about theirs, yoga spirituality in this military state. And I wonder for the thousandth time if this supposed nourishment of the soul actually changes a soul, or sustains it just enough to keep people ticking over as humanity recedes.

▦

Another hour later, stomach on empty, I passed through more iron gates, and at the heart of well-tended grounds found myself in front of what looked like a huge temple. The building was pink, apart from soft turquoise on a few small spires, and constructed of repeating geometric shapes set under the clear blue sky. From its centre shot up the long stem of a giant mushroom shape with a short hat on top, and a pathway leading to the entrance was flanked by tall palm trees. In hope of finding a shop or café, I rolled through the grounds towards a few outbuildings. As he heard the sound of my tyres on the gravel, a man looked over from a greenhouse where he was lifting crates of plants in tiny pots. Loading the crates onto the rear of a bicycle, he brushed dust from his waistcoat, from which string and bags and secateurs stuck out. He looked at me, left me to speak first.

'Hello... is there a place here that I can buy food?' I asked.

He looked a little longer, and then pushed a curl of greying hair up off his forehead and back into the tangled nest on his head. Right away it was strange, I remember, the way he looked at me dispassionately, a little suspiciously, and yet the words he said – so oddly blunt – were also the most hospitable.

'Sure, you can eat with us.'

He waved to where two younger men were sitting silently on a low wall, biding their time.

'They will show you to dinner,' the man said, disengaged, as he walked away with his bicycle and flower pots.

Approaching me the two men, dressed in jeans and T-shirts, almost in unison stuck out their hands for me to shake.

'Where are you from?' asked one, tall and lean, his skin pale, with a wispy beard that was jet black on his cheeks.

'Britain,' I replied as he turned away, his expression distant. 'You?'

'From Russia.'

He began to walk off as the other man, short, Mediterranean in appearance, offered his hand with a smile.

'I'm Tamer. From Tel Aviv.' He laughed. 'How did you find this place?'

'I don't know. I just turned off the road.'

The Russian walked ahead as I left my bicycle and went with Tamer, wondering what or where it was I had found. We moved towards a large hall where tables and chairs were assembled.

'It is a very unique place,' he said kindly, 'but there are some rules.'

'OK…' I answered, sceptical.

'There is no talking at dinner. And if you want to eat more, you just raise your hand. OK?'

At that I smiled to myself. A travelling cyclist, relieved from the obligation of making polite conversation at dinner, and fed as much as I wanted simply by raising my hand? That I could manage.

⠿

Tamer is on one side of me and an old lady sits opposite, her face behind the bottle of olive oil, a light red vinegar, the small container of salt and a pepper mill. She has a knitted jumper and gives an awkward smile as she pulls herself closer to the table with a screech of chair legs. There must be about a hundred of us in the room, a few helpers at the margins, standing to attention and ready to serve. Opposite me is a middle-aged man, balding, plump. The Russian is two seats beyond Tamer. A young woman walks in, sits further down the table, hair in a plait and a blouse that, just barely, reveals the shape of her breasts. A dozen male heads turn towards her, necks rotate, as the helpers walk in with bowls and trays and set down the meal. We all take it in turns to serve one another conscientiously. Tamer drops a roast tomato stuffed with brown rice on to my plate. I give a grateful smile and then look at his plate to see a larger one. In return I give him a spoonful of aubergine, smaller than the one I give myself. *Is everything grown here?* I whisper. He nods and we lower our heads again.

The food is good. The stuffed tomato, boiled potato a waxy yellow, olive oil and pepper dripped over the top. Steamed leaves, something like chard, dark green in colour with white veins. Salad. I reach for the last of the aubergine in the tray but am beaten to it. Someone does my work for me, raises their hand. A woman in an apron comes over to us, silent, takes away the tray and returns with it a moment later, refilled with new piles of glistening purple. The hall is silence, only the tapping of cutlery on crockery and whispers of condiment requests.

'Can you pass the pepper?' I ask Tamer, who reaches across to it and hands it back with another question, quick and quiet.

'How long have you been riding?'

'Some weeks.'

'It is OK?'

I chew food, weigh my words. 'Not bad. It started off…'

'Excuse me.' The woman opposite looks up from her plate, a sharp nose points accusing at us. We look back, quizzical, boys in a classroom.

'*Shush*!'

After a while the plates empty, the hands stop going up. Tamer gives a nod to check I'm OK, done? I nod back, together we get up and I follow to a kitchen where we drop knives and forks into a bucket of water, stack plates.

'You want tea? Coffee?'

I nod, follow to an urn in the corner with a tower of glass mugs in front of it. There is a box of mint from which Tamer makes his tea, the smell exploding as the tap is opened to let out hot water that lifts in a burst of aromatic steam. I take coffee grounds with a spoon, add them to the bottom of the cup and as the hot water falls in to form first mud and then fill the cup, out comes the smell of coffee cut with cardamom.

In the courtyard, small groups stand in happy conversation, looking more at ease now they are out of the dining room. The woman who had sat opposite us gives a smile as she passes Tamer and me, sitting on the wall, the sun so beautiful and everything kissed with happy light. Younger men and women mingle shyly in front of a picnic bench, as if there is some immutable courtship playing beneath a slightly extreme set of rules. Tamer and I sip our drinks, laughing at how I wound up here.

'It is very funny that you found this place.' Tamer gives a warm smile.

'It's crazy! The tanks, then the yoga and this, so close together.'

'This is Israel!'

He laughs, spreading arms in welcome and spilling a little tea as he does so. We relax, as if here we are alone in understanding a shared truth. Both of us are open to it, but still think odd the strange ritual we have just been pressed through.

'Why did you come here?' I ask.

'I had to. I needed a change. Tel Aviv is like no other city. It is twenty-four hours. Non-stop. It is full-power. There I used to go out at midnight. The drinking. The partying. It was too much for me, so I left. I had to get out, I had to. I went to walk the *camino* in Spain. Then I come out to the desert. First a kibbutz called Samar,' he points south, 'then I go to Sinai. Then, last, I come here.'

I look at him, imagining this person out and partying, where here he looks so tired in even the sunlight of a late afternoon and already in need of sleep. I look at his soft eyes and wonder if in them I can see all our collective burnouts, our breakdowns.

'And you? Why did you come here?'

'I'm trying to figure something out, I suppose.'

He looks at me, wanting more, and so I clarify.

'Palestine. Israel. Someone said I should write about it, a book.'

'If you want to understand this, I think you need six books.'

I look at Tamer and decide to trust to his nature, the gentleness of his eyes, the ease with which he smiles. I will speak plainly.

'I know the history is complicated, but the reality is simple, isn't it? The Palestinians need to be free.'

Tamer sighs a deep sigh, a sigh with a hole in it, a tired hunger that sighs almost as if it has forgotten what it desires but knows others have it.

'My generation, the young people, we are tired. This government has no policy for peace, only more settlements. There is zero policy. We are tired because we have nothing that even resembles hope. When Rabin was killed, we were only children.'

He breaks off. 'You know about Rabin?'

I nod and he continues. 'That was the last time there was hope. We still have energy, I think we are still willing to fight for peace, but peace is a long way from us.'

'You think it has a bad effect on people, all this war? The threat of war?'

'Yes. Of course. But it's not so simple, we feel vulnerable here. In 1973... we almost lost it. When the Arab countries invaded us, and our army wasn't prepared, we really thought we could lose it, that we could lose our country.'

He waves back towards where out of view the tanks are still stationed, performing drills in their clouds of dust and turning gun turrets.

'And so all of this, it's kind of necessary, even if now we are stronger.'

We sip our drinks as the crowd in the yard thins and the shadows grow longer. Tamer begins to say something, then stops uncertainly, then decides to go ahead.

'But, if I were eighteen now, I would not go to the army. The army has so much bad influence on our culture, all of it.'

And in his voice, you can feel him hurting, a tone that quietly announces the reasons he is out in the desert.

'The army is what says the Israeli man has to be an elite commando or he is nothing.' Tamer waves his hands and pulls a face of pained disgust to say that this is bullshit. 'He has to be this hero, this special unit guy.'

And I look at him, with his slightly sunken shoulders and wide eyes, a little startled at the world, as if because his heart is not hardened. Tamer is one of those souls troubled by that cursed vision that the world should be fair and could be better. In his wide eyes, shining with something not quite tears but hinting at them, you see the size of the boy's heart, so that even without his saying it, you know that he never wanted to be a commando, and even if he had wanted to be, he perhaps couldn't have. We sit together and I think of the young life next to me, I wonder what will happen to it next. If he can repair his spirit, if the desert air and the silent mealtimes will be enough. I look down at my coffee, the sediment and whatever fortune it holds, concealed there at the bottom of the cup.

'You have a place to stay tonight?'

'No, but I wanted to ride further, I think.'

'Then go to Samar.'

'Samar?'

He smiles. 'The kibbutz I used to live on. Samar is the opposite of here. You are at Nedar Samorot, and this place has rules. Samar has no rules. Here it is good, but it's different. Samar… it is a lot of fun.'

I feel intrigued but exhausted. 'Even for a tired cyclist?'

'There are no rules. You just go there for whatever you need. It is maybe another thirty kilometres south, on the road to Eilat. They will feed you, give you a bed.'

'A bed sounds good. Thanks for the advice.'

'After that, where are you going?'

'I dunno. Maybe Jordan, maybe Sinai.'

His eyes sparkle and his voice goes far away, so that again I sense he is one of those spirits for whom the world is all too tender and so simultaneously all too sad.

'Sinai,' he breathes it out and his eyes glaze. 'You must travel there, or at least you must go and see it.'

'Why?'

'Because… because it is the most beautiful place on earth. The sand. The beach, the mountains, desert. All together.'

And he smiles. 'Tell me you'll go there and see it?'

I nod.

'You promise?'

To Samar

The road tilts due south, through the last stretch of the throat and on towards the exit of Israel. It spits me out of the folds of mountain, through the dusk silhouettes of ibex, their horns curled back and hooves rattling over tarmac as the road shoots out the gorge. Sheer, rugged cliffs watch over me and the road points down, all the way down into its corkscrew. Riding south I think of Tamer, and sad though it is, from somewhere I smile at those words of his that give me quiet optimism…

'We are still willing to fight for peace…'

…it keeps ticking over in my mind as I pedal, the words going round on the chain under me. The sentence takes hold, for the word 'fight' is seldom placed alongside – but ordinarily in opposition to – the word 'peace', and it is a cause for hope to have people say out loud that *peace* does not simply arrive, that it does not get bought or ordered in. Peace is not off-the-shelf, it has sweat in it. Peace is a struggle, getting to peace is hard. The path to peace might sometimes be violent, or at least have the threat of violence over it, in order to ensure the justice that peace requires is finally delivered. Perhaps it is cruel of me, but somehow it gives me hope to see an Israeli hurting like this for his nation. Tamer is further proof that placing your head in the sand is not possible if truly you want a complete life, if you want to live without a troubled soul. They were in some ways quite different, his conventionally handsome face and olive skin, next to her, pale, slightly awkward, but in Tamer's eye was a look of sadness, but also of unstoppable principle, that reminded me of Adi.

On the flat below me stretches the southern reaches of the Jordan Valley, where a new road is being built, widened, under what looks like round-the-clock construction. Floodlit. Engines throb, generators, work gangs press on. Steamrollers, their drums shining, roll. Pirouetting diggers dance atop mounds of earth and dump trucks shift aggregate. A warning light flashes, revolves, and an alarm sounds as a truck reverses. A surveyor walks with a tripod and measuring instruments tucked under his arm. Pedalling through, looking at it all, so non-stop, again I see that Israel learned how to build a country but not a society. In the brutality and unflinching purpose with which this place was constructed, in the extirpation of heart, Tamer and Adi and so many like them have been flattened by these steamrollers. Israel might have been built, but as I see their faces I understand that, without the Palestinians, they will never learn how to live happily. This place may be the refuge for the Jewish people, but if something is built on fear of what waits outside, it is only a prison.

░

Samar is set back from the road, past a giant shed where a vast herd of cattle belonging to another kibbutz moo and shuffle. The whole place stinks of shit. The night is down, only a few lights illuminate the settlement nestled under mountains, as again I pedal through heavy, half-closed iron gates.

Following the path, I ride towards buildings with white lights shining, one building larger than all the rest and containing a dining hall. A man carrying a crate of vegetables crosses the entrance just inside the doors and in front of two large refrigerators. Without seeing me, he heads into a kitchen with industrial sinks. His hair is long, black and grey, thick curls held in a ponytail. He wears boots, sunglasses hooked to the collar of his shirt, forearms tense with the weight of the crate. The man's skin is the shade and roughness of someone who works the land. He looks over as I get from my bicycle, walk up.

'Hello. I'm cycling through.' I pause, suddenly uneasy at what I'm asking. 'Someone at Nedar Samorot said maybe I could stay a night here.'

He puts down the crate and steps over, his body bounces a little, as if he's on the edge of a dance and it's all cool, groovy. He sticks out his hand.

'Hi. Yeah, I guess we could do that. I'm Nir... but here they call me Hilmi.'

He sounds oddly disappointed about this.

'Which do you prefer?'

He reflects. 'You know, people always called me Hilmi back home, but I came here to be someone else. Eight years here and I ended up with my old name again. I guess it stuck.'

I smile, thinking to myself that this might have been an awkward conversation, confession, but somehow, on a kibbutz, it seems nearly ordinary.

'I guess we can't escape who we are.'

▦

Nir-who-can't-not-be-Hilmi leads me down a path. I push my bicycle past a few small houses with lamp-lit porches, some with coloured lanterns hanging from the beams of a low roof. I follow a few steps behind as he gives a guided tour, gesturing wildly with long arms.

'There are the young people, over in the caravans. They come and volunteer here. A few months. Some stay. Then here are the families, they get some more space, many stay for years, because they want their children raised in the kibbutz way, where everyone helps raise the children and we all are family.'

My pannier pushes through a bush and invisibly releases a thick cloud of rosemary into the night. We draw towards a small row of what resemble holiday chalets, compact, that appear through the pines. Nir/Hilmi stops in front of the door, a sturdy metal thing as over-engineered as every other entrance in this country. On it is scrawled a message in something like black crayon, waxy and the streaks of each letter pockmarked by the texture of the door's surface. Across the top of the door is a length of string with feathers hanging off it, a final feather hangs down longer and more elegant than the rest, and below the makeshift dreamcatcher are stiff, angular letters of Hebrew:

האור לא ינצח את החושך עד שנבין את האמת הפשוטה: כדי להביס את חושך צריך להעצים את האור.

'You can stay here tonight,' he says, resting on the handle.

'Thank you,' I say, hand on my heart, happy at the prospect of a bed. I point at the door, a little surprised he hasn't told me. 'What does it say?'

Nir/Hilmi looks at the door, almost with a start, as if he has somehow forgotten about it. He nods his head in a way I realise he does when he is becoming excited, he bounces in his boots, all groovy. He gives a sad smile, goes full confession as another episode of his life comes spilling out.

'My ex-girlfriend, together we lived here. She put it there for me when she left. I was a different person then. It was difficult for her. This is an old Hebrew saying. Let me think, I guess it means... *Eventually there comes the time you realise you must stop fighting the darkness and instead make the light shine brighter.'*

And I look at Nir, who can't escape being Hilmi, as he stands beside these beautiful words. I look at this man, with his long, curly hair in a ponytail, his baggy jeans and work boots, his slouch, his awkward but happy, irrepressibly gentle way of being. And as he remembers, he gives the unmistakable smile of someone who had his heart broken once, but it's OK now, because time heals and life is beautiful enough that, if only we let it, things can be made new again.

Plantation Peacocks

He told me that next morning I should head to the plantation to meet them for breakfast. Down to the highway, under it, along the track. I'd see it, can't miss it. Five hundred palms in perfect rows.

They were gathered around a table when I arrived, a patio decorated with mosaic tiles. Inside was a kitchen, a man and woman cooking, passing pans of food to be taken by those eating. A man sat on the step of a tractor, holding a cup of coffee, steam winding up in the sunlight as he gave a wave and a young man with hair shaved close came up to me, arm out.

'I'm Gal.' We shook hands and he gestured to a place at the table. 'Please, join us. Hilmi said you were cycling through. I always wanted to go on a journey by bicycle.'

'You should,' is all that I say, wondering inwardly which stack Gal will one day join: those who do or those who always mean to, itself the one way you always find out if a person ever truly wanted to in the first place.

I take a seat with a nod of thanks. Gal passes me a plate and I fill it with scrambled eggs, salad, a stir fry of noodles, food to keep people working all day on the plantation. People leave me to it, talk at ease with one another around the table, a mixture of experience and newcomers. I overhear an introduction from one of the recent arrivals, moving here to the desert after growing exhausted as an activist against racism in Tel Aviv. Gal eats beside me, silent but looking over, and I feel I should make conversation.

'How long have you been out here?'

'Six months almost. First I came for just one month, but I stayed.'

'It seems like a good place to spend time.'

'I didn't know what to do with life. To live at home, to move away, to get a job, to study more, to join the army. My family didn't want me to join, and I went to an Orthodox school, so I didn't have to.'

Younger than Hilmi, but with life less figured out, he shares it all, right off.

'It's good not to be involved maybe.'

'Maybe, but now I feel bad about this.'

'I was at Gaza a few days ago. It would be sad to have to go there and shoot protesters, I think.'

Gal nods, replies, 'Only the violent ones are shot, who put us in danger.'

I look at Gal. Nice kid, but glazed eyes.

'How can anyone put you in danger when they are the other side of a fence and a wall?'

'For me, they are very restrained. The Israeli Defence Forces have the most well-trained soldiers in the world.'

Gal repeats the army line, but beyond the state propaganda, I suspect I can hear his guilt talking. Because he wasn't there, he pays his dues to the military in other ways: Gal will do this national service forever. I remember the look, born of actual experience, in Tamer's eyes as he said the opposite.

'I don't think that's true,' I say, feeling a firmness come over me. 'I met soldiers who had trauma, it sounds more complicated than that, more violent.'

Gal strokes his chin a moment, pondering. 'I like people who are interested in complexity.'

I listen to him, and for a moment I worry that something in the

Israeli middle class, and perhaps even the tradition of thought in which Jewish culture can be so steeped, has a love of intellectualising that might be at odds with ever ending this thing. I wonder if, without knowing it, it is mere play that Gal indulges in this bright morning. Some intellectual recreation, a bouncing ball for the brain made out of a dense knot of human suffering lived by Palestinians.

'I think we must resolve the situation. There I agree. And because we are the powerful, the responsibility is with us. We must do this.' And then Gal laughs in disbelief and says, 'But some people in the world believe in cutting off Israel altogether, in boycotting us!'

Without thinking, I reply in earnest.

'Yes. That's what I think.'

And for one glorious moment, a total confusion settles on both of our expressions. Two actors sit together as humans, but with different political positions floating above our heads, abstractions, carrying a policy that we should not engage, that I will disengage from Gal even if I sit in front of him on his own kibbutz. For a moment I can see very clearly how the world is at once human beings and also abstract systems of ideas. The two things might be distinct from one another, but if you can reshape those abstract systems, you can make it so that some human beings become entitled to actual lives that are better or worse. I hear it again, for the first time since Haifa: *Exit, loyalty, voice.* And it feels like the equation is becoming clearer to me. The world must *exit* from the abstraction of Israel – it must boycott its system of apartheid. The humans living under these abstractions must continue to use *voice* to talk back and forth, but on terms that remind Israel of its humanity and speak of what it has done to the Palestinians. Loyalty? What loyalty can be shown to a state that has suspended all of its human loyalty to those obliged to live under it? Were Israel to lose the power to make sure of it themselves, my only loyalty to them is that they should never be treated thus.

Interrupting the silence, I pick up as Gal forks eggs from his plate.

'Where do you think you'll go after the kibbutz?'

'I'm not sure yet. Maybe I travel like you, with a bicycle. Maybe another kibbutz. I have to make some choices, but not yet.'

I smile. 'That sounds good. It's a privilege to have choices.'

Gal shoots back, finger in the air, 'But also it is a burden!'

'Yes,' I say, the sentiment not totally untrue. 'But mainly a privilege.'

Quietly we finish our breakfast and Gal goes to the kitchen, returns with two cups of coffee.

'You want to see the plantation?' he asks, offering a cup my way.

Together we step through a small clearing, next to which empty crates are stacked high, awaiting their cargo of dates from the palms towering overhead. A few armchairs are in a circle around a battered old table and the blackened remains of a fire. Through the clearing step five peacocks, their long blue-green tailfeathers shining almost metallic in the sunlight. Gal and I stand next to one another, looking down the columns of the palms, this setting like some great architecture of nature. The morning sun moves in swirls of white mist between the shadows of each trunk, and the peacocks step from us, out to where pampas grasses stand like feather boas shining bright at the base of every tree.

'It's a beautiful place,' I say, meaning it.

'Yes, it is. We do things differently here. We don't use the same chemicals as other places. The pampas, the plants, we don't cut it back, we let the floor of the plantation stay wild. That means bugs grow around the trees. They eat the pests and the peacocks eat the bigger pests.'

'It's a good balance.'

There's a peace in the air, the plantation glowing with silence.

'We do OK. After seeds, labour, machinery, water and electricity, and shipping… nine million shekels net profit on our date harvest. That's more than a million euros to go back into the kibbutz, to make sure we can stay here. Not bad for one plantation.'

I make an impressed face. The blue neck of a peacock is standing glorious and proud against one of the pampas chandeliers. Gal and I watch with our cups of coffee, the rest of the kibbutzim still sitting around the breakfast table, the sound of conversation and laughter moving back and forward. Gal looks at me and says proudly, 'We don't work hard here, we work enough.'

Soon after that I rode out of the plantation and back to the road, where the holiday homes and boxlike hotels of Eilat began coming into sight. Ahead of me were signposts pointed for the Taba crossing with Egypt on the right and the Jordanian border on the left. A small delivery truck was parked up, and as I pedalled by I saw the driver unroll a prayer mat in its shadow. I smiled to see his direction of prayer following the highway, with Mecca no longer in the east, but only a few hundred miles distant and to the south.

In that same direction I moved onwards and out of the country, carrying the sense that maybe something in the kibbutz could save Israel, or once could have if it could be found again. Gal's words stuck with me – 'we don't work hard here, we work enough' – and perhaps it was that same spirit that was needed to save all the world. It was not as if the kibbutzim were different altogether, but there was something special in them. Gal was susceptible to the same propaganda that filled the rest of the country, Tamer was traumatised by it, others ran from something, and others still carried the strangely aggressive rudeness of Israel with them. But Gal was not in a hurry, and he was looking for something. He lived for the sun on his face, for the honest life, and then as now, riding into Jordan that day, I had to find a faith that it is only in this state of being that humans can see their right priorities, and so maybe also their mistakes.

Saudi Frontiers

The traffic discipline weakens. I hear the sound of Arabic spoken at the roadside, the smell of fruit coals as someone smokes *hookah* nearby. A familiar place, the bustle of a community returns. The memory of the Israeli border official recedes, scowling at me from inside his armoured booth as he said with contempt, 'Jordan? Why you want to go to Jordan?'

People sell food, sell trinkets from small kiosks, a hustler tries to get a couple of tourists on to a tour, departing tomorrow for Petra. It occurs to me that in this part of the world, public opinion is often referred to simply as 'the Arab street', and part of me thinks that might be a romantic orientalism, but then another part thinks it quite true, for nowhere else in the world does daily life seem to exist quite so much on its roadsides.

As I pull to the kerb, a woman in a light pink hijab stands proudly at the sign beside her shop, selling scarfs, soaps, ornaments.

'Where you cycle from?' she asks.

'From Israel, but I'm British.' I point to the distance behind me, where the demilitarised zone and its high fences separate the two countries. She makes a face of amazement, eyes open wide.

'From Israel?!'

I nod with a smile. 'Are Israel and Jordan... friends?'

She pulls an awkward but friendly face, as if I'm asking a family secret that people prefer not to discuss. A few men drinking tea in a neighbouring café look over.

'We signed a contract, and now things are OK. They can come here. We can go there. In Aqaba there are some restaurants where Israelis cannot eat, where they are not served. Well, just one like this, because the owner is Palestinian and he will not cook for them. But it is OK.'

She pauses, smiles, presses her hand to her chest.

'Really, many of us are Palestinian. *I* am Palestinian. My grandfather came here to Aqaba in 1948 from Hebron. But I don't know anything about Hebron.'

⠿

Moving south of the city, the highways sprawl, wide but empty. Drifts of sand are swept to the centre on gusts of passing traffic. Burst truck tyres scatter the familiar debris of most of the world's frontier roads, where – again, as I am used to – the borderlands between two places are neglected rather than contested. A stray picks its way down a path leading from the road, its tail so far between its legs it limps. The highways are deserted, save for the occasional almost-empty car or full bus. Along the coast are underwater sites for tourist divers, where the wreck of an old US plane and sunken boats dot the shoreline with a submarine universe. Outside some of the larger resorts there are tourists, wandering back up the beach to the hotel bar at the day's end, their skin red and bodies clad in white cotton dressing gowns. They walk slowly, clutching towels as they move side to side, like zombies from the sea.

The port and its docks pass by at the roadside, and as I ride, I see freighters waiting to be loaded, containers hoisted high as cranes roll on huge tyres along the quay, lowering cargo into holds. A grain ship unloads and golden flumes are unstoppered, so that millions of seeds are poured like liquid into the holds of a growing line of trucks. Across the road, a mountainside is being quarried away, and long-limbed conveyor belts and machines rise with the dust of clinker for a French cement company that processes and ships the earth of Jordan to turn a profit for a company listed in Paris. Over my shoulder the gulf glistens, while the sky turns purple and the sun, all dressed in gold, finally exits.

Slowly, I pedal up high hillsides, where the road cuts through short but steep mountains. Signposts confirm my direction for the Durra frontier, the southernmost point along this Jordan coast just fifteen miles long. Ten kilometres appears on a sign, then five, and then there comes a rattle of electricity from a pylon on the hill I crest. And then, there it is, unexpected, but perhaps no surprise.

On the border there stands a red-white chimney, a candy stick belching smoke above a grid of lights and runways. It is with the sight of a refinery, aptly enough, that after barely an hour of cycling from Israel, I have reached the Kingdom of Saudi Arabia. Here is enough. Forbidden to cross into Saudi Arabia at any land border, here I stop.

Spellbound in the new night, I look down at it… that beautiful beast, this tiny monster. Perhaps it is only fitting to see such a thing on the Saudi border. Below me the refinery stands and ticks as if a nervous system, and there I see it in a circuit board of lit roads, of smokestacks, of floodlights, the cerebellum, the frontal lobe. Headlights of tankers snake through the twists and turns, shuttling with their tiny messages of cargo and taking energy either out into the world's body to be burned, or their empty vessel back to the refinery to be replenished. Pipes line the roads, run along footbridges, contort and knot where they fracture and crack the chemicals into newer mixes, blends that burn differently, that thin or thicken heavier and lighter crudes, and that will be set to sea for export and different purposes around the world. No journey of these lands would be complete without the presence of oil, the commodity that made, but mostly ruined, an entire region. I wonder what will happen to Israel without it – not because Israel has oil – but because in a world of oil, Israel has been a useful staging post for the West in the Middle East. As people move to cities, the remaining cars turn electric, and with power grids fed by tides and winds and sun, I wonder what will become of a country so embedded with hostility and fear towards the peoples and cultures it settled among. Will it cease to be so dear to the West, and will it survive if it does?

Below me, out of sight, somewhere is the end of a pipeline that brings thick unprocessed oil to Aqaba from the fields of Iraq, where the derricks line the desert and work endlessly as the oil *pumps, pumps, pumps*. Back through the desert, out of sight in the heavy night, I know the flames go fluttering like flags above a battlefield, flaring the excess gases from the rigs and the non-stop century of *pump, pump, pump* where gases from each barrel that was extracted and burned sit in the atmosphere, heating this earth in which rivers flow no more, seas retreat, and when the rains finally fall they do so with such hot ferocity that they do not replenish the earth and its crops but wash it all away. Pulling out of my morbid fascination, like looking at a corpse, I avert my eyes, for the refinery is too dark a beast. Below is that which replaced an entire social nervous system, a brain for all the region. Give me a moment, allow me explain.

Of that black gold, first you must know that once oil had automated all power, force and energy, the spirit of combustion would encroach on the spirit of the human. The worker who was once needed to lift a stone or fell a tree, even the miner who with a pick pulled the power of coal from the wall of a mineshaft – both became redundant when the liquid energy in oil offered tyrants the chance to replace the power of people. With this new and plentiful energy, willing to flow towards wherever it was directed in a pipeline, still more human endeavours were to become automated. Computer systems removed the human who had worked the production line, who had held the abacus, the ledger… who had worked the presses of the factory floor. With energy abundant and technology replacing the functions of a human brain, what was left was the chance to make a society in which the human – and with it all the creativity, rights and ingenuity – was for the first time no longer needed for prosperity.

And so it was that in those places where this black energy was found, the true richness of a society – its freedom, its creativity and spirit – was not just allowed to fall bankrupt, it actively had to be bankrupted, for otherwise it would demand a fair division of the land's riches. For a tribal family, a hereditary monarch or a foreign oil company, such sharing is impossible. And so, oil gave these countries the opportunity, or the curse, to attain vast wealth without creativity, education, innovation or – most crucial of all – rights. Piles of money could grow with little need of workers, meaning rulers could become rich without sharing that wealth, and without the competing interests and compromises that previously had been essential to form an effective state. Authoritarians and oil will always be friends because, to prosper, the authoritarian does not have to give anything to his people, and instead must learn only the best methods of oppression that oil can buy. Without the power of oil, a society needed some justice, because the people could refuse to lend their productive energies to their leaders. With oil came a new and colossal power, one that left no further need for the energies of those who once were able to refuse consent.

Out of this evil bargain, brutality flowed across the Middle East and beyond. The entire Muslim world – Palestinian, Turkish, Balkan, Iranian, Saudi, China's Uyghur, Malcolm X's Nation of Islam – all lost a piece of their liberty because the heartland of Islamic thought was itself lost to a century of oil and war and repression. Left in these hands, Islam was used as an emblem rather than a faith, its only function the extent to which it could be enlisted as a tool in the oppression. Where Muslims or Arabs might have looked to these lands for leadership, dignity and support, they found only corruption. To keep the system running sweet, the profits of oil were recycled back into Western banks, real estate and – in dizzying quantities – weapons, so that Arab minders in Washington, London, Paris and Berlin kept their palms crossed with silver.

In truth, the brutality of this arrangement worked for Israel also. For it is easier to do business with a few tribal princes than a democracy of millions that muddles its way through to the right answers and the necessary compromises with its neighbours. Saudi Arabia, just as Israel became, was always a national bet that the spring of freedom can simply be held down firm. Not only the hope, but indeed the only plan for survival, is that this spring should never be released, for the further it has been pressed down, the more forcefully it will uncoil. The lie goes that Israel is the only democracy in the Middle East. The unspoken truth is that not only is it not – more importantly – it would fear the prospect of one.

▦

Down through the night, from above the refinery, I descended towards the port and town, riding out from the thick smoke burning up into the sky. Behind a high bank I pulled my bicycle and laid down my bed for the night. The acrid smell cleared, the wind pulling it away to the south, leaving only the shifting shapes of smoke illuminated in the lights.

On the beachfront far below, I watched a group of men – barely dots – gathered in front of a floodlit café, seated around a hookah pipe of hoses, chambers and bubbling water that smoked with the humbler industry of its own small refinery. On the narrow waters of the gulf, a red-blue flashing light circled on top of a patrol boat, drifting as a silent shadow on the water. In a tracksuit and flip-flops, a man stepped out onto the forecourt of his beachfront kiosk, where a small group of friends sat together. His hand held a length of rope, and on its end a metal tin with a few smouldering coals for the hookah inside, the tin showing pinpricks of orange light where holes had been punched to allow an airflow. A sense of peace prevailed, silent but for the waves on the sands, lapping rhythmically as I— *cr-cr-crack – cr-cr-cr-crack – cr-crack*. Loud. Gunfire. From high in the hills opposite, sudden and violent. Like a car crash of light it hit the dark sky, shot adrenaline. Slow my heart. Across the gulf, from the far hill, whether it was in Israel or Sinai – whichever side of whichever fence – came a short crack of bullets in response, as machine guns spoke in dark hills and the fire-fight conversed in sparks of white before, once again, the guns fell silent and the waves went lapping, lapping, lapping. Steady – *red-blue, red-blue* – the patrol boat pressed on through the gulf. The man with the tin of coals on the end of the rope scarcely looked round towards the sound, and began to swing the rope, rotating it fast into a figure of eight so that the night air blew hard through the holes in his tin and across the new coals for the hookah. He let his shoulder go limp, and round and round that tin drum flew on the end of its rope, coals glowing orange, glowing white, glowing red, throwing their own sparks, casting their own trail of light that flew out in the darkness.

There was a meteor shower over Sinai that night, and one after the next I watched those rocks burn up and fall to the desert, redrawing the sky with new light as they crashed and collided with the atmosphere. And my soul was heavy, but I smiled, because again, the universe commanded it.

Eritreans

Across the Gulf of Aqaba, I see Sinai opposite as the world begins another day. I see the ruddy brown mountains in shadow, see them flash red as the dawn hits their tops, see them stand crimson against sky so blue. I watch the sun pull the cloth of shade off Sinai, and Tamer was right, it is beautiful. My road feels almost over, and for weeks now I could sense the energy slipping from me. I'm tired, my legs weary, and a part of me is ready to submit to this view and die in its arms tonight. Across from me, I realise, is the sort of landscape you would want to invoke when telling people the Ten Commandments of their new religion have been handed down. Within my very vision I can see Egypt, can see Israel, I sit in Jordan and Saudi Arabia is over my shoulder. I realise for the first time that the only other place I have ever known so many cultures, so different, to exist so close, is Europe, and a part of me enjoys a moment with my faith that the Middle East, West Asia will one day know such harmony too. As I look out across the four states, the land reminds me that the worst thing about borders is that they legitimise the human failing of not caring about people elsewhere, even when they are very close.

As the sun rises on the red mountains opposite, it feels clearly as though what passes for politics in this place is a defiance of the earth's beauty. Israel to the Palestinians, the ruling family of Saudi Arabia to its own people, Egypt's generals, the gangsters of its deserts. The people of these lands demand freedom, and they will go on demanding it because the soul commands it. Like the bicycle cresting the descent to Jericho, or the notes of the piano lesson falling innocently to the street below, that shade of red as dawn hits the mountain earth of Sinai is perfection. With a lump rising in my throat, the words form silently a second time in my mouth. The shade of red, as dawn hits the mountain earth of Sinai, is perfection, one more evidence to all who witness it that the world in its very nature is a better place than the cruelties they are asked to live under. Eventually all tyrannies fall, because ultimately those denied freedom are always more determined to change the world than those who deny it can muster the energy to keep it ugly. For now, people just have to pick the right side, and then push.

Looking across Sinai, it is here, finally, that I should tell you that story from Eritrea, as I promised. It was the story that waited also at the gate of that Ethiopian Church in Jericho, a story that once walked up through the Sinai Peninsula, and that I then found in an unlikely backstreet of Tel Aviv. And I watch as a line of sun traces the tips of the mountains, gleaming bright, like the metal runners that held the shutter of the industrial sliding door to that old factory unit, where I stepped into a large room with two large windows in its far wall.

Draped between the windows is the cloth of African textiles, brightly coloured in blues and pinks, with tropical fruits and birds flying from trees and flowers. In a far corner is a kettle, and cups are draining next to a sink. There is a low table with a few sofas beside it, and everything glows in the sunlight pouring through the windows. Against them stands the perfectly African silhouette of a woman with her hair bound up neatly in a scarf, who is wearing a long skirt wrapped tight and high around her hips and falling loose around her feet. With a broom she works the floor, silent as she sweeps, moving in front of the soft colours of crocheted baskets – blue, grey, yellow and rust – stacked on shelves all around. Running in from an adjacent room comes a small girl, no more than a toddler, and she chases after the sphere of a pea green balloon. On her face is the delight that with only the slap of her tiny palm she can push it high through the air, as if in all this solid, stubborn, adult world, this balloon alone responds precisely to the force of her. Seeing me, the child stops in her tracks, then runs over to the side of another woman and clings to her leg, so that two impossibly wide eyes, half afraid and half curious, stare at me from above her mother's lap, where a basket is taking shape, and a crochet hook works through a reel of red cotton tape that winds down to the floor.

Two more women appear from the next room, walking and talking, speaking English and together making plans for the day. A younger woman, Israeli, looks like a volunteer and is dressed in a large leopard print coat over a vintage denim shirt, frayed and fading. She has the palest of skin and black hair, striking in appearance but nonetheless somehow dimmed in the presence of the older woman, a nun, who looks unassuming in a knitted white cardigan, but has eyes bright behind her spectacles, and a great calm radiating from her. A small, white cloth is folded into a triangle that loosely covers her head, with wiry black hair turning grey and pushing out from underneath.

'Maybe we can start a shop with all the donations and sell them?' suggests the volunteer.

'Oooff, but that is a lot of work. What happens when we get donations nobody wants and have to spend hours organising them?' the nun replies with cheerful exasperation as the two women look up and see me, standing in their reception area.

'Can I help you?' the nun asks.

Framed by the wrinkles of age, unmistakable and proud, is the faded ink of a cross, the four points of the Ethiopian Orthodox Church tattooed pale green on the brown skin of her forehead, the rich colour of East Africa. Her voice is direct but kind, her face wide open with trust, but I do not really know what I want here – I just followed a stranger's advice to visit. Is my curiosity taking up time no different to the unwanted donation of an old sweater? She goes on looking at me, waiting patiently before offering her hand in welcome.

'I am Sister Aziza.'

I smile a hello as we shake hands and I explain myself.

'Someone told me this was the place to find out about African people in Israel, or about people who came through Sinai.'

Aziza laughs. 'Everyone wants stories, but nobody buys anything!'

She speaks with a kindness that in even a short time together I'll come to recognise as her radiant personality.

'The baskets are really beautiful,' I say, gesturing at the wall of baskets stacked neatly on shelves behind her, woven in the colours of the earth, the trees, a moody sky.

'Thank you. We started with crochet of small things. Kippah, key rings. Then we started making baskets, now sometimes we work together with other businesses to make designs they like… large laundry baskets, other things. First, we just used materials given to us by a factory, off-cuts from T-shirts, clothes, you know.' Aziza points to radiant spools of cotton colours. 'Now we make more, so we have to buy materials. First, we looked after thirty women, now two hundred, but I don't know how we can keep going.'

The volunteer in her leopard print coat excuses herself, walks over to the corner and fills the kettle at the sink.

'How long have you been working here?' I ask Aziza.

'Long time. I trained as nurse. Before here, I was in Sudan, Juba… but eleven years now I am in Israel. I was destined to come here.'

'You're Eritrean?'

Aziza nods. 'Years ago, one day I go down to the park, what is it called?' She lifts her voice, in the direction of the leopard print volunteer, 'Near the bus station?'

'Levinsky,' comes the reply.

'In Levinsky Park I go there and find many women from Africa. They have been badly treated, they are depressed, they are sleeping outside. There are women who have been sexually abused, raped, who are pregnant maybe and they do not know who raped them. Many people need medical help, very bad condition. We have some people without eyes, some with maybe one arm, with many injuries. I know one man who lost both hands,' and Aziza holds her arms in front of her, crossed at the wrists, 'because for long time he had been tied up with ropes while he was tortured.'

'They come through Sinai?'

She nods solemnly.

'Some pay to come here, others walk through the desert. Some Christians from Eritrea get pilgrim visa to visit Jerusalem on a tour, and when they arrive, they disappear into Israel. They are many nationalities. Some are Somali, some Eritrea, Sudan, Ethiopia. One man from Chad.'

'Who are the gangs taking them hostage?'

'They say Bedouin. Some Bedouin may be involved, but it is not them. This is professional business. A few Bedouin maybe take them to a house, but they cannot organise something like this. Money is being sent from all over the world... it is coming from Europe, America, Canada. The torturers find family and they must send money to buy freedom for their relatives. They say they have doctors to operate and take out organs for sale. Sometimes thousand dollars ransom, ten thousand, most I heard was thirty thousand.' Aziza shakes her head defiantly. 'This cannot be Bedouin, because Bedouin have no money.'

'Someone told me about the organs, being taken and sold,' I say.

'Many people talk about this, this "organ harvesting" they call it.'

Aziza grimaces before trailing off and I wait with those two unlikely words, spoken by an Eritrean nun, with her faded cross tattooed as a mark of faith on her forehead. And it feels almost incomprehensible that such words might leave her mouth and mean what they mean.

'Most people say to me that the organ harvesting is just a threat. They tell the prisoners they will do it. They say "you are worth more to us dead".' But this I have not seen. We had one man come here and say he had it done, they took a kidney, but we were not sure and in the end it wasn't true.'

'How do you know?'

Aziza puts a hand to the small of her back. 'We checked.'

'And?'

'Two kidneys.'

She gives a chuckle at this surreal stock-take. 'As soon as we heard this man's story, a journalist come from the USA. He gets on a plane to us, straight away. But man has two kidneys, so no story.'

I feel myself standing in the same spot as others before me, so that I consider first whether or not I am a cliché, and second why we write and why we read. Am I here to transcribe a life-and-death message to the outside world, or am I one more vulture ready to fly?

'And when people get to Israel from Africa, is it better for them here?'

'In Israel they used to just leave them in the south, in the desert. Now they bring them to Tel Aviv and put them by the Ayalon Highway. They do not give any social security, no refugee status. I have one woman, diabetic, from Eritrea and very bad condition.' Aziza places flat palms across her middle. 'She needed amputation to save her, so now she has both legs removed. Twenty-five years she was in Israel, cleaning. Every two months she gets new permission to stay two more months. She has no rights, protection, security. Twenty-five years. She loses her legs, so I have to put her with sisters in the convent, but many are homeless.'

I listen in silence as Aziza turns and busies herself, folding a length of material and placing it over the back of a chair. She looks up, opening her arms in resignation, her voice stern but somehow not critical, so that by the power of her faith she remains without judgement for any of that sheer sin she recounts.

'Let us be honest, it is a racist country. If you are not a Jew, they do not want you.'

Aziza goes on folding lengths of cloth, making a neat pile on the chair.

'Even if it is racist, do people want to stay here because it is safe?'

She shakes her head. 'The number is going down, because life is so difficult. Every two months they must go and get approval renewed, like a visa. Everyone wants to go somewhere else. Last year we have a woman's child, one year old, attacked with a knife to the head.' Aziza pauses for my stunned expression. 'Thankfully she survived.'

'Attacked by an Israeli?' I ask.

'Someone new here, an immigrant from Russia, I think. But there are so many problems. Israel refuses to give refugee status and people need money to live but cannot get jobs without status. We used to have many women clean hotels, shopping mall, and then at the end of month boss refuses to pay wages because they have no rights. Africans have few friends here.'

She turns from me and towards a photo: a tiny, printed shrine stuck to the wall. It shows a young girl with her phone, its camera outstretched at arm's length in front of her. Posing, curly hair tied back in a ponytail, like any young girl anywhere, she takes a photo of herself among a group of friends.

'You hear about this girl?' asks Aziza.

I shake my head.

'She is the daughter of Eritrean woman here, her name is Sylvana. She killed, by her mother's ex-partner, last month.'

Sister Aziza points to the photo on the wall, the evidence of the life snuffed out. Her voice wavers.

'She was in her thirteenth year. Twelve. She did not even get to thirteen. She was such a happy child, so much love she has. When she died, that week, that very week we were making hats together for a protest about violence against women.'

We stand in front of the small memorial of this small community, the image of the child framed beside the stacked baskets. For the only time in our meeting, a small light flickers in Aziza, a moment of doubt.

'They found the man. He's in jail?'

'Yes. He is in jail… but what good is this? What do we care? It is too late now, she is gone. She is not coming back.'

Aziza looks at the photo again, then turns back to organising the baskets. She gives a little smile in reassurance to me, and then moves over to the sofas, takes fabrics from their backs and begins folding them anew. I stand and watch the preparations for a new day in this small, embattled sanctuary of hope. I watch the girl still playing with her balloon, the mother crocheting with a thick, hooked needle and a reel of cotton, a basket taking shape in her lap, its colour that same gorgeous red of all the earth I've cycled. I watch the face of the woman as she crochets: so peaceful, a proud forehead, a scarf wrapped tight and high to hold back her hair. I see the child, grinning, her milk teeth pure white and each the size of a tiny pebble. She looks over at me, all smiles and cheeks beside her mother's basket, growing stitch by stitch, taking shape as the reel of cotton is pulled out and makes its way as a random tangle across the floor, ready to be pulled through and given new form. And as I watch these stitches being made, I hope that it brings her some healing.

From across the room, the woman sweeping up leans her broom against the sofa, takes a cushion from it and holds it in one hand, beating it with the other so that it becomes plump and full while a soft thud echoes through the air. There is a slowness to everything, the deep calm of a harbour in a storm, where a scene carries significance simply in its normalcy. The young Israeli volunteer reappears, giving what looks like a tour to two visitors.

'So in the 1950s Israel was a big part of getting the world to agree to the Geneva Convention, and rights for refugees, because of the Holocaust and all of that... now we have one of the lowest rates of helping refugees. In Europe, most refugees from Eritrea get status to stay. Here it is less than one per cent.'

Somehow the statistic hits me more lightly than the words 'the Holocaust *and all of that*', spoken as if the Holocaust, referenced in passing, is only one among many details of history. Something about the woman's tone though sounds not casual, but brave and strong. Hers feels like a rare voice in Israel, one that does not wish to be defined by that past, refuses to be anyone's victim, but which will take history and use it to demand more of her country and the world.

Bursting through the middle of the tour, the child chases after her green balloon, then runs back to the side of her mother, at work with her tiny hook. I watch as the woman unreels a spool of cotton that works up from the floor and into her lap, meeting with the galvanised point of the needle, so that in front of me I see a thread become a basket. I watch Sister Aziza blowing at a steaming cup of tea across the room. And I watch the crochet hook, the woman sweep, the girl in leopard print, the child now hiding, now chasing her balloon. And I think of those famous words of the anthropologist Margaret Mead:

'Never doubt that a small group of thoughtful, committed citizens can change the world. Indeed, it is the only thing that ever has.'

A half hour later I prepare to leave, carrying the two small baskets that are all that I can fit in my pannier. Two women sit next to one another, talking softly and smiling as they crochet, so that I see the lengths of cotton stamped with their words, and the emerging baskets become a sort of cassette tape, recording the conversation. The child with her green balloon sits to one side, feet dangled off the front of an armchair, oblivious to all that has been discussed, the weight of the adult world she's to inherit. I walk over to Aziza to say goodbye.

'The children being born here… is it easier for them here than for their parents, can they integrate?'

'For them it is often harder because here is all they know,' Aziza says sadly. 'They know Hebrew, but they cannot understand why they are not wanted. For the parents, at least they know this is not home, and so it makes more sense.'

She stands in front of me, arms folded, sad but strong, indomitable, undimmed… a human light that leads us on, and in a land where faith does such harm, in Aziza it seems like the only way to understand her resolve to do good.

'Your faith, it must keep you going.'

Again she just smiles by way of answer.

'Do you work with others too?' I ask. 'With the Palestinians?'

'Of course! I live in the West Bank, Jericho, a Bedouin village near there. I work with the Palestinians, the Bedouin. It is very difficult here for Bedouin.'

Seeing again the cross on her forehead, I have a memory of a similar sight, that same cross from the Jericho street: the green, yellow and red on the gates of the Ethiopian church I'd stood in front of, so recently but so distant.

'I saw your church, in Jericho. I was there.'

She smiles with the fondness of home. 'Yes, that is my church, but I live in a village outside Jericho, with the Bedouin.'

'With Muslims?'

And at this Aziza straightens, levels a finger at me. She breathes in and prepares to give me the sort of unforgettable statement that you hear rarely in your life but once you have done will never forget.

'There is no difference. There is no Christian, Muslim, Jewish. It is we who feel we must divide God. It is we who give our different names to God, but there is no absolute true religion, there is no one faith. All there is is respect, and love, and without that there is nothing. So, a long time ago I say to myself, "Aziza, I will be a seed of peace. That is what I will do," I say this to myself. "I will be a seed of peace."'

And she smiles at me one last time.

'And you,' she instructs, 'you must be a seed of peace, too.'

Part VI

EXIT

THE WALL

Hebron

Hebron

In green uniforms, outside a bus station a group of conscripts with kit bags re-boarded their bus, wearing a mixture of kippahs or pigtails on their heads. The door shuddered closed with a hiss of pistons, and I watched the wheels begin to turn, to roll like the reel of a film that rewound my journey through the country. North of Eilat and back into the desert. North into the sand that turned to dry mud. North where the mud grew tufts of grass and then became a scrubland that moved gently over and down the rising hillsides of the land. There were only two stops that I made, and I was tired, so very tired. Tired of the injury Israelis had detached themselves from, of the frustrated dignity with which the Palestinians and the Bedouin were left to face it. Everything was etched in faces, in land, in walls and fences and blockades, each of which showed again the simple truth that a landscape can never lie.

My wheels turned it over and over until, finally, back inside occupied Palestine, on the horizon a few large apartment buildings reared up ahead. Signposts directed me off of the highway and up a slight incline on the road moving north. A conscript called to me to halt and, marching my way, shouted something in Hebrew. The kid had an anger to him, a tiny evidence of what I'd once been told: that Hebron was a special case, the furthest-claimed city from the agreed borders of Israel, deep inside Palestine and populated by a particularly zealous, aggressive minority of settlers. As a result, the army sent only a certain kind of soldier there, those who could be relied upon to defend a more aggressive form of Israel's apartheid.

'Where you going?' The boy shouted a second time, and with acne on his face and a rifle over his shoulder, he strode out from beside a cube of concrete, placed as roadblock.

'To Hebron.'

'Why to Hebron?' he shouted again, tense, a temper so weirdly quick to rise in him, the tendons pulled taught, ribbed all around his neck, like a sphincter that had shat out a head.

By then, I no longer knew. Dumbfounded by all this rage I pointed ahead.

'To visit. Is it that way?'

'No, that way,' he lied, pointing west as I gave a wave of thanks, rolled on.

Ready for the end of my road, in me nevertheless was that promise made back at the start of my ride, to Mohammad, that I should visit Sohaib and the cyclists of Hebron. And so it was that I leant my body and tilted the handlebars slightly east, and pedalled up into Hebron, the second-largest city of Palestine.

The traffic grew in the streets, a few bicycles rolled down an enormous hill, and passing through the edge of a crowded market, I saw soldiers in black uniforms, wearing berets and with shades across their eyes and guns across their fronts. For the thousandth time, my mind boggled at the constant presence of military force that Israel had put upon the Palestinians, and then I neared, and saw on their shoulders an embroidered badge with the flag of Palestine and the name of the Palestinian Authority. In some way it amused me, showing that regardless of the uniform you dress them in, the side you proclaim them to be of, armed soldiers on the streets always boil down to the same thing. At a roadside I stopped and opened my notepad, took out the scrawled number on the scrunched-up till receipt from Ramallah, and called Sohaib.

⠿

Fighter jets pass overhead, a quick scream. My head follows them, still instinctive. Sohaib scarcely moves, as if it were nothing more irregular than a fly in a far corner of the ceiling. One of two mechanics fixes a chain on an old bicycle, winding the tool to fasten a rivet in place. A young man, tall and lean, in a helmet and full Lycra, steps inside on his cleated shoes. The bicycle shop smells, as always and as everywhere, of rubber. Outside the sun beats down, so hard you understand where the expression came from. It beats, it pounds, it presses down on your head. It pours into your body and from inside you grow so hot it seems to be kicking. You crave the cool.

'Now it is hot, but maybe we can ride later,' Sohaib tells me, then places a hand on his clean white shirt, pressed, stiff collar. 'I don't have my riding clothes with me, but perhaps someone will want to. I'm just taking a break from work.'

'You work in Hebron?'

He nods. He's clean shaven, with neatly cut hair. He seems kind, welcoming, but with a distance to him, as if not giving himself away.

'Cycling is just my passion. I started the club, but because of checkpoints, sometimes it is hard to ride on the roads. We get stopped all the time.'

'Someone told me it was difficult here,' and I lose what to say, 'like that.'

Sohaib gives a quizzical frown, gently making a point.

'Hebron was always difficult. In 1994 a settler killed thirty Palestinians in the Old Town. A Jewish settler to Israel from the US. Goldstein. I was a boy. We all knew people who died. After him, after Palestinians were killed, the Israelis started removing us from the town. They say for security, but it was to try and make us all leave. Now the centre is a ghost town, not everyone is allowed in. I am, because I can prove my family have history there, so the Israelis give me a number to allow me in.'

He laughs a brave laugh, which on some deeper level I hear and admire, for the laugh is disbelieving but does not give in to sarcasm or disdain. It is not a laugh of the gallows.

'Can you believe it? The Jewish people put a number on me, like the Nazis did to them.'

We look at one another, but in some imperceptible and silent moment my eyes must let slip a reaction, and Sohaib shuffles. In his comparison I realise that I feel unease, for where I am from it is seen as unacceptable to equate Israeli brutality against Palestine to Nazi Germany. And yet, who am I to police the language of an Arab man who has no guilt for the Holocaust, and who sees in his own life some of those methods he knows were used against Jews by Dutch, Germans, French, Hungarians? Who am I to deny him his comparison, to say that a comparison is somehow more offensive than the blood of his relatives, the sores from Israel's handcuffs? There is a pause, then Sohaib points out of the window towards the horizon.

'Three kilometres from here, there was the other massacre. June 1936. People here were fighting with the British. The British took fifteen men into the fields, the middle of the day. They tied them there without water for days and said they would leave them until they told them where the guns were. And they didn't know where the guns were. So they left them to die. Some of our grandparents, they were alive. They told us the story, told us about seeing it.'

Sohaib looks across at me as he finishes the story. I'm silent.

'I'm sorry,' says the Palestinian, politely to the Brit.

'It's fine.' I say. 'It's the history.'

His quiet apology pulls on my guts. The man reporting the massacre of his community feels compelled by manners to apologise for interrupting polite conversation, so that again I oblige him to suffer my awkwardness as well as his history. I shift the subject.

'The Palestinian Authority, they have some control here now?'

'Not exactly. Israeli military is everywhere.'

'But the Palestinian Authority can do some things, has some power?'

'It is not a perfect organisation, but it is still new. Your country, you have three hundred years' history in your government. We, we have thirty. The PA it has little control.'

'Would the settlers ever leave Hebron?'

I ask it with some hope, like it's plausible. Hebron isn't like the hills beyond Rantis, the edgelands. It is the centre of the West Bank, it is like France occupying Munich. Sohaib looks sceptical.

'Abraham was born here. Hebron is mentioned many times in all the holy books. The settlers who come here will never leave. We try to raise awareness. But we have many restrictions on us, not just on cycling. When Israel attacked Gaza last time, I put a post on the internet. I use targeted advertising for my business, so when one Israeli unit killed a lot of people, I put some shekels to advertise the post in the region the general in command is from. Alian was his name, from the north. Druze, he is an Arab, but he fights for Israel. I targeted it on Facebook, saying something like "Do you see what your sons do to us?" That was all. In Israel people don't normally see what happens with the bombs, so because of this, Alian had consequences at home, people ask why he does it.'

It sounds like a glimmer of hope.

'That's good.'

Sohaib raises a finger, has not yet reached his point.

'Then, one day I am in a taxi and they stop us at a checkpoint. They put me in the back of a car, they handcuff me. They take me, question me. They blindfold me. They take me to a prison. Facebook accepts 95 per cent of Israel's requests for information on Palestinians who use it.' Bit by bit he gives out the information. 'So I was the first Palestinian to be arrested by Israel for a Facebook post. It is not all Israel. My lawyer, he was an Israeli, a good man. But now, now they make it so hard for us to do anything.'

'How long did they hold you?'

'Some days.'

'For a Facebook post?'

Sohaib nods.

'You have family?'

Sohaib nods. I leave it. I think my heart breaks again, but what good is my broken heart to anyone here?

'Are you glad you did it? Would you do it again?'

He shrugs. I sense it is like being asked if he's glad he breathes. Sohaib is a reluctant radical. The best kind. The safe kind, trustworthy, the radical who simply wants a just life, but knows he needs politics to get to that. None of this is for fun. I realise that even my questions, no matter how delicately put, are offensive, for each question emphasises how his dignity was violated and not that here all along was a man – dignified – who the outside world cares for only when he becomes a victim.

'You have a lot of questions.' Sohaib smiles, puts his palms on the tops of his neat, pleated trousers, like that's enough for now.

'Sorry,' I say, embarrassed.

He shakes his head, dismissing my apology.

'You should go on a tour in the Old City. I am with an organisation against the settlements. We try to show people what happens here. I can take you to a group if you want. Leave your bicycle.'

Ghosts

The town was deserted all right. Nothing but dust and soldiers adorned those streets, but in the old frescoes and shopfronts welded shut, you could still imagine what it once was. I saw crowds, imagined storeholders with fruit and vegetables, the joyous calls of wares. Cafés with tea and coffee, a baker with *knafeh* and children outside his shop, eating with delight, holding cutlery too big for their small hands and sitting on small chairs still too big for their bodies. And then I looked at the reality, and saw only the cubes of concrete, the soldiers behind gates of sheer metal, the flags of the battalions that occupied the city for Israel, empty but for its sadness.

A young man led a group of five of us, gesturing right and left while we headed towards a covered market. He passed a building with a green shutter down across its front, black graffiti scrawled hostile across it in Hebrew.

'This says "*Gas the Arabs*",' he said, walking on. 'We have two thousand soldiers here for six hundred settlers. The soldiers are supposed to protect Palestinians from settlers too, but they do not.'

We pass through a stone arch into a covered passageway sloping downwards, immediately cooler and shielded from the sun. Ahead are shadows set next to perfect white stone, where the light gets into a courtyard. A woman sits on the doorstep of her shop, selling spices and a few stone bowls, some ornaments and ceramic pomegranates. The passage of the old town leads us forwards under a wire mesh with plastic bottles, dusty shards of wood and torn bags resting on it. Sohaib's friend points up through the littered hexagons of the mesh, where the sky is a honeycomb of blue and a settler block towers over us.

'We had to install the wire because the settlers throw things, they throw their rubbish down on us.'

And he says it so simple, matter of fact. And I look at him, with the wisp of a moustache, soft hair above his top lip, not yet stubble. This is his youth and here he is, taught that this is his place in the world. The boy points to a guarded checkpoint beside a shop, where a man sells *keffiyeh* and other garments, a few trinkets – badges and magnets – of Palestinian flags. He invites us to have tea as soldiers mill around beside us, arms rested on their guns. The young man gestures.

'I cannot pass this checkpoint.' He points to a building five metres from us but on the other side of the guarded metal barriers, then loops his arm around. 'If I want to go there, I have to walk that way round, fifteen minutes. This is our everyday here.'

Outside the store I wait, unsure of whether or not to leave, to make my own way to the house on the hill overlooking Hebron, which Sohaib says the group will head for anyway. Tea is served as I stand, watching that street so eerie. Another member of the group comes up to me, his black skin the only one of ours not showing traces of sweat. He is dressed in a linen dashiki with its African tribal patterns proud and bright. He holds out a camera to me, gripping it where the lens meets the body.

'Excuse me, can you take my photo, please?'

'Sure,' I say, taking the camera as he retreats to a low wall and smiles.

I capture him, a couple of times. He with his arms folded, rucksack straps, the colourful band of shields and feathers embroidered around the neck of his dashiki. I give the thumbs-up and he walks back, thanks me.

'Where you from?' I ask.

'South Africa,' he replies, 'but here training as a human rights lawyer.'

'Did you have problems getting into Israel, as a rights lawyer?'

He shakes his head.

'It is easy for a South African. Israel and South Africa were very good friends, at least under the apartheid. Maybe nobody told them we changed government!'

Deep, soulful, he laughs. And I smile, for the sound of it defies this place.

'Does it feel similar, South Africa and here?' I ask.

'Oh yes,' he replies as if mine is a stupid question. 'Many similarities. Zionism is the same as apartheid was for us. When Israel shows images of the land it is always empty, just like the flower in the desert with no people there. If they show people, they are always showing Arabs as servants. Apartheid was exactly like this. In South Africa now, we feel the Palestinian struggle. It is the same fight we had.'

He looks at me, perhaps senses my dejection and then adds, 'But they will win... just like we won.'

###

The group continued on their tour as I made my way alone and slowly up the hill Sohaib had told me to head for. At the top, just as he had said, an old house stood, shabby but proud where it watched over the city. I neared a checkpoint, a soldier holding his gun, surrounded by giant cubes of concrete and looking bored. Something in his face had learned to be indifferent to his surroundings, but with interest he sat up as he saw me approaching, interrupting his monotony.

'Where are you going?'

I pointed up the hill. 'That way.' I paused. 'You having a good day?'

He shrugged. 'Job is job.'

Along the road I went on, passing the steep blocks of the settlement housing. Outside of one house a pickup truck was pulled in with the engine running and bonnet up, and red-black jump leads snaked across the ground towards another vehicle with its bonnet also lifted and a settler attaching the large metal clips of the leads to a flat battery. Fair-skinned and fair-haired, in work boots and work jeans he dusted his hands off and made his way with loping strides back to the first vehicle, wearing a kippah and a loose white shirt. And something in it caught my eye right away, for it wasn't only his fair complexion that looked like it came from elsewhere. So many things about him reminded me of something I'd seen before and in a different place. And I considered a moment, and then realised that here in Hebron was an image of the United States. He was Oklahoma, he was Kansas, he was Missouri: that same mixture of populating the frontier, rugged-work hillbilly and religious calling. In that man charging a flat car battery, in the sun-baked leather of his lolloping boots and the hard denim of his jeans, for just a moment I walked past a scene that made flesh the commitment of US conservatives to the state of Israel.

Outside a fortified yard, guarded by a heavy gate with a sheet of metal reflecting the heat from it, I caught the eye of another conscript, Mizrahi, his dark hair lifting into curls, eyes piercing. We looked at one another a moment, his young face, held there in his booth, surrounded by more concrete and holed up in the heat with a gun. And here was his youth. Whether or not he needed it, I gave a smile of my commiseration, but into it he seemed almost to scowl, with a dull anger in his eyes, as if I had offended him. It was then, in that instant, that I remembered Aharon, and the conversation about his Hebron military service in the garden at Neta's house, recent but so distant, with the feeling of the rock from its slingshot still stinging in the back of my head. Aharon had looked at me with the same intensity, skirting anger.

⠿

'What about the occupation?' I ask Aharon, the two of us sitting next to each other, below the garden wall. 'Is there anything you can do about it?'

'We can't end it. The occupation is a system of control, and if you don't have faith, trust, you need such a system. The occupation became its own logic.'

'Was that what it was like in Palestine, in the army? A system of control?'

'The army was many things. Jumping out of planes was good. I miss it. But most of the time was just sitting in a hot checkpoint in the middle of Hebron.'

His tone hardens.

'That was tough. Long days. And if a Palestinian guy wants to make a joke, he better make sure he includes me in it. When he comes through my checkpoint, if he's laughing then it needs to be like he's laughing *with* me, not at me. If he wants me to make it hard for him, he needs to know I've got four hours there and I'll make him sit with me. I don't mind ruining his day.'

'I think you're a proud guy,' I say to him, 'I think you like your freedom, like not being told what to do. I don't think you'd accept that for you.'

'I know. But we all have to play the game sometimes, man. I have people I talk to who I can't say certain things to. My boss, my landlord... even if I think he's an idiot. So if someone thinks he can make a joke at me, then...'

'But they have this every day, all day, just because they're

Palestinian and you're Israeli. You're not their boss. You have no right to that power over them.'

The adrenaline of the rock comes back to me, turns to anger, like for once I feel I have some small right, born of experience, to say something rather than just ask another question.

'The Palestinians don't get to leave the army, go out into their desert, go travelling to help with their trauma. They don't just do three years of it. They see how some of your soldiers can shoot them dead, for fun.'

Aharon knows the guy I'm referring to. He knows the whole world saw the same footage of the Israeli soldier execute a man, Abdel Fattah al-Sharif, murdered by a soldier in 2016 as he lay face down and disarmed on the Hebron streets. Aharon's face goes serious.

'This soldier, Azaria, who kills a man. Shoots him in the head when he is on the ground. Me, my friends in the army, we want this guy locked up forever. To send a message that you can't do that. That this is not the army. We have all been in his situation, we would not do what he did.'

His tone drifts away, and it is like he is talking more to himself than to me.

'I know we did a good job. Those boys were some of the best.'

Aharon laughs.

'But you are right. We're better than this, I know.'

And he pauses and again he laughs, only this time with the presence of a brokenness. With a tone in his voice that I cannot understand or describe, Aharon says simply:

'Really, really, we're just losers.'

⁞

Along those same Hebron streets I made my way through winding, dusty white passages beneath the heat of that day. My legs ached, the movement of walking now unfamiliar to my returning cycling muscles. I squinted a little, for everything was so bright in the sun. The sky was so pristine, peerless as the ocean, and against it the occupation held firm, pressing back in its own wearying intensity. Through olive trees and flowing grass, up the hill to the house I went. The feathery ears of the grasses leaned heavily towards the ground, so that they stood like golden quills, stuck in the earth against that sapphire blue sky, waving freely with a whistling sound akin to running water. Again, I thought to myself how beautiful it all was, and how beautiful it all could be. Emerging up onto the last outcrop of the hill, outside the old house and facing the far side of the valley where the city grew, a couple of mattresses were laid on dusty earth. Sunflower seeds and a few other signs showed the remains of people who had gathered to spend time there, up above their city, set so brave but so besieged.

Watching over the house was a ragged Palestinian flag, leaning on the wind but defiant as it went on fluttering. A mature olive tree stood at the centre of a garden, the building behind it marked with Palestinian flags and the affirmations *Youth Against Settlements* and *This is Palestine*. Approaching a table with a small plate of hummus and pitta on it, a young woman stepped barefoot from the open door, her skin fair and her long, light brown hair in a bun on top of her head. She looked up at the sound of my footfall, and her face was high cheeks and two piercing eyes, something between green and brown in colour, and she looked straight at me and in an American accent said hello.

Elle

We sit across from one another and she places a glass mug of coffee in front of me. The familiar aroma of cardamom drifts up. She wears a long-sleeved white sweater, pulls the sleeves down into her hands and holds the seams of each cuff between her fingers and palms. She pulls her arms around herself in a half-hug, one knee up on her chair, then leans across to her own tea, leaves of mint floating in it.

'I came on a term abroad trip. To Jordan, but I met so many Palestinians there and it affected me, so I wanted to come, to see. You know. Do more.'

'That's amazing,' I say, trying to sound encouraging even if we both know it's but a drop of hope.

'In my university department there's like six people in our Justice for Palestine group. Out of six hundred. And you compare that to something like AIPAC, the American-Israel lobby…'

She trails off, rolls her eyes at herself, embarrassed for knowing what's right in a world that so readily does wrong. I look at her, wide-eyed and innocent, and wonder what we are doing to our children, when as adults we are expected to quietly unlearn the moral truths of right and wrong that as children we were taught. I wonder what happens in a world where young people are trained to be ashamed of their conscience, where it becomes embarrassing to have morals, because you know your society only ignores them. Elle takes a breath, gives a smile that is forced but not insincere.

'But you know, at least we have one.'

'You have to start somewhere. What do you do when you're here?'

'Take photos, mostly. So there are images ready when something happens. Technically, the Israeli soldiers are supposed to be neutral, to protect the Palestinians from the settlers. But they don't. This week the army welded shut the front of a house with a mother and her children still inside. They said there was an exit for her at the back of the house, but the woman said it was too dangerous to climb out that way with a kid.'

'Why do they do it?'

'Harassment. So that eventually people leave. The Palestinians were demanding they open it, but then the soldiers left because some Israeli children arrived. Military law says the army can't be present around children, but the settler kids have been taught that by their parents, so they know to use it and they show up when it's useful.'

I shake my head as a rattle on tin interrupts.

'What's that?' I ask.

'Settlers, probably. They throw rocks at us quite a lot.'

I get up, step around the corner and see a metal fence and the garden of a settlement creeping up the hillside opposite, the blue and white of an Israeli flag hanging on its pole. I turn back to Elle, point up at the top of our hill, where the Palestinian building stands over us, shabby but proud.

'Where did they get this property?'

'A Palestinian family was pushed out, and when the house was abandoned, the Israelis started to break it up. They cut the electric, pulled out water pipes. We put it all back in when the family gave us papers for the building, but someone has to be here permanently or they restart demolition.' Elle nods upstairs. 'So I'm here for the month, with the settlers as neighbours. We try to organise things from here. Things for the community, or to help people resist when the army or settlers try to remove them.'

'How do they get funds to keep it going?'

Elle winces. 'People in Hebron don't have much money, but they give if they can.'

'And donations from the Palestinian community, or internationally?'

Elle gives a short laugh, like it's an unfortunate question.

'It's hard. Paypal is banned for Palestinians, but it's allowed for settlers.'

And as with Sohaib's Facebook post, or the emails I deleted before flying here, you see the architectures of oppression moving into the cyber, digital world, those places where oppression can be confirmed with the press of a button in front of a screen and where no protest can be heard, no eye looked into, and no strength of force or will can stop it. The chance to resist is still there, but the gaps into which that chance must force itself grow smaller.

'They figure it out, though,' says Elle, as if offering reassurance. 'It keeps going.'

I point up at the Palestinian colours, fluttering on this hillside overlooking all Hebron.

'The settlers must hate that flag.'

Elle just smiles, and I look at her. I wonder who she'll be in twenty years. She is dressed in slacks, cotton loose around her ankles. She looks like she could have just padded on tiptoe straight out of a Martha's Vineyard lounge, her brown hair tied up in its knot, her voice with the measured tones of high society, well brought up. I know that I'm older than her, but I sense the age less from her appearance than her manner. You can feel that she doesn't understand why the world is like this, but knows it's not yet her world, it belongs to the adults, and so on some level she doesn't yet expect it to be entirely as she wishes. When we are young, convinced that it's all wrong but aware that we still have more to learn, on some level our brain tells us that some of that waiting information may yet explain it all, make sense of everything being upside down. I recognise that look in Elle because I know that's how I used to look once, before you realise that, no… that's just it: the world *is* upside down, but nobody says so.

With time I know she'll change. There's no avoiding that, but how will she change? The more years you spend on the planet, the more entitled you become. Time steeps in you and you grow, you find your voice, stop accepting less than you know the world could be. You realise that it only got made this way because others said it was fine to do so and nobody shut them down when they did. I look at her calm eyes, that green-brown, looking back at me, determined but with the uncertainty, the pondering of youth and a mind that knows it must keep asking questions, but questions that are difficult because they are being asked of a place that does not make sense. I look at her, this girl from New England, here on a hill overlooking Hebron, and twenty years from now, I think Elle's still going to be demanding answers to the questions she's starting to ask. Looking at her, you can see her heart, it's strong enough, Elle's in it for the long haul.

We Ride

In time I begin to suspect that Sohaib has reached the Age of the Excuse, immediately pre-middle age. This moment in life is a worldwide phenomenon, where the enthusiasm for cycling becomes more the enthusiasm for talking about it, where the excitement is more for the bikes you own than where you ride them, the coffee stops between the pedalling. It's been a long day. I sense him looking out for reasons not to ride, and there is something so beautifully mundane and universal about how he goes about it, the same instantly recognisable reasons dispensed from Hebron to New York to Sydney. A last-minute work obligation, a mechanical gremlin, it's getting late. The potential route we could fit in, perhaps, could be shortened. Eventually we hug parting farewells, will ride another time.

Standing in the shadows, shyly, in the corner of the room, Sadam is another matter. The kid has been milling around all day, anticipating this moment. Sadam is young, has youth, energy to burn. His road bike has been all set to go since noon, his Lycra uniform ready on his tall, lean frame. If this were a European Grand Tour, I'd say Sadam has the body of a great climber… long limbs, legs up to here, a physique that would let fly in the mountains. He paces the tiled floor with the tap of his cleated shoes, itching to ride, just waiting for one of the adults to show up and actually put their wheels where their mouths are.

I'm game, ready to go. I walk up to him, my nose the level of his chin, where his wraparound sunglasses hang at the zip collar of his jersey and catch the light of the last sun diving into the room to get out of the heat. He has the thin stubble of a young man, and in his eyes the quiet of the road cyclist, a discreet sort of passion that is experienced mostly in solitude. We're cut from a certain cloth.

Whatever his normal routine, with the evening light filling the sky, glowing orange through the window, I feel that Sadam likes the idea of a road mate, a companion. His English is little and my Arabic less, but we know there is one thing we both understand. He steps up to me, I point to the bikes.

'Sadam. We ride?'

He smiles, nods.

'We ride.'

⸪

We ride, and the road moves under us, we the two styluses, side by side on its black vinyl playing towards the end of the record. Together we climb the long hill out of Hebron, a straight drag where the stallholder calls out the last of his produce, where the plums dropped from their crate squash yellow into asphalt, where an old lady cleans her fourth-floor balcony, pouring a bucket of water across it, setting a cascade of light waterfalling down, spilling golden marbles into the air before they land and roll across the road. I ride behind Sadam as the gradient lifts, watch as he rises out of his saddle, dances on the pedals, the bicycle going left to right beneath him while his body points straight up, unmoving and cast in black against the gold sundown and the silhouetted trees that line this long avenue.

Listening close, I lean in as our bicycles talk to one another, as they converse: my tyres with a deeper thrum to the near-silence of his thinner rubber, the springs of his cassette engaging – *tic, tic,*

tic – as Sadam stops pedalling and freewheels, the wind hitting soft against my pannier, the spokes of our four wheels threading the air. Sadam points at me.

'You ride Jerusalem?'

I nod, point at him. 'You?'

'I, Bethlehem.' He turns his forearm and places it parallel to his handlebars, barring his own path with a wall. 'Bethlehem. Army.'

I nod a sad understanding as he rubs his thumb at his finger to show nothing there.

'I no permit.'

⠿

We ride. And the countryside starts to open, and the hills in their wan light yawn gently at the concrete garrisons the Israelis threw down on their backs. I catch up with Sadam's back wheel, hug it, suck it, pulling from it whatever tempo I can scavenge from his pace-setting at the front of our road crew. I pull alongside and point ahead.

'How far Bethlehem?'

He looks for the words and then instead at his hand, lifts it from the bars and uses fingers as he says, 'Two. Three.'

'Twenty-three?'

He nods, and I wonder what more I can learn of my road mate beyond his bicycle and our destination.

'In Hebron… what's your job?'

Sadam repeats 'job', before his tongue answers instinctively in Arabic, and then finds and settles on the nearest word of English: 'School.'

'Teacher?' I offer, but the word doesn't hit home.

'*Hoca*,' I try, the old Turkish word, from Persian but also in Arabic, for a religious instructor, and so a colloquial name for a teacher.

'Ahh! *Hodja*,' and Sadam nods a little, moving his head not disagreeably, like it's near enough. *Hodja* will do.

We ride on and I return the conversation to numbers. 'How old are you?'

He shakes his head. 'No.'

I point to myself. 'I am three-three.' I point to him, speak slowly, 'How old are you?'

'Ah. I two-three. Two-three.'

'Same Bethlehem,' I smile.

And Sadam nods.

⠿

We ride, below the concrete cylinder of a watchtower above the road, below the razor wire, beside the blue-white Israeli flag daubed clumsily in paint on the concrete tablets of a sentry post, where a uniformed teenager sits, reclining in his chair with sun on his face and a semi-automatic rifle set in hot black across his middle. I look over at Sadam, riding beside me. The shadows of our bodies moving, legs turning inside rigid bicycle-frame silhouettes cast perfect on the concrete balustrade that flanks the road, spokes fading a shade of grey as they blur and then with growing speed spin out of sight altogether. Our shadow bodies lift up and then fall flat against a field of vines, landing high on green leaf then low on red earth, then green leaf, then red earth. The gradient eases and, *clunk*, our gears drop, our chains move down a sprocket in perfect sync as together we both read the same road in the same instant. Sadam's slender face shines with the beginning of a sweat, his eyes again with that patience of the road cyclist, redoubled, his nostrils flaring a little with each calm, rhythmic breath. He looks over, smiles.

'Fr-Frida…'

The sound thick, but I get the name of a day.

'Friday?'

He nods, points ahead of us, north, up the road. Sadam points at the future. 'I, Haifa.'

'Haifa?!' I point to his wheels. 'By bicycle?'

Sadam nods, proud with excitement.

'One hundred kilometres?' I ask. 'One-fifty?'

He nods back, slightly sideways, lips downturned in a look that says near-enough.

'But permit?' I put my arm flat to my handlebar in our sign for checkpoints. 'Army?'

Sadam shakes his head. He gestures knowingly to his wheels in that same point Mohammed once made, of how soldiers assume only Israelis ride road bikes and so by riding them Palestinians too can steal themselves some liberty.

'No passport.' He smiles quiet, points below him. 'Bicycle.'

Together we laugh as Sadam picks up speed, spins a high gear into a long climb leaning up in front. Above us, a military-guarded shopping mall stands at the summit, a consumer fortress watching over the Holy Land with its offer of a new faith. Adherents pull in and out, parked up to join the shining windscreens and bodywork across the stretch of asphalted earth. Sadam breaks away from me and I watch him from a growing distance, his figure getting smaller, again out of the saddle, attacking the climb and the gap that opens between us somehow shows Sadam in the truest form of life. For a moment I see him, beneath the arcs of cirrus glowing gold with sun, and he is simply timeless: a young man riding a bicycle through his land, immune to the idea that someone else says this land is not his.

At the top of the climb I brake, roll to a halt and refill water from the bottle strapped to the back of my bike. I drink, feel the cold press down through my chest, and up ahead I see the dot of Sadam pull over. His thin, towering figure stands at the kerbside, one foot down, a shape of blue-black Lycra at the foot of the hill just descended. I clip back into my pedal, press down and roll after him, watching as he too clips cleat into pedal with a crack – loaded – and begins to spin, not wasting a moment as I swoop past and he accelerates up to my speed until once again we ride side by side.

'OK?' he asks, with a thumbs-up.

'OK!' I point to my bottle. 'Water.'

But I see that his face has lost its ease and that a grave look of fear has taken it.

'Next time water,' Sadam waves a frantic hand, 'no stop.'

He points around us, as if checkpoints lurk everywhere, not only those positioned across the land but also the checkpoints Israel has placed inside his mind, inserted there with a fear that they can maybe spring from nowhere to hold a sudden mortal power over him.

'Here many settlements.' Sadam holds up three fingers. 'Three time… *el jeish waqafni.*'

'Three times?' I ask.

'*El-jeish waqafni hon talat marrat.*'

…and his voice stays in Arabic, so that instead he points at the ground and then at himself, and he has none of the necessary words of English but it is all written and spoken loud from his eyes. I ask him, 'Army stop you here three times?'

I say it for him, and Sadam grunts a yes, nods, relieved that I get it, his face relaxing a little before he says it again, a kindly order mixed with a request.

'We no stop.'

▦

We ride, putting on a sprint, escapees, a chain gang, like the two of us must work together in a breakaway from the pack, the *peloton,* the occupation on our wheels but for one of the two riders the stakes so cruelly high. In my mind, over and over the thought does laps: he only wants to go for a bike ride, he only wants to go for a bike ride, the kid just wants to go for a bike ride. In the lapse of concentration, I fall behind, then realise I must pick up the pace and get on with the job at hand. Damn, but the kid is quick. Sadam can really ride, and I wonder if the outside world will ever get to see as much, will ever see him on the roads of Europe, riding the *Tour*, the *Giro*, the *Vuelta*. I wonder if the Israelis would let him travel to the prospective trial with the cycling team in France, in Spain, the Basque country, Haute-Savoie. Up on his pedals, Sadam's feet turn perfect, effortless circles, circles without a single rough edge of impact or friction, no up-down but round and round in sheer geometric bliss. I see the watts coursing through his cranks and along the road the blue of the globe thistles throws sparks at us, like sapphires exploding in the maquis, like the flash of old newspaper photographers at the Tour de France. We share pace-setting duties, get into a time-trial motion so that we orbit one another and constantly rotate to overtake the rider in front. Sadam pulls out from behind me to ride by and lead and I pull out from behind him to ride by and lead, and so collectively we begin to ride faster, accelerate the pace of the other and then rest a moment in the keyhole, the slipstream they punched into the atmosphere for us to follow. And right now, we speak exactly the same language and share the same goal, the aim to get a time so fast that Sadam can get the hell out of here, or rather, get *here* back. Saddam moves ahead once again, but this time he's really putting on a spurt, wants out, launches himself off the front. A gouge in the tarmac opens before him and he hops it, both wheels momentarily off the ground and Sadam's arm pointing in an arrow behind him to warn me of the crater coming up. I weave, dodge its crevasse, try to accelerate and regain his wheel but he's about to drop me, the bit between his teeth, the legs moving faster to a blur, a song of motion sings.

⠿

We ride, but Sadam pulls ahead, opens a new and bigger gap, terminal this time, so that I watch once more as he moves into the near distance and now I am no longer riding with him but only watching him. I can feel the sadness of his fear seeping into my heart, split like so much cracked asphalt. The tears do not form in my eyes but instead they flow back down inside me, drying my spirit with their salt and settling a sadness that I know will and must last until its cause has passed.

I watch as Sadam pulls out towards the centre of the road, leaning wide and high around a hillside before it throws itself at the horizon. The road rears up, like some ramp that will launch Sadam into the sky where a moon almost full, sad and cratered, rises slowly. I watch as he saws at the road, making quick turns to feel and savour that movement of the bicycle under him, cutting crescents that align with the wisps of cirrus pulled into arcs by the winds across this dusk. A last sunlight gleams in his wheels, the flash of his cranks burns bright, like Sadam has been dusted with something magic, needs to pick up such a speed that he'll hit this ramp just right and then can lift up into space above this land at last. I watch him, darting, at play, just as the swallows swoop in, swoop out, and I think and feel in my blood that Sadam rides in a fashion instantly recognisable to any who have ever known what it is to love riding a bicycle.

He leaves me, dropped at last. I see Sadam, riding in the cloak of his shadow, as if the image in a reel of film and he the only shape that did not develop when the acetate was lifted, dripping, golden orange from the tank in a dark room. I gasp a moment at the scene closing out in front of me, I drink it down for I always wanted to record it, to record the spirit of that vehicle I loved and can see so clear in front of me now. I grit my teeth, pedal hard at the road, but really I know that I grit my teeth not to ride it but so that I can write it, so that I can write this just so, and so that nobody could ever see or ever dream of seeing this as anything but what it is: the boy riding a bicycle through his Palestine, riding a bicycle until there comes that day when he does not have to do it in secret, with nothing to hide and with none to stop him because the Palestinians, in body just as they already are in heart, will be free.

Dome of the Rock

One last place. I had to go there, you have to, but you only find that out after you visit. Through the white limestone of the old city, cool against the heat, I make my way down, going lower beneath the sinking steps of hewn rock. Each side are stalls, proving the immutable laws of commerce as Israeli shopkeepers sell Palestinian trinkets – *keffiyeh* and prayer beads – and Palestinian-Israelis sell kippah and fridge magnets bearing the blue and white of the Israeli flag. So long as each trader can make their money, profits take priority over the struggle, or perhaps, they are the struggle.

Down through the complex I pass the Muslim Quarter, the Armenian, the Christian, in this ancient city belonging to all of the faiths and constructed so many centuries ago, way ahead of its time, with the principle that equal access to all places made most sense. A man leans on a chair turned backwards, one leg crossed over the other as he swings beads in his hand and, outside the mosque, young men watch the street from where they sit and they stand and they huddle in a line over his shoulder. From a bakery I move in and then out of bursts of baking flour, of cakes coloured with the yellow of saffron waiting in heavy steel trays scattered with almonds. The sun disappears as the complex goes deeper, and only white lamps reflecting off the limestone now glow in these underground passages that break back to a daylight edging in up ahead.

And it must be the most beautiful thing I've ever seen.

⠿

I don't want to turn from it, like leaving a loved one, where you have to go but know the next thing you see will be less beautiful. Its golden dome shines, sandwiched between the blue tiles and the blue sky, designed and constructed with the most joyful certainty that each day above it the sun would shine and there would be no clouds in that sky so blue. The golden dome smiles, and my heart feels so happy.

Through the courtyard, to a washing point where taps protrude from marble, I remove my shoes and the water runs cool over the vein at my ankles, drawing the heat out of my body and bare feet, out of my blood. The marble beneath the tap has been smoothed away, pushed, worn gently back from where the stream of water flows and hits hard stone. I pull water over my face, washing away the miles ridden, preparing me, cleaning me before the last depart. I pull the water out of the beard that grew, place my head under the tap and push my fingers through hot hair turning wet and cool. I look at that smoothed stone, and something about stone removed by mere water feels reassuring in this place, a reminder that – drip by drip – things disappear, and small acts will erode a solid edifice. Two other men wash their feet, their faces, beside me and before prayer. One sits motionless, upright, a palm on each knee, then moves a hand to massage at the back of his neck. A young woman, a tourist leaving with a camera, takes our photograph from behind, then steps quietly on so that I'll wonder where we'll live on in her own life: a hard-drive stamped with the imprint of our data, an image on a screen, a printed photo on a mantelpiece or wall. Or she'll never look at us again.

Beneath the Dome of the Rock, shining in the sun, a group of armed guards seem to melt away, as if there is a presence here gentler than they are hostile. As if the creation of beauty and meaning will forever rebuke, softly but completely, all thought of violence. Above me stand the domes and circles of the mosque, the repeating patterns of its tiles. All of it, endless and without right-angles, seems to convey an idea of eternity, a structure without the binds of nation states or codified laws, but still strong, still solid and full with meaning. Looking up at it, I see the road and the land behind me, and I wonder how long it will be before a state called 'Palestine' comes about. Will it share its name with Israel when it does, or will the idea of nations anyway fade from importance before that time? Will it one day be announced that conflict has been resolved in West China District 14, or will there come a day when 'a Palestinian' is a word stripped of its original meaning and used simply to describe one who fights successfully for freedom against near-impossible odds?

Beneath the Dome of the Rock, shining in the sun, from somewhere I know not, happy but also sad, a great tiredness takes me. Looking up at that mosque, more beautiful than anything I have ever seen that was not made by nature, it seems to show a little of how it feels to be a Muslim in this world, or to have any part of you at all feel like it is Muslim. Surrounded by a land in which your spirituality is unwelcome, hesitantly, you make your way inside its walls. And there, on the inside, you look up at the Dome and in yourself feel such a peace and such a joy at this sight, that it is impossible to believe that this feeling is so invisible, and so misunderstood, to all those who stand outside of it. The sadness fills you, but so too the beauty, and so you keep your spirit, and draw out the same force by which, quietly, you know you will continue.

Take-off

The closing miles roll beneath me, a cold wind coming from the sea as seasons change and a new weather takes watch of the land. My metal water canteen is scratched at gently by the reaching twigs of a roadside bush, the leaves stroke at a pannier bag, a stone disturbed by some small animal crackles down a rockface and a truck passes close so that, from somewhere on its tailgate, there comes the chime of a chain holding a bolt that has not been slotted away. Loose it hangs and *tink, tink, tink* comes to my ears, as the truck plays a few notes and for only a moment, privately, the truck sounds as delicate as a xylophone. And again, I wonder if, with all the languages of peace corrupted, maybe music will be a language that helps teach us how to talk again.

In front of me waits not even a day of Tel Aviv, but already everything behind and up ahead has taken on the form of a collage. Of a chaos, stitched together by my turning legs with the road endless underneath them. I know that the hours waiting in the city will pass in a blink. I will see the adverts, all the adverts. Of couples pirouetting together in underwear, *Live Your Dream* written next to their embrace. I will see stationery shops selling high-quality paper and rubber stamps customised with your own personal insignia, the girl with *Winnie the Pooh* tattooed on her forearm in an adult souvenir of childhood. I'll sit with a last coffee, I'll watch the battery-powered scooters zip beneath outdoor speakers playing easy-listening electronic music. People all around will be looking at their phones as more adverts roll on the buses and on the bus stops, so that once again I will see a world of capital and consumerism where, like anywhere under capitalism, you can buy anything except that thing you want most of all, because the tragedy is that peace is valued only where it is between the world's rich. I will pull up a chair in the city, will take my place, will watch the feet of restless strangers tap the pavement, watch their fingers tap thighs in this atmosphere set on edge by something more than just caffeine, a place all but anaesthetised but not beyond that sinking feeling that just won't sink, because one Israeli life might remain valued to a dozen Palestinian, but what if you're that one?

Along a familiar path I will leave the fading, painted road markings for a last time, passing the run-down, rusting bus station at Levinsky, where the Eritrean men wash bicycles and the poor sell their goods in the quest to stay only as poor. I will watch as people promenade, living that metropolitan dream, but the *dream* part here it is more literal than I'm used to, for this truly is not reality. Not exactly a lie, but a place so heavily moderated, edited, that once you have stepped outside of it for a while, to return is to see it as unbearably fake. I will remember those words, spoken to me by that kind woman in the Golan, and as I ride they'll come back to me while I watch revolving doors on shopping malls and a voice repeats in my head, 'Many of the Palestinians don't have to leave their cities… they just live quite a normal life inside them.' And she spoke of Palestine, but perhaps more than that, unintentionally, she described Israel, for the Palestinians live with fewer illusions of being free.

Eventually I will be gone. Pedalling, always pedalling, I will take my final ride to the airport, where an aeroplane drops from over palm trees and a gutted ruin, no different to how it all started all those miles before, with only the road still loyally unchanged. At the airport they'll swab everything, all of my belongings sniffed by a mechanical nose tuned for explosive residues. They'll stuff my sleeping bag in that poor machine's sniffer, old socks and underwear right under its conk, and here – I'll think to myself – here was a job that, of all of them, none wept to see automated. Some kid will take off my shoes and stroke the soles of my feet for whatever it is he wants to be sure is not there, and from the corner of my eye I'll see officials pass my black-bound notepad first for swabbing and then for sniffing. I'll notice that they'll leave the notepad closed, dust off its cover for traces of dynamite, but they have no fear of these words and letters and tales inside, as if such things hold no danger, no power. I'll be offended by this judgement, pitched against my own faith that within those pages are held stories, and that stories alone can truly make a world shake or a heart budge, even if only a little. And as I pack my belongings away again, I will wonder, are they right, or am I?

On the far side of the aisle, waiting anxiously in fear of the final call, will be those two young girls who went through maximum security with me on our way out of the airport: one of them – Bengali and brown-skinned – strip-searched before being let through, her friend on a Dutch passport but the child of Iraqi refugees. And all they wanted was to see Al-Aqsa. I'll watch as they stand nervously, and while the guards scroll through photos showing no more than two smiling friends in mud masks at the Dead Sea.

Numb to everything… to the rounds of searching, the sit down, the stand up, the sit down… at last I'll make my way down the tunnel to the aircraft. I'll wonder how long this story I wrote will last, how it will age and if the miles ridden were worth it. I'll wonder if someone will do a peace deal, if the stalemate will grow more painful or less. And somehow, whatever happens, how these words age in the test of time, somehow it will not concern me too much, because today it was the truth that I finished writing, only that. Just as I found it at the roadside, and a truth now destined to meet with one of two fates. If the troubles of the Palestinians and the Israelis are solved well and soon, then I would not much mind having my words made void by such an outcome. It would be a pleasure to see them turned quickly into only a warning from history: an outline of what we do to the vulnerable when we have power, and a reassurance that some will always resist this, simply because their spirit commands them to. The second fate in which these words will age poorly is less happy, but maybe more important, for a sad part of my soul understands that money and violence is employed to reorganise the land behind me with a new history that is chosen by the powerful. If that story prevails, if it becomes the accepted version of history, one that leaves this one dated and builds a world without room for those random acts, where Abu Bakr tells a stranger on a bicycle to remember his razed village of Imwas, then still I will not be sad for the fate of these words. At the very least, they will remain the truth. And what else was I to write?

Looking out the plane window it will finally come to an end, above a tarmac not a bit like my humble roadside, but so crisp and sheer, with runway lights rushing towards the beach and then the sea. I will feel sorry for those stories that stick inside of me and never made it onto these pages but still burn keen. The city goes flooding by, blending into one, and I look over at the jet engine, the fuselage, three of them in a line off the bottom of the wing. Beads of water run fast along the window. The wheels turn below, solid rubber, and finally I hear the engines roar, the plane lifting, engines heaving and at the centre of the fuselage I think I can maybe make out the past and the future, thrown together by the turbine turning, as it roars, and it roars, and it roars.